The Universal Laws of God

The Universal Laws of God

Volume I

Dr. Joshua David Stone
and
Rev. Gloria Excelsias

Writers Club Press
San Jose New York Lincoln Shanghai

The Universal Laws of God
Volume I

Writers Club Press
an imprint of iUniverse, Inc.

For information address:
iUniverse, Inc.
5220 S. 16th St., Suite 200
Lincoln, NE 68512
www.iuniverse.com

ISBN: 0-595-21334-0

Printed in the United States of America

Epigraph

The Sermon on the Mount

Matthew 5-7; Luke 6, 11

And seeing the multitudes, he went up into a mountain: and when he was set, his disciples came unto him: And he opened his mouth, and taught them, saying,

Blessed are the gentle, for they shall inherit the Earth.

Blessed are the merciful, for they shall be shown mercy.

Blessed are the pure in heart, for they shall see God.

Blessed are the peacemakers, for they shall be called the children of God.

Blessed are those who are humble, those who are just, those who try to do right, those who suffer persecution—all of them will be rewarded in the kingdom of Heaven.

Do not keep your good qualities hidden, but let them shine out like a candle lighting up a dark house. When a lamp is lit, it is not put under a bowl, but placed where it can brighten the whole room.

I am not here to destroy the law, or contradict the words of the prophets. I am here to uphold them, for it its essential that the law be obeyed.

You have heard it said, you shall not kill. But those who keep murderous thoughts in their minds are also to blame. You must be able to forgive whoever has made you angry.

The old law speaks of an eye for an eye, and a tooth for a tooth, but if someone strikes you on the right cheek, it is better to turn the left cheek so that he may strike that, too.

It is easy to love your friends, but it is as important to love your enemies also, and be kind to those who turn against you.

You should never boast of your good deeds, but do them secretly. You cannot value both God and money.

When you pray, do not do so in the open where everyone can see, but alone in your room. Talk directly to God, and say what is in your heart. Pray using these words: "Our Lord who is in Heaven, holy is your name. Your kingdom is coming. We will obey you on Earth as you are obeyed in Heaven. Give us our daily food. Forgive us our sins, as we forgive the sins of others. Do not lead us into temptation, but save us from evil."

Do not worry about what you wear or what you eat and drink. The birds in the air do not sow wheat or store it in barns, and yet the heavenly Lord feeds them; the lilies of the field do not spin or weave, and yet not even Solomon in all his glory was as magnificent as one of these.

Do not condemn: as you judge others, so will you yourself be judged. Before you criticize the speck of sawdust in another's eye, first remove the plank of wood in your own.

Ask, and it will be given to you; search, and you will find.

Avoid false prophets; beware of the wolf in sheep's clothing.

Anyone who hears my words and follows them is like the wise one who builds a house upon a rock. When the rain comes, and the wind blows, and the floodwaters rise, the house will stand firm. But anyone who hears my words and ignores them is like the foolish one who builds a house upon sand. When the storm comes and the waters rise, the house will fall, because the foundations are built only on shifting sand.

Contents

Introduction

This book that you are holding in your hands has the potential to totally revolutionize your consciousness and change your life forever, if only you have the eyes to see and the ears to hear! It contains the essence of *The Easy To Read Encyclopedia Of The Spiritual Path*. The Kybalion teaches, "Every cause has its effect; every effect has its cause; everything happens according to law; chance is but a name for law not recognized; there are many planes of causation, but nothing escapes the law." Every jot and tittle of the law will be fulfilled, as Edgar Cayce put it. Everything in God's Infinite Universe is governed by laws, and once we learn to live and walk in harmony with these laws, life shall change in untold, unseen, and unthought ways. We each have come to collectively create a fifth-dimensional society and the Seventh Golden Age. We have come to collectively build the New Jerusalem. We have come to see and fulfill God's Revelation to John when He said, "I am the beginning and the end. I will make everything new once more so that God and the people shall live together. There shall be no more pain, nor sorrow, nor death, for all such things will have passed away." Then an angel took John to the top of a high mountain and showed him the holy city, the new Jerusalem, whose walls were of jasper and whose streets were made of gold. Through the city ran the River of Life, whose waters were as clear as crystal. Here there was no need of sun by day nor of moon by night, for in the city dwelled God and his Son, and all who came there walked in the light of their glory! Nelson Mandela in his famous speech of 1994 said, "We were born to manifest the glory of God within us. It's not just in some of us; it's in everyone. And as we let our own light shine, we unconsciously give other people permission to do the same." We are living in the most exciting times in Earth's history, and the stage is all ours! It is time for each of us to shine our light and take our rightful place. We have come to collectively dream the impossible dream and reach the unreachable star. Let this be our quest, to follow that star! Following the Universal Laws of God, as outlined within these pages in the easiest and most practical manner possible, we shall each become a beacon of light to the world and we shall each learn once more to celebrate life in our every thought, feeling, word, and action—living life in all its glory. Let's stop dreaming our lives and start living our dreams, so that we may see what "no eyes have yet seen," hear what "no ears have yet heard," and conceive as "no mind has yet conceived" what God had prepared for those who love him. "Keep therefore the words of this covenant, and do them, that ye may prosper in all that ye do." (Deuteronomy 29:9)

The Universal Law of Affirmations and Visualizations

Every thought we think, positive or negative, is an affirmation. Every word we speak is an affirmation. Every action or behavior we take is an affirmation. Used in a Psychological healing context, affirmations are specifically designed to program a desired feeling, behavior, or habit into our subconscious minds. The continuous process of pushing the negative attitudes out of the mind with our personal power and then repeating the new positive affirmations into the subconscious mind is the main key to reprogramming the subconscious mind, and also maintaining self-mastery. Affirmations are a total key to developing every attitude and behavior demonstrated by one who is in Buddha/Christ/Melchizedek Consciousness. For affirmations to develop certain key attitudes that pertain to self-concept and self-image, please see *Soul Psychology*. Every thought and feeling you allow into your mind is not only an affirmation and visualization, but once accepted into the conscious mind, it imprints itself on the subconscious mind like a tape recorder or computer! It will then attract and magnetize that! The subconscious mind is always attracting and magnetizing. It is just a matter of what you allow it to magnetize and attract. Now the question is, Why do affirmations and visualizations not always get the results people want? First, most people don't realize that every thought you think, feeling you feel, word you speak, and action you take is an affirmation. Hence, everyone is doing affirmations and visualizations every moment of their lives. Second, most people are not aware of all the programming that currently exists in their subconscious mind from this lifetime and all their past lives, which is functioning as an affirmation and visualization already programmed into the subconscious from the

1

past. Third, most people do not have 100% mastery of their thoughts, emotions, negative ego mind, lower-self desire, and inner child, and are not thinking and feeling with their Spiritual/Christ/Buddha Mind at all times. So what happens is, Lightworkers use positive affirmations and visualizations, which is good, however, they are having to counteract an enormous amount of programming that is already functioning all the time as an affirmation and visualization. Plus, all the positive or negative daily self-talk which is the inner dialogue that goes on all day in our consciousness. So the positive affirmations and visualizations definitely help, but be sure to clean out your subconscious mind and conscious thinking, and work on gaining full mastery of your daily thinking, feeling, speaking, negative ego, inner child, lower-self desire, and so on. Above all else, deny any thought not of GOD to enter your Mind! Ponder on this! This is a golden key to life!

*   *   *

The Universal Law of Appropriately Responding Rather Than Inappropriately Reacting

Whatever happens in life, you want to respond rather than react. A response is a product of the conscious mind, when you choose how to deal with the incoming energy. A reaction is a product of the subconscious mind. If someone judges or attacks you and you let the incoming energy go right into your subconscious mind, solar plexus, or emotional body, you will either be hurt, withdraw and cry, or lash back. You are letting another person be the cause of your emotions. We are hypersuggestible when we don't make a choice about how to respond. In reality, we all are invulnerable psychologically. This is a very profound statement. To be invulnerable means that we can't get emotionally hurt unless we choose to be! See *The Universal Law of Feelings and Emotions*. Don't go on automatic pilot! Be conscious and respond rather than react! An integrated Ascended Master responds and stays in his self mastery!

*   *   *

The Universal Law of Ascension and Integrated Ascension

Ascension begins when you take the beginning of the sixth Initiation. This is called the Ascension Initiation. It has to do with achieving approximately 83 % Light Quotient in your Spiritual Body! All Initiations are basically focused on the amount of Light Quotient you are currently holding. The first step is taking this Initiation which means you have to go through the seven sublevels of that Initiation to take you to the sixth Initiation and completion of the seventh sublevel! This would mean the completing of your Sixth Initiation and Ascension Initiation. Once you take your ninth Initiation and the seventh sublevel, which leads to the beginning of the tenth Initiation, it leads to the full completion of Planetary Ascension and the beginning of your Solar Ascension! After Solar Ascension comes Galactic Ascension, Universal Ascension, Multi-Universal Ascension, and the full realization of Cosmic Ascension! Well, all Initiations are just levels or percentages of Light Quotient in your Spiritual Body! So really Initiations are speaking of the evolution of your Light in your Spiritual Body, but that is all! Which brings us to the subject of Integrated Ascension. Integrated Ascension refers to the understanding that it is not enough to just achieve your seven or nine Levels of Initiation and build your Light Body or Light Quotient, you also must integrate your Initiations into your Mental Body, Emotional Body, Etheric Body, Physical Body, and into your Earthly Life! Ascension and your seven Levels of Initiation or beyond have nothing to do with Psychological development or Physical/Earthly development! A fully Realized Ascended Master on a Planetary Level is the Master of the Spiritual Level, the Psychological Level, and the Physical/Earthly Level, and is balanced and integrated in the three! To understand what it means to integrate your Initiations into your Four-Body System, please see *The Universal Law of Integrating One's Twelve Levels of Initiations Into One's Four-Body System*. So you also must integrate your Initiations and become an Integrated Ascended Master. And no one will be allowed to move into their Solar, Galactic, Universal, Multi-Universal, or Cosmic Ascension process unless they do this! There is a ring pass not at the seventh Initiation for those who do not address this issue. Also, even if you do pass the seventh level of Initiation, if you don't do your Integrated Ascension Work you will have to reincarnate back to the Astral or Mental Plane to complete this work even if you have achieved liberation from the Physical/Earthly Plane. The seventh Initiation is the "Liberation from the Wheel of Rebirth". Once we complete our seven levels of Initiation and our nine levels of Initiation and integrate them into our Four-Body-System, we are allowed to begin taking our Cosmic Ascension Initiations! To fully realize God we must take 352 levels of Initiation. It is impossible to take all of these Initiations in a Physical Body! The First Cosmic Initiation is the Tenth, which is an Earthly Solar Initiation! Then the Eleventh, which is an Earthly Galactic Initiation! Then the Twelfth, which is an Earthly Universal Initiation! These Initiations keep continuing until 352 are achieved! These Cosmic Initiations are much larger in scope than the Planetary Initiations! Well, what about Physical Ascension? Physical Ascension is the process of turning the Physical Body completely into light and returning it to the Spiritual World! However, this is not required to become a fully Realized

Ascended Master. It is just an option, and most choose not to do this! It is an option, however, that is not even realistic to consider until you fully complete your Twelfth Initiation! In terms of Physical Ascension, you can Physically ascend and leave for good when your Spiritual Mission on Earth is complete, or you can Physically ascend and remain on Earth to continue your Spiritual Service Work! This allows you to travel back and forth from the Spiritual and Earthly World and in a sense live in two places consciously simultaneously! Now, there is also what might be called Multi-Dimensional Ascension. There are many lenses to Multi-Dimensional Ascension. The first is that it is not just you who are ascending, it is your twelve Oversouls, your Mighty I Am Presence, and your 143 other Souls, or Soul Extensions, who are ascending with you as well! Also ascending is your entire monadic family! So, from this lens, groups of, onads are ascending together at higher and higher levels. At the Solar Level is one grouping of monads, at the Galactic Level a much larger grouping of monads, at the Universal Level an even larger group, at the Multi-Universal Level a larger grouping yet, and at the Cosmic Level or the 352nd level of the Godhead, all monads are grouped together! Add to this the fact, that the Mineral, Plant, and Animal Kingdoms are in an Ascension Process as well! The Earth Herself is in an Ascension Process! So is the Solar System, the Galaxy, the Universe, the Multi-Universe, and the Omniverse or Cosmos, that is God on all levels and all Dimensions of Reality! If you look at Multi-Dimensional Ascension from God's Perspective, there is no such thing as Personal Ascension! There is only GOD Ascending! All of Creation is Part of GOD! This is the Supreme Multi-Dimensional Perspective! We are all Ascending for GOD! We are God! Well, this is the good news! The other news is that the most common form of Ascension is what might be termed Disintegrated or Fragmented Ascension! The first part to start is that a great many Lightworkers are much more developed in their Spiritual Bodies than their Psychological Self. Often this manifests with people not knowing how to properly own their personal power, love themselves, keep up their bubble of protection, control their mind, emotions, energies, and master their Physical Body! They are often victims instead of causes of their reality, are run by the subconscious mind and by the inner child. And one of the biggest problems is that they do not understand the difference between Spiritual/Buddha/Christ Consciousness and negative ego/fear-based/separative consciousness. They do not fully understand and do not fully apply the Spiritual understanding that our thoughts create our reality, our feelings, emotions, behavior, and largely, what we attract and magnetize into our lives! The negative ego is creating havoc in a great many Lightworkers. When one is not fully right with self, this begins to contaminate all channeling, psychic work, healing, and Spiritual teaching. The work begins to be contaminated with wrong motivations, personal agendas, negative feelings and emotions, power, fame, greed, selfishness, false pride, lust, lower-self desire. This is rampant in the New Age Movement and religion! And this is why the concept and ideal of "Integrated Ascension" is so important! There are three Levels that each person must master to become truly a full-fledged Ascended Master—the Physical/Earthly Level, the Psychological Level, and the Spiritual Level! Each Level is unique and has its own set of laws and Spiritual practices that must be adhered to! The key is to master all three levels and then keep them integrated and balanced at all times! See *The Universal Law of Integrated Spiritual Growth on all Three Levels: Spiritual, Psychological, and Physical/Earthly*. Ascension really is the process of anchoring your Higher Self and Mighty I Am Presence into your Physical Body in an integrated and balanced way and hence achieving your levels of initiation. It is also a process of achieving a 99% Light Quotient level on a Planetary scale. It is also Self-Mastery on a Spiritual, Psychological, and Physical/Earthly level in service of God and Unconditional Love. It is the balancing and integration of your Seven Rays, Seven Chakras, Twelve Archetypes, Twelve Astrological Signs, and Twelve Sephiroth of the Tree of Life. It is the fulfillment of your Spiritual mission, contract, puzzle piece, personal blueprint, and Divine Plan on Earth. It is the full embodiment and demonstration of God and Unconditional Love on Earth and a life dedicated completely to service of one's brothers and sisters!

*   *   *

The Universal Law of Attitudinal Healing

It is our thoughts that create our reality, and there is always a perspective of life that will bring you inner peace no matter what your outer situation. This is the science of Attitudinal Healing. Think with your Christ Mind and you live in a reality that is based on oneness and love. Think with your negative ego mind and you will live in a reality that is based on separation and fear. Our thoughts create our feelings. And there are only two emotions, love and fear. All other emotions return to this basic core. Fear based emotions are expressions of the negative ego, love based emotions are expressions of the Christ Mind. The ego perceives itself as separate, and therefore fear arises as it tries to protect itself. When you view all through your Christ Mind, you see all as one, so love based emotions arise. So you see, your experience of life depends on whether you interpret life from your negative ego mind or from your Christ Mind. The process of accomplishing attitudinal healing is very simple. Imagine that you are surrounded by a golden bubble that protects you from the outside world and other people, and also protects you from your own subconscious mind, in other words, imagine that all of your thoughts, feelings, impulses, desires, and images are outside your golden bubble. All of what is termed the content of consciousness is outside the bubble. The idea, then, is that every time a thought, feeling, or impulse arises from your subconscious mind, you stop it at the gate of the bubble. If the thought or feeling or impulse is positive, loving, Spiritual, balanced, Christ-like, of God, then let it through the bubble and into your mind. If the thought, feeling, impulse, or desire is negative, selfish, fear-based, imbalanced, and not of God, then push it out of your mind. *A Course in Miracles* states, "Deny any thought that is not of God to enter your mind." It takes twenty-one days to cement a new habit into the subconscious mind. After twenty-one days it will be automatic to think with your Christ Mind. It will be easy. It will be a habit. The idea is to fill the subconscious mind with positive Christ-like habits and get rid of the egotistical ones. This process is called the science of attitudinal healing. Be aware though that most people have never been trained in the science of attitudinal healing. Traditional Personality-Level Psychology, practiced by 90% of the psychologists, marriage/family/child counselors, social workers, and psychiatrists, will tell you that it is wrong to get rid of negative emotions. They believe that it is wrong to deny them. They hold that one should acknowledge them and then release them. Do you believe that responding out of anger, defensiveness, upset, fear, depression, attack, violence, and revenge are appropriate responses for a Son/Daughter of God? Look at the examples of the great Masters who have graced this planet, like Jesus, Buddha, Mohammed, Krishna, Gandhi, Mother Teresa, and others. Let this Mind be in you that was in Christ Jesus, Master Buddha, Mohammed, Krishna, Gandhi, and Mother Teresa, and the peace that passeth understanding is yours! Ponder on this!

*   *   *

The Universal Law of Balance and Integration

Integration and Balance. These words hold much power, but no power is achieved unless you strive to attain these goals through daily use in your lives. We must learn to live in balance and integrate God's wisdom into our consciousness! It must become part of our beings without conscious forethought. It must become an automatic unconscious action. How does one achieve Integration and Balance? How do you stay in balance when everything around you seems to be out of balance? This is the time when you focus on your Divinity! This is the time when you focus and tune into God. This is the time when you need to remember your God-given Divinity and know in your being that God will take care of everything within His divine plan. Now, this is all well and good but how can I really learn to do this? Where to start? You start with yourself. "Your Thoughts Are Things And As You Think, So You Are!" You must realize and understand that your thoughts are the first items to be addressed. Changing your thoughts should be the first priority in your life to change your realities! For it is your thoughts that create your reality! You must learn to handle what you can and do it always remaining in the Christ/Buddha/God Consciousness. This is how you achieve balance in your life. It is in this way you shall integrate love and light into your Four-Body System and all of your Light Bodies. You must attain balance in all areas of your earthly life. You must become a Master in all areas of your lives and live in the Spiritual/Christ/Buddha/God Consciousness! You must learn to balance and integrate the Mental/Physical/Earthly/Psychological aspects of your lives! You must be devoted and dedicated, owning your personal power 100%, using your free will choices to constantly keep your thoughts in balance and integrate these principles into your daily lives and into your total beings! Always, no matter what happens in your lives, focusing on your Spiritual/Christ/Buddha/God Consciousness! Always adjusting your thoughts the instant something happens and focusing only on this Consciousness! This simple process will help you to live a life in balance and integration.

*   *   *

The Universal Law of Balancing and Integrating Each New Light Body

It is not enough to only work on one aspect of Ascension and building Light Quotient. You must learn to build each Light Body and level of Ascension in a balanced and integrated manner. What does that mean? With each level of Light Body come very specific life lessons associated with it. You must learn these lessons and live these lessons before you will be allowed to move up the Spiritual ladder. It is not merely enough to request from the Masters your acceleration of Light Quotient and expect to receive it unconditionally. Although the Ascended Masters are ready and willing to dispense this to you at your request, they are more interested at this time in developing your Integrated Light Body as opposed to just your Light Body. Integrated Light Body means you are balanced in all areas of Christ/Buddha/God Consciousness. You are balanced in the Spiritual, Mental, Emotional, and Physical/Earthly aspects of life on Earth. So, as you strive to achieve a new level of Light Body you must realize that you must clearly be focused on achieving integration and balance in this new Light Body. You must learn to focus on integrating the new Light Body into your being, and balance the new Light Body with your existing structure. What does this truly mean to you? As your Spiritual lessons come with each new Light Body, you must learn to live these lessons with sincerity and devotion. "Devotion is not a uniform to be worn on certain days and then to be put aside." (Sai Baba) You must integrate these lessons into your being and they must become a part of your consciousness. It is not enough to be Spiritual if you do not have control of your emotions, your negative ego/fear-based thinking or you have abusive behaviors within your Physical/Earthly existence. How does one achieve this balance? Through the right use of your "will" and the right use of your "power." You have total control over your "will power." You are the Masters of these gifts. These are the God-given gifts of free will. It is through your free will that you make the choices to learn your lessons and live your lessons with devotion and sincerity. There are no shortcuts to this process. You certainly will fool no one but yourself if you think there are shortcuts on this path of Ascension and building Integrated Light Bodies. You must take it one step at a time and build your Light Bodies in a fully integrated and balanced fashion. Ponder on this!

*   *   *

The Universal Law of Balancing and Integrating Heaven and Earth

God Realization cannot be achieved if the Heaven and Earth sides of self are not balanced. Some Lightworkers get way too heavenly and celestially focused and ungrounded. Other people on Earth get way too materialistic and third dimensionally focused. If a person is too Earthly and too grounded they will have blind spots to proper development of their Spiritual life. If a person is too heavenly they will have blind spots as to how to function effectively on the Earthly plane. Spiritual people and Lightworkers must come to love and appreciate the Material Universe and the Earth and see it as one of GOD's Heavens. They must recognize it as one of the "Four Faces of GOD"! The Four Faces of GOD are the Spiritual, Mental, Emotional, and Material Faces. Lightworkers often forget about the Material Face of GOD and think it is less than or not equal to the other faces. Listen carefully! You will not achieve true full God Realization if you do not integrate the Material and Earthly Face of GOD. Remember God's words when He was talking with Moses, "Put off thy shoes from thy feet, for the place whereon thou standest, is holy ground." The Earth is Holy Ground! Your Spiritual mission is to create Heaven on Earth. Your Spiritual mission is to become the Mighty I Am Presence on the Earth. Your Spiritual mission is to manifest your Spiritual mission and Spiritual puzzle piece on the Earth. GOD is as much in the Physical as He is in the Spiritual. You will literally miss out a quarter of GOD if you do not fully understand and demonstrate this. For always remember, the purpose of life is to demonstrate God and Integrated Ascension on the Physical/Earthly Plane, not just in your Mind, or your Feelings, or on the Spiritual plane! You are meant to demonstrate GOD in all your Bodies, the ones in Heaven and on Earth. Namaste!

*   *   *

The Universal Law of Balancing and Integrating the Eight Spiritual Quotients

The Cosmic and Planetary Masters, contrary to popular opinion, are not into "Ascension", they are into "Integrated Ascension." They are not just into "Christ Consciousness", they are into "Integrated Christ Consciousness". The path of true GOD Realization is the path of integration, balance, moderation, synthesis, and synergy in all aspects of self and in all things. If you strive to score high marks on a percentage basis on these following eight quotients, you will be well on your way to becoming an integrated Christ and achieving Integrated Ascension. The eight quotients which would be the new ideal for the understanding of Ascension in this next millennium are: Light Quotient, Love Quotient, Wisdom Quotient, Melchizedek/Christ/Buddha Quotient, Transcending of Negative Ego Quotient, Service and Spiritual Leadership Quotient, Integration and Balance Quotient. Your Light Quotient is the amount of light that you are currently retaining in your aura or 12-Body system. Some of this light is created by your own thinking, feeling, and demonstration of the Presence of GOD in your daily life, and some of it is built by calling to GOD and the Masters to have them channel it into your aura. Your Love Quotient is being increased by calling on GOD and the Masters to infuse you with Love Quotient from the Spiritual Plane. Ask for a Love Shower! On a Psychological Level, your Love Quotient is built by demonstrating unconditional love in your daily life, in all your personal and impersonal relationships. You cannot realize GOD without this quotient, regardless of your level of Initiation. The next ingredient to becoming an "Integrated Christ" is the development of your Wisdom Quotient which is divided into Psychological and Spiritual Wisdom. Building your Spiritual Wisdom Quotient means building your information banks in your subconscious mind. When channeling, you are utilizing the information in your information banks from this life and past lives, hence you will be a better channel of information for the Masters if you fill them. Another way of building your Wisdom Quotient is to call upon GOD and the Inner Plane Ascended Masters to anchor and activate from the Celestial Realms "Light Packets of Information" from some of the different Ashrams of GOD. This type of wisdom will build your Wisdom Quotient, however, you will never truly realize GOD unless you develop Psychological or Psycho-Spiritual Wisdom. This is the most advanced form of the Wisdom Quotient, and when learned and mastered, will allow you to utilize the Spiritual Wisdom you have gathered in a much more efficient and useful manner. Without Wisdom you cannot maintain Unconditional Love, and also cannot use your power appropriately at all times. Balancing the Love and Power takes Great Wisdom! Part of building your Wisdom Quotient, of course, is demonstrating and practicing the Wisdom of GOD! So, the ideal here is to build your Psycho-Spiritual and Spiritual Wisdom Quotient simultaneously. After having discussed the Love and Light/Wisdom Quotients of GOD, it's important to equally balance and integrate the Third Flame of GOD, which is Power! Now this quotient has two levels: owning your Personal Power and surrendering to GOD's Will. You cannot retain Unconditional Love in life, or attain any true Psychological Wisdom if you don't learn to own your Personal Power. If you don't own your Personal Power, then by the laws of energy you automatically give it to other people, life situations, and give it to your mind, emotions, Physical Body, subconscious mind, lower-self desire, inner child, subpersonalities, and negative ego though system. The Spiritual Path is the Path of Self-Mastery. You cannot be a master if you don't own your Personal Power. You cannot be a cause of your reality through your thoughts if you do not own your Personal Power. The second level of building your Power Quotient on a Psychological Level is learning to let go of the negative ego's will and instead surrender to GOD's Will in all things. Have preferences and strive for them with all your heart, and then also surrender to GOD's Will. the third level of building your Spiritual Power Quotient is to anchor and activate the power packets of information from the different ashrams of GOD. The fifth and sixth major Spiritual Quotient to become an "Integrated Christ" are to transcend negative ego thinking, and to only think with your Melchizedek/Christ/Buddha Mind. These two quotients focus upon the joyous vigilance you keep on a moment to moment bases of denying negative ego/lower-self thoughts from entering your consciousness, and replacing them with thoughts of a Christed nature. To say it in Jesus' words, "Deny any thought not of GOD to enter your Mind!" Or as it is written in the New Testament, "Let this Mind be in you that was in Christ Jesus." The seventh major Spiritual Quotient is to develop your Spiritual leadership and Spiritual service Quotient. It is a natural by-product of the Spiritual Path, as you Spiritually evolve and move through your seven levels of Initiation and Ascension development process in becoming an integrated Christ/Buddha to at some point begin to fully claim your personal power, full love, full wisdom, and Spiritual Leadership and find your Spiritual puzzle piece in the Divine Plan as to where you can best be of service to your Brothers and Sisters in the world. The first step is to become right with self and right with God, and to become whole and complete within self once this is achieved. The second step is to then claim your Spiritual leadership. Service is not just a job, it is every moment of your life. The main Spiritual service is practicing the Presence of God every moment of your life, in every thought, word, and deed. Did not Jesus say, "The greatest among you is the servant of all!" The eighth Spiritual quotient is the Integration and Balance quotient which requires the integration, balance, and synthesis of all you have learned in life about self and the world. It requires the balancing of your Three Minds, your Feminine and Masculine, and Heavenly and Earthly selves. It requires the proper parenting of your inner child, the integration of your Seven Rays, twelve major Archetypes, and the learning to think with your Christ/Buddha Mind rather than the negative ego mind. Strive to score high on these eight quotients, and you will be well on your way to becoming an integrated Christ and achieving Integrated Ascension!

*   *   *

The Universal Law of Balancing and Integrating the Feminine and Masculine

It's important to learn to balance the Feminine and Masculine aspects within self. This is one of the prerequisites to achieving Ascension. Balancing the Feminine and Masculine energies is another way of approaching the clearing of the negative ego. Whenever these two complimentary aspects of Self get out of balance, negative ego qualities develop. As with the Archetypes, Rays, Astrological Signs, Houses, and Planets, they each have a negative and positive expression. Every man and every woman needs a balance of both of these energies within themselves. This is called androgyny. When this balance is lacking within ourselves, we usually seek it outside of ourselves in another. Hence we have the father-daughter relationships and mother-son relationships, or variables on this theme. If a person is too Feminine and too overidentified with their Emotional Body and right brain, then they will automatically develop enormous numbers of blind spots in their Masculine side. They will have extremely poor Spiritual discernment. They will likely be very poor in business and mathematical areas. They will likely be very child-like and have blind spots in being more adult and impersonal. They will also have a great many blind spots to the negative ego's thinking because when the Emotional Body is too much in control the negative ego automatically becomes the programmer. Hence, an imbalance of your Feminine and Masculine energies manifests as negative ego emotions and feelings rather than Christed dmotions and feelings. Imbalance equals negative ego, which equals lack of Godliness in that moment. One can, in truth, never lose their Godliness for that is beyond what can be lost. One can, however, lose one's realization of their Godliness in any given moment, which is us falling into glamour, maya, and illusion like in a bad dream. On the other side of the coin, if someone is too Masculine and identified with the Mind, they will have blind spots to the appreciation of the heart energy and feeling energy. They will have blind spots in romantic relationship functioning. They will have blind spots to their own criticalness and judgementalnesss. This issue of balancing the Feminine and Masculine obviously relates very much to balancing one's Four Bodies (Physical, Emotional, Mental, and Spiritual) and the need to balance one's Three Minds (conscious, subconscious, and superconscious). This need for balancing the Feminine and Masculine could be seen in Carl Gustav Jung's "Theory of Types" in which he said there were four types of people: the intuitive, feeling, thinking and sensation/function type. People tend to lean towards one or two types within themselves, however, the ultimate is forever balance. In astrology and Chinese medicine they speak of the need to balance the four elements: fire, water, air, and earth. In nature we see this balance again in the four seasons: winter, spring, summer, and fall. We see this need for balance in the left and right brain. One side of the brain is not better than another. One needs both sides to fully realize God, and to clear away negative ego. The Masculine side provides the power to master your energies. The Feminine side will provide the ability to listen to the intuitive guidance that is always forthcoming in every situation. This will also allow for the blending of the First Ray and Second Ray. This is the blending of the Power and the Love with the Wisdom. Power without love is like Nazi Germany. Love without power is to become Emotionally dysfunctional. A woman likes a man who is strong but sensitive and loving. A centered man wants a woman who is loving and sensitive but who can be strong and powerful. More and more, these two sides of ourselves, which might be considered the ultimate Archetypes, are coming together. The key to our society changing is for this merger and integration to first occur within oneself. The ultimate example of this in our universe is the Lord Melchizedek, our Universal Logos. So again, this ties in with the need to balance the Four Bodies and Three Minds and coming into a proper relationship with the inner child in firmness and love. These are core aspects and the nuts and bolts of the Spiritual Path. The Spiritual ideal is to become Psychologically androgynous. Learning to achieve this is absolutely essential to achieving God Realization. God Realization cannot be achieved if this is not done!

*   *   *

The Universal Law of Balancing and Integrating the Four Faces of GOD

There are Four Faces of GOD: the Spiritual, Mental, Emotional, and Physical/Earthly face. Most often new seekers to the path open up Spiritually with an incredible opening of some kind. Over time however, if the person's psychology and consciousness isn't addressed, in some people problems can take place. Especially those who begin opening to talking with their Spirit guides. If their psychology is still very much personality centered and run by the negative ego and victimized by the Emotions, it will attract more Astral and Mental plane entities rather than the Ascended Masters. In the beginning they may be Spiritual but over time this psychology of the person will draw and attract its frequency and attunement. Being developed Spiritually but not being fully trained in Spiritual psychology creates corruption, personal agendas, self-centered motives, and corruption. Now the reverse of this process is where a Lightworker develops themselves Psychologically but not Spiritually. Some approach the Spiritual Path through the Spiritual door and some through the Psychological door. Those who choose the Psychological door often get involved with traditional psychology and/or fragmented under-standings of Spiritual psychology. Why? Because Spiritual and/or Soul Psychology is so poorly understood in our world. Traditional Psychological theories will actually cut oneself off from their own Higher Self and Mighty I Am Presence. For example, there are a certain number of Spiritual teachers who believe in their psychology that they have to bal-ance everything. Balance is a wonderful thing, however there is one thing we do not want to balance in life and that is negative ego consciousness versus Christ/Buddha Consciousness. Remember, "GOD equals man minus ego!" Sai Baba said "minus" ego, NOT "balance" ego. They are opposite philosophies of life. Balancing the two would be like trying to balance forgiveness and holding grudges, unconditional love and condi-tional love. Holding this philosophy, they may be doing wonderful work on a Spiritual Level, but their psychology is completely corrupting their work and ultimately it contaminates every aspect of the work because their foundation is totally off-kilter. If one is off-kilter in self and one's psychology, it is impossible for this imbalance and off-kilteredness not to exist in their channeling, clairvoyance, healing, Spiritual teaching, Spiritual science work and in relationships. The lack of understanding of the negative ego and the need to transcend it allows the negative ego to run rampant in their personal, professional, and Spiritual lives. The dan-ger of the person coming through the Psychological door is that they get stuck in a particular Psychological theory, and this creates a certain lens they get stuck in for seeing life. What happens is this type of person attracts and magnetizes people and Lightworkers of a similar imbalanced philosophy yet still Spiritual. They think they are getting healthy feedback from others but really what they are doing is just attracting a small group of people who keep collectively reinforcing their Psychological neurosis. It is only when we see life through the full spectrum prism of Soul and Spiritual psychology, and are able to demonstrate this self-mastery in our daily lives, can full integrated Self-Realization and God Realization take place. Now, the third aspect is the Physical/Earthly Level. Some Lightworkers become highly enamoured with the Spiritual Level and become too ungrounded and create Physical health problems. They may be highly Spiritual, however they may not eat right or exercise. They may drink too much coffee or smoke cigarettes, which eventually takes a toll on their Physical health. They may eat too much sugar or not get enough sleep. All their energy is in their higher Chakras and very little energy in their lower Chakras and this will take a toll on the Physical organs and glands in the Physical Body. Another way this problem manifests is that the person is raising their frequency Spiritually at an astronomical rate, however, if the Physical Body isn't evolved at a similar rate of growth in terms of raising the frequency, one can and will get sick a lot. This is a type of cleansing crisis to raise the vibration and frequency of the Physical Vehicle to catch up with the Spiritual Vehicle. So the question is how does one raise the frequency of the Physical Body? This is done by eating a good diet, Physical exercise, sleep, grounding one's Spiritual energy, holding and demonstrating a proper Spiritual psychology, connecting with nature, practicing the Presence of GOD on Earth and creating Heaven on Earth in your daily life. If one does not take care of the Physical Body, one can develop chronic Physical health lessons which greatly impede one's Spiritual and Psychological progress. Life becomes much harder when the Physical Body is not supporting the Spiritual and Psychological work. Take care of your Physical Body as well, for as you know it is the Temple of the God you are. Sai Baba has said that our Physical Bodies are a house rented to us by God. We live in the Physical Body as long as God wills it, and we pay God rent by demonstrating faith, devotion and Spiritual sadhana or Spiritual practice. Imbalance can also occur in the Physical Body if the Psychological Level is not addressed properly. The subconscious mind runs the Physical Body; this can be clearly proven by the practice of hypnosis. Most people don't have mastery over their subconscious mind, emotions, and negative ego. This causes too many negative thoughts, negative emotions, and too many negative orders given to the subconscious mind which will cause it to manifest all kinds of Physical health problems, pain, and illness. Every thought you think manifests in the Physical Body. Every emotion you feel manifests in your Physical Body organs and glands. Your psychology totally affects your Physical immune system. If you do not have a healthy Psychological immune system over time you are going to have a weakened Physical immune system. So, people are often sick, fatigued, exhausted and not in good Physical health because of overidentification with the Spiritual, improper psychology, improper care for the Physical Vehicle and then living in a world filled with Physical pollutants such as smog, petrol chemicals, chemical pollutants, drugs, pesticides, imbalanced ozone layer, polluted water, polluted air and polluted Earth, caused by imbalanced psychospiritual relationships to the Earth in the mass consciousness of the world. It is actually amazing that our Bodies function as well as they do, given all the abuse they take. In conclusion, always remember that God lives as much in the Physical and material universe as He does in the Emotional dimension, Mental dimension, and Spiritual dimension. It is absolutely essential that we pay our rent to all Four Faces of God in a balanced manner. This includes working to revamp our Earthly society and civilization as well as taking care of the Earth Mother and nature. As we enter the New Millennium and the Seventh Golden Age it is now time for Lightworkers to fully ground their Spiritual Paths on Earth and dedicate their lives to transforming our civilization and society into a fifth dimensional, fully functioning society on Earth. For too long Lightworkers have waited to ascend and escape Earth. This New Millennium, Aquarian Age, and Seventh Golden Age now teaches us just the opposite. Love the Earth, love nature, and love our society and civilization and make it reflect God in a similar manner that His other three faces reflect on a Spiritual, Mental and Emotional Level. It is now time to manifest GOD on Earth and in our society and civilization. It is not God's job and it is not the Inner Plane Ascended Masters' job. It is our Spiritual assignment and mission for we are the ones inhabiting Physical Bodies. Transforming our Earthly civilization into one that functions fully on Spiritual principles in all its countries and institutions is not an easy task. It is, however, what we have collectively come here to do. Let us now take hold of the sword of Archangel Michael in a balanced manner and courageously and joyously realize our destiny and fully realize the "Great Souls" that we collectively are!

*   *   *

The Universal Law of Balancing and Integrating the God/Goddess Within

This is a new Spiritual ideal and balance for Lightworkers to focus on. The Divine Mother, the Lady Masters, the Earth Mother and the Goddess Energies have taken a beating in Earth's history. The patriarchal nature of our society has caused them to recede into the background. Finally, the return of the Goddess has come! And we each have a part to play by integrating the God/Goddess within ourselves whether we are female or male! No one will achieve full God Realization without learning to balance the God/Goddess within! The Goddess Energies, although in truth fully balanced and integrated from the "Full Spectrum Prism Perspective" of the Divine Mother, classically have to do with the proper integration of unconditional love, compassion, feminine nature, feelings, the Earth Mother, the Nature Spirits and Devic Kingdom, Spiritual joy, Spiritual passion, Spiritual enthusiasm, Spiritual desire, and the proper integration of the inner child. It is the understanding that on the right and left sides of God are the Divine Mother and the Divine Father. They are on the two sides of the Cosmic Tree of Life as well. Creation cannot be understood or realized without fully integrating the God/Goddess within. Ponder on this!

*   *   *

The Universal Law of Balancing and Integrating the Horizontal and Vertical Planes of GOD

There are two planes of GOD that need to be fully mastered, balanced and integrated in order to become a full-fledged Ascended Master and Self-Realized Being. There is the vertical plane of GOD and the horizontal plane of GOD. The vertical plane deals with one's direct relationship to GOD and the Masters. The horizontal plane deals with one's relationship to your Brothers and Sisters on Earth and to Earth life in general. What often happens in Lightworkers is that they become more developed in one of these planes to the slight neglect of the other. There are those who become very introverted and focus their lives on GOD and their Spiritual Path, however, in doing so they isolate themselves from other people. On the other extreme there are those people on Earth who are immersed in Earth life and in relationships of all kinds, however, are a little weak in their vertical development. They may spend all their time with people in socializing and working at their job, and may not, in essence, spend enough time cultivating their relationship to GOD. Both of these paths, in truth, are not good. It is easy to be Spiritual when you live in a cave. Master Jesus taught about the importance of living in the market place. Or as Sai Baba so aptly put it, "Hands that help are holier than lips that pray." It's very important to get involved with Earth life and be of service. GOD's Plan is it to create Heaven on Earth, and this cannot be done if Lightworkers do not get involved with Earth life. On the other side of the coin, if you get involved with Earth life and do not properly cultivate the vertical plane, the demonstration you will be doing on Earth will not be as pure and refined as it could be to your own Spiritual Path and to others. Some of the tendencies to be more vertical or horizontal stem from past lives. If you had many lives as a Buddhist, ascetic lives, or Hindu lives or lives as a Priest or Priestess, there may be a subconscious tendency to be more horizontal. On the other side of the coin, if you have had most of your past lives immersed in Earth life then the opposite is true. The most important thing is to try and be balanced in this life. The true goal of life is to be an integrated and balanced Spiritual Master!

*   *   *

The Universal Law of Balancing and Integrating the Seven Rays

This law stresses the importance of mastering and integrating the Seven Great Rays of GOD. These Seven Rays make up what is known esoterically as the "Personality of GOD!" GOD's Personality is divided into three parts and seven parts. GOD is first divided into the Trinity of GOD, which of course is GOD, Christ, and the Holy Spirit, GOD being the Creator, Christ being the Eternal Self we as the Sons and Daughters of GOD are in truth, but are in the process of realizing, and the Holy Spirit, which is the Voice of GOD and the "still small voice within," which speaks for the Atonement or the At-One-Ment. Each person was created by God under the auspices of one of these Seven Rays! Said in another way, their monad, or their Mighty I Am Presence is under the auspices of one of these Rays. This Monadic Ray does not change! Each incarnation, the Soul Ray, Personality Ray, Mental Ray, Emotional Ray, and Physical Body Ray do change, to help the incarnating Soul develop new and different aspects of self! These Rays have an enormous influence on the incarnating Soul, even more than any Astrological influence. So, our Ray readout tells us how GOD created us and what we came into this lifetime with. The goal is to integrate and master all of them. People who have not started on the Spiritual Path are dominated by the Rays of their Physical, Emotional, and Mental Bodies. As the person develops a more self-actualized personality, then the Personality Ray becomes dominant and the three Body Rays (Physical, Emotional and Mental) become subordinated to it. As we continue to evolve, the Personality Ray becomes subordinated to the Soul Ray which in return will become subordinated to the Monadic Ray. This process continues throughout the steps of Initiation, with each successively higher Ray becoming dominant over the previous one. This hierarchical order proceeds step by step to the Godhead! In different lifetimes, the Physical, Emotional, Mental, and Personality Rays change to allow the incarnating personality to develop a more holistic perspective. All of us need to exhibit the qualities of each of the Seven Rays. All of us need personal power, love, activity or action, artistic sensibility, scientific development, devotion, and business acumen. Although we incarnate with a certain Ray structure, we need to integrate and master all the Rays. If we are deficient in any one of these, our whole personality will become imbalanced. Each Ray, although characterized by a specific quality, is in truth whole and complete within itself and carries within it the qualities of all the other Rays. And in blending with the other Rays, an even greater whole is created. Well, since everyone comes into incarnation with one Ray influencing their monad or Mighty I Am Presence, there are eight different types of Ascended Masters. The first seven types spring forth of the first Seven Rays, whereas the eighth type of Ascended Master is the type that knows how to master and integrate all Seven Rays and hence truly demonstrates the full nature of GOD on Earth! The First Ray type of Ascended Master is highly developed in their Personal Power, God's Will, Spiritual Leadership, and may achieve their Ascension working in the field of politics, government, international relations. Also, in leadership, in a business, as soldier, explorer, pioneer, or executive. The Second Ray type of Ascended Master is highly developed in the Love/Wisdom Aspect of God, and will achieve their Ascension usually in the field of being a Spiritual Teacher or Educator. Also, in writing, public speaking, television, radio, and so forth. The Third Ray type of Ascended Master is highly developed in the quality of Active Intelligence aspect of GOD. This is an aspect of Wisdom and Intelligence that is very active in the Physical world. This could be in the area of business, finance, economics, or they could be serving as organizers, diplomats, or bankers. The Fourth Ray type of Ascended Master is highly developed in the quality of Harmony and Beauty. This type of Ascended Master achieves their Ascension most often in the Arts! Being an artist, musician, composer, architect, and so on. Any area dealing with the Arts, and creating more beauty and harmony in the world! The Fifth Ray type of Ascended Master is highly developed in the quality of Concrete Science! This type of Ascended Master achieves their Ascension working in one of the great many scientific professions. They may be a doctor, psychologist, chemist, mathematician, metaphysician, surgeon, inventor, lawyer, and so on. The Sixth Ray type of Ascended Master is highly developed in the quality of Devotion and Idealism! This type usually achieves their Ascension as a priest or minister. Also in philosophy, philanthropy, missionary work, or as reformer and healer, to name but a few! The Seventh Ray type of Ascended Master is highly developed in the quality of Ceremonial Order and Magic! This translates into development in the qualities of organization, structuring, alchemy, invocation, and freedom! This type of Ascended Master you usually find serving in the area of restructuring society in some way, or in business and economics, as priest, doctor, nurse, or sculptor to name a few! The Eighth type of Ascended Master is the "Integrated Ascended Master" who may still have a profession in one of these areas, but they do it fully operating out of Mastery and Integration of all Seven Rays! No matter what your Ray Configuration, and no matter what your Astrological Horoscope, and no matter what your Numerology is, you must develop all Seven Rays, all Signs of the Zodiac, all 22 Numbers of God, all Twelve Archetypes of God, all the cards of the Tarot Deck, and develop Mastery on a Spiritual, Psychological, and Physical/Earthly Level. If you do not do so, you will be filled with blind spots and see life through a limited lens! Now, there are Planetary Rays, Solar, Galactic, Universal, Multi-Universal and Cosmic Rays. Not only is it possible to call forth and utilize the Twelve Planetary Rays, it is also possible to call forth and utilize the Ten Lost Cosmic Rays. The Twelve Planetary Rays consist of the Seven Rays spoken about plus the Five Higher Rays which are combinations of the first Seven Rays with a touch of Source Light, or white Light, that gives them a luminous quality. They have only been recently activated in relationship to humanity's evolution. (Ray Eight: Ray of cleansing; cleans out characteristics and qualities within self that one no longer needs and wants to get rid of; green-violet luminosity. Ray Nine: Ray of joy; Ray that begins to attract the Body of Light; also cleansing function; greenish-blue luminosity. Ray Ten: helps to facilitate the Soul merge experience and to code the pattern of Divinity into the Physical Body; allows the Body of Light to be fully anchored into one's being; pearlescent-colored luminosity. Ray Eleven: deeper cleansing function; bridge to New Age; orange-pink luminosity. Ray Twelve: Ray of anchoring the Christ Consciousness on Earth; summit of all the Higher Rays; combination of all the Rays with a sprinkling of white Light and Christ Consciousness; golden.) Now, part of understanding this *Universal Law of Balancing and Integrating the Seven Rays* is also that each Ray has a higher and lower expression. This is because the Rays, although created by GOD, can be misused and corrupted by the negative ego/fear-based/separative thought system. Each of the Rays can be used in service of the negative ego or in service of the Soul. Your goal should be to overcome and transcend the lower aspects of all the Rays in order that you are free to manifest each Ray's highest potential within your Being.

Glory and Corruption of the First Ray: One either owns their personal power 100% in total service of GOD and unconditional love plus surrenders to GOD's Will. Or one owns their personal power to hurt, control, and manipulate others for reasons of selfishness and does not surrender to GOD's Will but consciously or unconsciously follows the will of the negative ego mind; the negative ego has you either surrender to GOD's Will and not own your personal power or it has you own your personal power and not surrender to GOD's Will.

Glory and Corruption of the Second Ray: Ability to unconditionally love self and others at all times, and the Psychological wisdom it brings to help one do this in all situations and with all people. Or conditional love, being overly loving and not having a backbone, being overidentified with the guru role, being a know-it-all, since the Second Ray is that of education.

Glory and Corruption of the Third Ray: Wisdom to put out our God Consciousness into demonstration and action on and in the Earthly world. Or being overintellectual, lack of proper integration of one's feelings and emotions, being run by the mind instead of being its master.

Glory and Corruption of the Fourth Ray: Creation of harmony, unity and oneness at all times with self, and in relationship to others and one's world, creation of the arts in glorification of GOD. Or—on a Psychological Level—the negative ego thought system creating disharmony and conflict within self which would manifest in conflict with others.

Glory and Corruption of the Fifth Ray: On a Psychological level, the use of the mind in a scientific way for the purpose of healing all aspects of a person and our society. Or being overintellectual and cut off from one's feeling and intuitive nature, worship of science, rejection of religion, too much focus on concrete mind, and not allowing oneself to tap into the abstract mind, the Higher Mind and intuitive right brain mind.

Glory and Corruption of the Sixth Ray: Devotion, Spiritual passion, enthusiasm, joy, idealism; glory of sixth Ray makes us strive for the highest within us, and pursue excellence at all times. Or, being overly Emotional, giving power away, being too idealistic to the point of being a negative perfectionist, lack of Spiritual discernment

Glory and Corruption of the Seventh Ray: Emphasis on freedom, Divine structures and systems within self and society that lead to even grater freedom within self and society, Spiritual alchemy, prosperity Consciousness. Or thinking that one is free when in truth they are run by the negative ego, Emotional Body, Mental Body, the inner child, lower-self desire, and the subconscious mind; misuse of structure (having too much or too little), use of magic without Spirituality, misuse of money, poverty consciousness; freedom is not giving free reign to one's negative ego, Emotional Body, and so on; this is not freedom, but being a victim; true freedom stems from total Self-Mastery of one's energies in service of GOD.

*   *   *

The Universal Law of Balancing and Integrating the Ten Sephiroth

The Tree of Life is composed of Ten Sephiroth or Spiritual centers. There is an Eleventh Spiritual center called Daath, which refers to the hidden wisdom that is opened when one attains higher initiate status, and a Twelfth Sephiroth—the Sephiroth of Synthesis. Each of these Sephiroth embodies a certain psychospiritual quality. Now, the Tree of Life can be used to help clear the negative ego. Each Sephiroth has a higher and lower expression. There is no lower expression of the Sephiroth of Daath, for it doesn't come into manifestation until the higher expression has come into play. People often end up identifying with one of the Ten Sephiroth just as people end up doing this with the Twelve Archetypes. The idea is to integrate and utilize all Ten Sephiroth in their higher expressions in a balanced and appropriate manner. One can imagine the Tree of Life as superimposed over the Physical Body and Etheric Body much like a Chakra System. When one Sephiroth is not integrated properly this will prevent the Prana from flowing properly through the Etheric Body which will create Physical and Psychological symptoms. Every person, when they come into this world, is usually predominate in one Sephiroth. This is the great Psychological work that needs to be done. Strive to embody all the Sephiroth in their highest expression.

Kether or Crown Sephiroth: Higher expression: person puts Spirituality as their top priority, but is also able to keep their Physical life in balance; Heavenly and Earthly life is well balanced. Lower expression: too heavy or over-identified with Heavenly energies at the expense of their Physical Body and Earth life; the Psychological and Earthly Levels are not integrated properly due to an imbalanced mindset.

Chokmah or Wisdom Sephiroth: Higher expression: person with innate connection to Divine wisdom who is realizing their potentials; Emotionally balanced and quite steady and evenminded; strong connection to the proper will/wisdom balance; connected to the Divine Father and the male aspect of Divinity; great occultist, psychologist or Master Spiritual Teacher; Lower expression: weak will function; wisdom on the level of the concrete mind rather than the Higher Mind and abstract esoteric mind; too conservative, limited in certain subconscious and conscious patterns; wisdom more of the personality rather than the progressing wisdom of the Soul and monad.

Binah or Understanding Sephiroth: Higher expression: one who carries the Divine Mother; great mystic; embodiment of receptivity, love, compassion, and understanding, with still the strong expression of the Divine Will; Lower Expression: person who is talking too much; not just compassionate but too empathic; mother is a co-dependent rather than a Divine expression of unconditional love and non-attachment; over-mothering, too selfless, not knowing how to take care of self. Kether, Chokmah, and Binah form a triad that the Kabbalah calls the Supernal Triad; they form the Monadic Level of the Tree of Life.

Chesed or Mercy Sephiroth: Higher expression: deals with emotions and feelings of unconditional love and compassion; mercy administered in a very balanced way; also deals with the Christ quality of justice and fairness; Lower expression: person feels like they have never been treated fairly or justly and that they are victims of mercilessness; they often think they are giving mercy, but, in truth, what they are doing is victimizing themselves.

Geburah or Serenity Sephiroth: Higher expression: discernment, self-control, and Divine Will (balance to Chesed); person is always centered and in the Middle Path; they are always at inner peace within themselves and at inner peace with other people; they are serene and are very much the peacemaker in a very positive sense of the term; good in political situations for they have the serenity and strength of will to remain clear and centered; excellent mediators and arbitrators; Lower expression: person who is undiscerning in life; problem making decisions; not decisive; they don't know how to retain their personal power; in essence, they are out of balance and are always struggling; no mastery over emotions, victimized by the outside world and other people; talk about the importance of being strong but not demonstrating it.

Tiphareth or Beauty Sephiroth: Higher expression: person who sees beauty in everything, rather like the fourth Ray type in its higher expression; they create beauty all around them; have the strength of beauty about themselves; Lower expression: vanity; instead of selfless interest in beauty, this is tainted by a self-interest in beauty beyond the quality of Godliness; they want everything to be beautiful for themselves not as a service for God and humanity. Chesed, Geburah, and Tiphareth deal with the Soul level of the Tree. If you are identified with the triad that lies below this one, you are identifying yourself as a personality or Physical Body rather than as a Soul.

Netzach and Victory Sephiroth: Higher expression: person who sees justice and triumph; if a person is just in this Sephiroth it may manifest only on a personality Level of self-actualization and not necessarily at the Soul or monadic level of victory; at the personality Level of victory, we might have the great athlete, conqueror, or successful psychologist; connected with the feeling nature; Lower expression: tyrant or dictator; person who always needs to win and be the "top dog," and is extremely competitive; they have not yet learned to transcend the negative ego game of superiority/inferiority complex; this type of person always needs to be right and is hence very self-righteous; they strive for victory at all costs, even at the expense of their own Soul; they make bad decisions when in a leadership role because of the negative ego; they always need to hide any sense of weakness or vulnerability because of their need to be the best.

Hod or Splendor Sephiroth: Higher expression: person who is a great organizer; since Hod is focused on the personality level, if not blended with other Sephiroth, it will remain more on the level of the concrete mind; opposite of Netzach; not focused on the feeling state, but on logic, thinking, and analytical perception on the personality level; Lower expression: person who is disorganized; they are often very limited in their perspective, and see life through a very small selfish lens and hence do not see the bigger picture; often striving for splendor but are doing so in service of the negative ego rather than the splendor of Spirit; grandeur versus grandiosity; misjudging self and others; weakness of the Mental function allows the Emotional Body to have too much sway.

Yesod or Foundation Sephiroth: Higher expression: person has made subconscious mind their servant and has learned to tap and utilize the unbelievable abilities of the subconscious mind; person is very strong in their convictions, has faith, and has mastered fear; they can go into the most difficult situation and handle themselves extremely well; often heroic; will often take a job no one else will do because they are so grounded and strong in their foundation; foundation of all advanced Spiritual work is a healthy psychology which has its foundation in the relationship between a person's conscious and subconscious mind; person might be psychic but not necessarily Spiritual if not blended; Lower expression: person is completely victimized by the subconscious mind; they are on automatic pilot and not conscious, vigilant, and do not have Personal Power attached to their conscious mind; are weak and fearful in all situations. Netzach, Hod, and Yesod make up the Lower Spiritual Triad; they deal with the personality level, and are only a reflection of the Soul level of existence, just as the Soul level is a reflection of the monadic level of existence.

Malkuth or The Kingdom Sephiroth: counterpart to Kether in the crown. Higher expression: person who can live like a king on Earth; when just developed in this one Sephiroth they are Physically very strong and healthy and function extremely well in Earth life; not necessarily developed on the Soul or monadic level; born with a very strong Physical constitution; good Physical capabilities; lesson of this type of person is to learn to blend the Soul level and then finally the monadic level into this Earthly function; Lower expression: person who is ridden with fears of Physical illness or is a hypochondriac; person who is fearful of money and Physical survival; preoccupied with First Chakra concerns; often very superstitious.

*   *   *

The Universal Law of Balancing and Integrating the Three-Fold Flame

Each person must own their 100% Personal Power in life to realize GOD and be successful in every aspect of life. Each person must own their 100% unconditional love at all times towards self, others, all kingdoms of GOD and the Earth, to fully realize GOD. Each person must own their 100% Psychological and Spiritual Wisdom at all times to fully realize GOD. It is when all three of these flames are operating at 100%, being perfectly integrated and balanced, that this aspect of God Realization can be achieved! Love, Power, and Wisdom need each other. All of us on the Spiritual Path certainly recognize the importance of Unconditional Love. The ability to demonstrate this, however, is easier said than done. The only way a person can be unconditionally loving at all times is if they have completely transcended the negative ego and all negative ego thinking and feeling. They secondarily must at all times think and process their reality from the Melchizedek/Christ/Buddha attitude system. There is also no way a person can be unconditionally loving at all times if they don't 100% own their Personal Power at all times, which allows you to maintain Self-Mastery and vigilance over your thoughts, feelings, emotions and energy. Without your Personal Power you will be a victim of your subconscious mind, Emotional Body, inner child and negative ego. There is no way you can be a Master instead of a victim or a cause instead of an effect in life, no way you can control the negative ego and remain in God Cosciousness if you don't own your Personal Power. On the other side of the coin, without Unconditional Love, Personal Power becomes a total agent of the negative ego and becomes a corruption of the highest order. These two Christ/Buddha qualities are intricately tied together! The third aspect of this trinity is Wisdom.

Wisdom is an essential ingredient and quality in the process of Self-Realization and successful living. To use your Personal Power always in an appropriate manner in every situation of life, and to remain unconditionally loving at al times and in all situations, takes enormous Wisdom. To constantly monitor one's every thought, feeling, word and deed and to keep your energies and Three-Fold Flame always appropriately balanced takes enormous Spiritual Wisdom, Psychological Wisdom, and Physical/Earthly Wisdom. To be joyously vigilant over one's every thought and impulse to make sure that one's motivations are always of highest order and not tinged by selfish desires and personal agendas of the negative ego, takes enormous Wisdom. It is only when these three qualities are perfectly balanced within self and within the sacred chamber of your own heart that true Self-Realization and full-fledged Integrated Ascension can take place.

*   *   *

The Universal Law of Balancing and Integrating the Twelve Archetypes

In William Shakespeare's *As You Like It*, it says, "All the world is a stage. And all men and women merely players." Archetypes are underlying mythic themes that can be found in all races and cultures at all times. The Archetypes are ageless roles or key stereotypes that exemplify different forms of behavior. In other words, the Archetypes are universal personifications of perennial themes. Every person fits into one of these Twelve Archetypes or mythic themes. And we are manifesting one or more of the

Archetypes every moment of our lives. It's a good idea to become familiar with them, for if we don't, we are opening ourselves to be victimized by their unconscious expression. The Archetypes, left to their own discretion, will attempt to monopolize our attention and expression. It's very important to understand that Archetypes don't reason. Each Archetype's primary goal is to express itself. By taking control of your personality and becoming the executive director, you can make them work with you in a cooperative manner. But they must have a leader. And well, son of a gun, you are the that leader, but you must own your Personal Power and maintain absolute Mastery and tough love, for the Archetypes are like children. If they don't take you seriously, they will not listen to you. So you really need to be conscious at all times and not live as if on automatic pilot. If we are not conscious, then mass consciousness, past lives, parental programming, and so on will determine our Archetypal expression at any given moment. We must strive to be not the effect but the cause! The ultimate goal of this science now is to enable you to integrate all Twelve Archetypes, along with all the Subarchetypes, with the Wise One as the main Archetypal theme during your last life. The Wise One Archetype, because its main role is to achieve complete balance, incorporates all the Archetypes within itself. The idea is also to integrate all of them from the perspective of being the Fair Witness or Observer. The conscious mind is not any of the Archetypes, but it chooses which role you need at any given time for the highest expression of God and service. When you integrate all the Archetypes you have infinite possibilities of expression and are not stuck in any one role. You have all of them available in their positive aspects when you need them. So, you are none of the Archetypes! Archetypes are roles that you are playing! Always remember, the real you is the observer self, who controls, directs, chooses, and causes. You can direct and control only what you do not identify yourself with. Whatever you, as the consciousness or "I", are identified with will be your Master. Identify yourself with only the Eternal Self for that is your True Self! Archetypes, past life aspects, and subpersonalities are all related. When God created us, these

Archetypal potentials were built into us from the start, like a psychic substructure. As we went through the reincarnation process, these past life aspects began to build up as we lived out one ore more of these Archetypal themes. In our present life all our past life aspects are manifested as our subpersonalities. So past lives manifest as programmed subpersonality expression in our subconscious mind. It takes some effort in the beginning to reprogram them, but after twenty-one days the old expressions will be working for us instead of against us. Like other Spiritual sciences, the science of the Archetypes is a tool for gaining Self-Mastery over the mind, emotions, and body in service of the Soul. Tarot might be the premier system of working with the Archetypes. Well, as always, the negative ego manifests the negative side of the Archetype and distorts each Archetype's true purpose as created by GOD. In a sense, the negative ego works through all the Archetypes just as the Soul and monad do. Hence, as with Astrology or the science of the Rays, and all the other Spiritual sciences, each of the Twelve Archetypes has a positive and a negative side. And the goal now is to reject the negative ego and lower-self expression and always attune oneself to the Soul and Higher-Self expression. The ultimate goal in your final incarnation on Earth is to integrate all of them and be victimized by none of them. It's important to remember that every Archetype or role has an opposite. This is why you can't in truth identify with any single Archetype but must embrace all of them from the position of the Witness self! To become an Integrated Ascended Master of the highest caliber, you must transcend the lower expression of each Archetype and only strive to demonstrate their higher expressions!

Destroyer Archetype: Higher Expression: Positive use of first Ray (power) to destroy the old and make place for the new, positive anger, used for destruction of negative ego in all its manifestations and to make positive change, healthy use of denial, very tied up with the Psychological issue of owning your Personal Power! Lower Expression: Destruction, glorified violence, abuse, control, domination, negative anger, power used in service of self, and criminal behavior.

Fool Archetype: Higher Expression: Risktaker, humor used in a positive and uplifting manner, superconsciousness, innovator, jumping off the cliff in service of the Soul as the ultimate healthy surrender in any given situation and lesson! Lower Expression: Scatterbrained and prone to the use of negative control and manipulation, being foolhardy and blind! "The fool who knows he is a fool is for that very reason wise. The fool who thinks himself wise is the greatest fool of all." (Shakyamuni)

Innocent Archetype: Higher Expression: Innocent perception, seeing life free from past programming, fresh and untarnished, positive side of being like a child, being innocent with the wisdom of the Wise One Archetype, purity, harmlessness, Spiritual discernment, Holy Encounter! Lower Expression: Being too naïve and childlike and lacking in Spiritual discernment, not being able to see darkness in self or others!

Magician Archetype: Higher Expression: True alchemists and transformers, magical in the way they can create change and transformation in one's Four-Body system (they do this by understanding Universal Laws at each level and applying them), egoless, true servant of the Divine, skill, diplomacy, self confidence and will! Lower Expression: Using one's Magician powers for the purpose of manipulation, to seduce others to follow oneself; false gurus, counselors; Black Magic!

Martyr Archetype: Higher Expression: Saint, Vow of Bodhisattva, the higher you go the more one realizes that the main reason for being here is being of service! Lower Expression: Person sacrifices but does so as a means to manipulate and control others, performing sacrifices as a kind of guilt trip, not realizing that there is a time to be selfless and a time to be Spiritually selfish!

Matriarch/Patriarch Archetype: Higher Expression: Tough love (love and firmness), proper use of Personal Power and Unconditional Love, Divine indifference in its proper relationship to compassion, parenting inner child! Lower Expression: Either weak father (not protecting the inner/outer child, being wishy-washy and totally controlled by the Feminine which turns the Feminine into its negative aspect) or the totalitarian, control-obsessed father (being over-protective, too militaristic, and too controlled by the Masculine); hence Feminine/Masculine imbalance!

Ruler Archetype: Higher Expression: Divine objectivity, fairness, wisdom, stability, all of us rule over our thoughts, emotions, body, subpersonalities, Archetypes, instincts, sensations, and intuition, and all of us will be put into positions of leadership as we evolve; Which kind of ruler will you be? Lower Expression: Tyrannical, dominating, and manipulative leader; drunk with power which may manifest as a superiority complex!

Seducer Archetype: Higher Expression: Spiritual salesperson who "sells" GOD, egolessness, oneness, salesman with pure motivations, positive use of self-talk (need to seduce inner child, subconscious, Emotional, Mental and Physical Body to cooperate), motivational speaker and ultimate Spiritual teacher! Lower Expression: Negative manipulation, bribery, molestation, narcissistic love of self, self-indulgence, and corruption; deceiver, the con man, the fast talker, the unscrupulous used-car salesman, the tempter or temptress, the amoral businessperson; negative Seducer Archetype uses everyone and everything to manipulate and seduce to meet its own selfish needs!

Seeker Archetype: Higher Expression: Adventurer, explorer, pioneer, wanderer, seeker who seeks the inner rather than the outer, the permanent rather than the impermanent, "See ye the Kingdom of God and all things shall be added unto thee"! Lower Expression: Person who seeks materialistic goals and gains and not the path of Ascension and Self-Realization; on the Physical level accruing money and material things; on the Emotional level seeking hedonistic pleasure and experiences; on the Mental level seeking of intellectual development of the concrete mind and not of the Higher Mind!

Servant Archetype: Higher Expression: Servant of God, the Masters and humanity, serving from wholeness instead of emptiness, from Personal Power, self-love, self-actualization, egolessness, and attunement to God, vow of Bodhisattva, "True pleasure is serving God"! Lower Expression: Servant of others from an unevolved state of consciousness which can manifest on outer level (i.e. wife who serves the demands of a selfish husband out of fear, lack of self-love and self-worth, or lack of personal Power and Spiritual attunement) and inner level (i.e. being a slave to drugs, alcohol, bad habits, obsessive thoughts, feelings, Archetypes, sexuality, food, the Physical Body, the negative ego, the desire body, the concrete mind, the child consciousness, or the subconscious mind); you are either a Master or a victim, a servant or the served!

Warrior Archetype: Higher Expression: Spiritual warrior, fighting for love, oneness, Christ Consciousness, for the good of the whole, owning your power, without owning the positive aspect of this Archetype you will be very ineffective in life and make yourself powerless, weapons are love, prayer, God..., "Life is a battlefield", "Get up and give up your unmanliness and get up and fight. This self-pity is unbecoming of the great Soul that you are" (Krishna to Arjuna)! Lower Expression: Unevolved Soul who is run by the negative ego and looks at life as a war; manifests as criminal behavior in its worst case scenario; on an Emotional level, being pervasive in terms of negative anger or abusive behaviors directed toward other people, animals, or even the environment; on an inner level it can manifest as abuse of self; on a Mental level as "attack thoughts" toward self or others!

Wise One Archetype: Higher Expression: True teacher who seeks to empower their students and make them equals; guide and teacher of all the other Archetypes (lifts all the other Archetypes into the Soul directed expression), fair witness or observer, you are in charge of the Archetypes and not the other way round, you are the president and director and will use each of these as tools! Lower Expression: Using wisdom to control others, to manipulate, demean, gain fame, for power, money, praise, or special status!

*　　　*　　　*

The Universal Law of Balancing and Integrating the Twelve Signs of the Zodiac

The Twelve Signs of the Zodiac need to be integrated and mastered as do the Twelve Archetypes and Twelve Rays. The fact that you are born under one Sign obviously has its influence as does your Ray Chart, however, this doesn't change the fact that all Signs need to be mastered. This is why we spend many lifetimes incarnating into all the Sun Signs to get the most complete view of Self. The Sun Signs then could be looked at as major Archetypes. As with the Rays and Archetypes, each Sun Sign has a higher and lower expression. If you are a victim in life and do not own your Personal Power, the stars will influence the type of choices you make. However, even if there are a lot of negative aspects in your total horoscope remember that you are God in truth, and God created the stars, the stars did not create God. There is no force more powerful in the infinite universe than your will. In this regard, you are the total master of Astrology. To realize God you must master all Twelve Signs of the Zodiac. The key as always is to develop yourself in the higher aspect of each of the Twelve Signs, and to transcend its lower aspects.

Capricorn—"I Use": Positive attributes are: patient, persistent, efficient, practical, ambitious, hardworking, integrity, strong, solitary and alone, dependable, purposeful, leadership, humility, confident, disciplinarian;

Danger areas are: clinging to past, and possible clinging to mother, false pride, self-righteousness, lack of empathy, cold, selfish, arrogant, street angel and house devil, materialistic; Key lesson is love and service.

Aquarius—"I Know": Positive attributes are: Mental pioneers, future focused, outgoing, involved detachment, impersonally friendly, confident, mind over emotions, work focused, home focused, individualists, creative, inventive strong-willed, leaders, organizers; Danger areas are: Mentally cold, cruel, critical, demanding, lacking in love or mercy, lack of self-control, difficulty at times in marriage; Key lesson is development of inner knowing that goes beyond just faith!

Pisces—"I Believe": Positive attributes are: faith, sensitivity, introspective, enjoys alone time, psychic, inner peace, compassion, devotion, musical, strong and deep emotions; Danger areas are: self indulgence, inferiority complex, unworthy, workaholic, restriction, limitation, moody, hard to understand, go with the flow attitude even if the flow happens to be negative; Key lesson is coming to a right relationship with self and God in terms of one's beliefs.

Aries—"I Am": Positive attributes are: self-directed, assertive, strong, pioneers, full of energy, filled with good ideas, leaders; Danger areas are: impatience, impulsiveness, arrogance, egotism, tendency to dominate; Key lesson is coming to a right relationship to self, and understanding one's true identity.

Taurus—"I Have": Positive attributes are: steady, kind, gentle, holds possessions and material things in great value; Danger areas are: over-possessiveness, jealousy, greed, fear of loss, stubborn; Key lesson is coming to a right relationship to the things you have or possessions.

Gemini—"I Think": Positive attributes are: logic, wit, humor, independent, liberty, facility in communication; Danger areas are: lack of concentration and persistence, extreme restlessness, two-faced, dramatize, neurotic, preoccupation with self, butterfly; Key lesson number one is developing a right relationship to your mind; are you the Master of your mind, or is your mind your Master? Key lesson number two is to harmonize one's Spiritual and Earthly life.

Cancer—"I Feel": Positive attributes are: mothering, nurturing, focused on house and home, passive, receptive, psychic; Danger areas are: too emotional, possessive, insecure, self-centered, selfish, sluggish in energy, Physically lazy; Key lesson is to develop a right relationship to one's feelings and emotions; are your feelings and emotions under your control, or are they running you?

Leo—"I Will": Positive attributes are: honesty, directness, dependable, faithful, dignity, self-respect, integrity, courage, energy, confidence, kingly; Danger areas are: inability to delegate authority, dominion over others and attachment to loved ones; Key lessons are impersonal love, coming from the heart, detachment, serving the Spiritual self rather than the ego self, and developing a right relationship to the use of will or power in one's life; is power used in a top dog manner for dominion over others, or can power and will be used in a Spiritual manner for unconditional love, equality, and for the highest good of all concerned?

Virgo—"I Analyze": Positive attributes are: idealism, affinity for details, work and service, focus, practical, down to Earth, importance upon home, refined, quite, gentle; Danger areas are: irritability, shyness, jittery, too cautious, inferiority complex, selfishness, difficulty in communicating inner thoughts and Feelings; Key lesson is developing a right relationship to the analyzing mind; in its proper usage there is the ability to correlate, digest, and collect facts in service of a Spiritual purpose; the negative ego side would be analyzing what turns into judgmentalness and criticalness of self and others.

Libra—*"I Balance":* Positive attributes are: friendly, outgoing, conscientious, just, will to do good, cooperative, focus on marriage, love, cohesiveness, travel, diplomatic; Danger areas are: people pleaser, and seeking approval from others, dominating beneath; Key lesson is the balancing of inner and outer worlds; sign of Libra focuses on relationships; there is a need to be involved with life but not to lose self in a relationship or life in general.

Scorpio—*"I Create":* Positive attributes are: strong, quiet, exterior, command respect, creative, resourceful, strong passions, not easily known, reserved, strong pride, Emotions do not show on surface, dynamic, majestic; Danger areas are: supercritical nature, judgemental of others, stubborn, vindictive, jealousy, resentful, sarcastic, lone wolves, rough time in relationships; Key lesson is developing a right relationship to one's creative energies; do your create energies serve your personality or egotistical self, or Higher Spiritual Self?

Sagittarius—*"I Perceive":* Positive attributes are: friendly, outgoing, optimistic, extroverted, sports, gambling, takes changes, independent, future focused, travel, direct. Danger areas are: superficial, procrastination, nervous, tactless, disorganized, undisciplined; Key lesson is development of intuition and understanding of the Higher Mind and Spiritual aspects of life.

      *   *   *

The Universal Law of Balancing and Integrating Your Chakras

Chakras are like non-physical organs within the Etheric Body, aligned along the spine corresponding to points along the central nervous system, and are associated with certain glands and nerve ganglia. At times one or more of these Chakras may be out of balance, which results in either Physical disease or Mental or Emotional distress. We have 330 Chakras that reach all the way back through the 352 Levels back to Source. They basically come in sets of seven, according to the Dimensional Grid with which they are associated: Third-Dimensional Chakra Grid—Chakras 1 through 7, Fourth-Dimensional Chakra Grid—Chakras 8 through 15, Fifth-Dimensional Chakra Grid—Chakras 16 through 22, Sixth-Dimensional Chakra Grid—Chakras 23 through 29, Seventh-Dimensional Chakra Grid—Chakras 30 through 36, Eighth-Dimensional Chakra Grid—Chakras 37 through 43, and Chakras 44 through 50 make up the Ninth-Dimensional Chakra Grid, to give you an idea. We have 50 Planetary Chakras, 50 Solar Chakras, 50 Galactic Chakras, 50 Universal Chakras, 50 Multi-Universal Chakras, and 80 Cosmic Chakras. It is possible to anchor these Higher Chakras into the Seven Third Dimensional Chakras that we are all aware of. There are three levels of understanding in the process of anchoring the Higher Chakras: installation, actualization, and accessing the Chakras' abilities, or utilization. Call forth to the Inner Plane Ascended Masters and ask for their help in anchoring, activating, and merging with these Chakras. How do you actualize the Chakras? It is basically done by living a God-inspired lifestyle. The third step lies in the ability to access the Chakras' abilities some of which are materialization of things, teleportation, and bilocation. Part of the whole process is asking for all chambers and facets of the Chakras to be opened and activated! Well, as you evolve Spiritually, your Seven Third-Dimensional Chakras will move into your legs, feet, and

Earth, and will be replaced by these Higher Chakra Grids. Now it must be understood that every thought you think is reflected in the Chakras. Every negative ego thought you allow in your mind will reflect itself in the Chakras as being overactive or underactive. This is why so many people have overactive or underactive glands. Their improper thinking causes the Chakras to be overactive or underactive, which causes the glands to be overactive or underactive. (1st Chakra: gonads, 2nd Chakra: lyden gland, 3rd Chakra: adrenal glands, 4th Chakra: thymus gland, 5th Chakra: thyroid gland, 6th Chakra: pituitary gland, 7th Chakra: pineal gland) It is only when you practice and realize the goal of becoming an Integrated Melchizedek/Christ and Buddha that your Chakras can truly be balanced. Perfectly balanced Chakras are a byproduct of becoming an Integrated Melchizedek/Christ/Buddha. It is only when we fully integrate and balance first all Seven Chakras, and in the course of our journey back to the 352nd Level the rest, that true God Realization can be achieved. There are some on the Spiritual Path who favor the Higher Chakras and think the first three are lower or unimportant. All Chakras are equally important! All Chakras need to be equally balanced. Those who do not fully balance and integrate their lower Chakras will not be right with self, which will corrupt their relationship to GOD, the Masters, all channeling, and a great deal of their Spiritual teaching. Neglect of the lower Chakras would also greatly decrease your energy level and could also lead to glandular, hormonal and organ imbalances as well as the potential of other Physical health problems. Learn by grace instead of karma, and heed the wisdom of that which is being shared with you here. In summary, the Chakras are another great key to understanding the nature of GOD. He built into us Seven Great Chakras, each representing another Divine Quality and aspect of the Divine!

First Chakra: Deals with importance of grounding, survival, and taking care of one's Earthly responsibilities as well as one's Physical Body! Negative ego's effect in terms of underactivity: overly focus on issues of survival, not having enough money to pay bills and eat, and possibly homeless issues. Also, instead of being able to focus on one's Spiritual life and service, just making it through Earth life and surviving becomes the focus. Negative ego's effect in terms of overactivity: being overly materialistic, too focused on money and business, having an improper diet, too focused on Earthly life, too caught up in the enjoyments and pleasures of Earth life, too grounded to the point of being disconnected from Spirit, and so on. The ideal is to get this Earthly aspect of life together so one can focus on higher Spiritual pursuits, taking care of Physical Body and developing mastery of prosperity consciousness.

Second Chakra: Deals with sexuality, procreation, creativity, and relationships with other people and one's Emotional Body! Negative ego's effect in terms of underactivity: non-sexuality can manifest as no energy being in this Chakra. If you choose celibacy which of course is a valid life choice for some, then adjustments need to be made to bring energy into these Chakras. Physical exercise, doing Hatha Yoga, stretching, certain Polarity exercises and most of all just being integrated Spiritually, Psychologically and in a Physical/Earthly sense will do this. Friendships and relationships will also help fill the energy in this Chakra. Also, those who are too closed in their feelings and emotions will have less energy in this Chakra. Negative ego's effect in terms of overactivity: overindulgence in sexuality which causes a weakening of the lydig gland, and will put a strain on the kidneys and other organs as well. Also, those who are too run by their Emotional Body, too focused on friendships and relationships, and too horizontal to the neglect of the vertical will have too much energy in this Chakra. Integration and balance is as always the key.

Third Chakra: Deals with the Mental Body and Emotional Body, the two bodies being intimately connected since it is our thoughts that create our feelings and emotions. The Third Chakra is also connected to our Personal Power and Will. It is connected to the proper use of our mind and the proper integration of our feelings and emotions! Connection to the adrenal glands! Negative ego's effect in terms of underactivity: caused by a person not owning their 100% Personal Power, not utilizing the full power of their mind, or not causing their reality with the use of their mind. Also, not causing their Emotional life by seeing and demonstrating that their feelings are caused by their thoughts! Negative ego's effect in terms of overactivity: too much adrenaline in our system which is not good for adrenaline is meant to be used for emergency energy only. Too much in the system will have a weakening effect, and cause "adrenaline exhaustion" which is why many people are tired so much of the time. This causes the body's energy systems to have to pull on other glands for energy, which over time can weaken them as well! Also, overuse of Will, Will Power, Personal Power will deplete person.

Fourth Chakra: deals with the importance of opening one's Heart and Unconditional love! Negative ego's effect: the Fourth Chakra remains in balance and focused on Unconditional Love when we think from our Spiritual Mind. When we think from our negative ego mind, the Heart Chakra becomes imbalanced, for conditional love, addictive love, anger, lack of forgiveness, and so on, have been allowed to enter your consciousness and are hence reflected in your Heart Chakra. Heart Chakra is immune system. If you see life with your Spiritual Mind, your Physical immune system will function much more perfectly. So Unconditional Love is the key to perfect health!

Fifth Chakra: Deals with the importance of communication! When this Chakra is in balance we communicate from our Spiritual/Christ/Buddha Consciousness. Imbalances would manifest as gossip, speaking judgementally about others, bad-mouthing others behind their back, breaking confidentiality, backstabbing, to name but a few. If you don't have anything nice to say, don't say anything at all! Negative ego's effect in terms of underactivity: undercommunication, "There are sins of omission or commission"! The key is to know when to talk and when to be silent. Negative ego's effect in terms of overactivity: too much communication. Overuse drains the thyroid gland. Person may process too much, or be too overidentified with service. May talk too much for they do not know how to quiet their mind, feelings, and emotions, or are not whole within themselves, or don't know how to just "be".

Sixth Chakra: Deals with opening our Spiritual vision (occult vision, mystic vision, and Psychological vision), is connected to the opening of all your Spiritual senses. See *The Universal Law of Opening the Third Eye*, and *The Universal Law of the Three Levels of Spiritual Vision*. Negative ego's effect: the key is not to underuse or overuse the Third Eye and Sixth Chakra, but to fully open it and keep it in balance with all the rest of the Chakras.

Seventh Chakra: Deals with opening one's Crown Chakra, and one's relationship to GOD, Christ, the Holy Spirit, our Mighty I Am Presence, our Higher Self, the Inner Plane Ascended Masters, the Archangels, and Angels, Elohim Councils, Christed Extraterrestrials, All Knowledge, Universal Mind, the Divine Mind, intuition, perfection, and God Realization! Negative ego's effect: overactivating and stimulating the Crown Chakra to the improper integration and balance of the other Chakras. Could result in improper grounding, all the energy being in the Etheric Body in the upper Chakras and not in the lower ones. This could cause headaches, not embodying the Physical Body, not grounding one's Spiritual mission on Earth, living in the Heavenly world, but not properly integrating the Psychological Level, or Physical/Earthly Level. If the Crown Chakra is not opened enough, the pineal gland will be understimulated or nourished. If the Crown Chakra is overactivated, the pineal gland will become overstimulated and eventually exhausted. Any Chakra that is over or under identified will create "blind spots" Spiritually, Psychologically, and in a Physical/Earthly sense, which is antithetical to God Realization.

        *   *   *

The Universal Law of
Balancing and Integrating Your
Four-Body-System

Everyone has four distinct energy bodies, each with a different and unique perspective: a Physical Body, an Emotional Body, a Mental Body and a Spiritual Body (which consists of many bodies, in truth). The Physical Body reacts instinctively and senses. The Emotional Body focuses on how we feel in any given moment or situation and might provide psychic impressions. The Mental Body gives us a logical perspective regarding what's going on and the Spiritual Body gives us intuition, conscience, and GOD's guidance. The ideal is to respect and listen to all four simultaneously. Often we tend to overidentify with one or the other. Some people feel life as their main function, others think about life and are less concerned with their feelings. Still others are so involved with their Spiritual Body that they don't take care of their Physical Body, or may not even care about thoughts or feelings either. And well, still others are caught up in their Physical Body, being completely cut off from their Spiritual Body, and maybe even intellectual pursuits. The Spiritual ideal and Spiritual balance here is simple. We all must be balanced in these four bodies. The mind must be balanced with the feelings. Each person must see and practice how our thoughts create our reality, our feelings and emotions. All people must see there are two ways of thinking and only two. You either think with your Spiritual Mind or with your negative ego mind, the ideal being to think only with your Spiritual/Christ/Buddha Mind. On the other side of the coin, we must also properly integrate our feelings and emotions. We must be Masters and not victims in life, and cause our feelings and emotions but simultaneously integrate them. This manifests as unconditional love, joy, happiness, bliss, compassion, Spiritual passion and enthusiasm, to name just a few. We also need to integrate our

Spiritual Body. This is the Spiritual Body of our own Higher Self and Mighty I Am Presence. The whole process of Ascension is to first anchor your Higher Self and merge, integrate, and become one with it, and then merge with your Mighty I Am Presence. The other key of course is to also integrate the consciousness of your Spiritual Body into your Mental, Emotional, Etheric, and Physical Bodies as well. Many just anchor it Spiritually and not Psychologically or Physically. For it is absolutely essential that each person achieve Spiritual mastery, Psychological mastery, and Physical/Earthly mastery and then integrate and balance these aspects of self. This is an essential principle of balancing the Four Bodies. Lastly, each person must balance and integrate the Physical Body. Eat right, exercise, get proper sleep and rest, fresh air, a little sunshine and so on. It's much easier to stay focused and keep Self-Mastery on all levels if your Physical Body is taken proper care of. The Spiritual Path is a lot harder if the Physical Body is not properly loved and cared for. It is a part of the Four Faces of GOD as well! How can you perform your Spiritual mission and walk the Earth as a fully integrated Mighty I Am Presence and integrated Ascended Master if you don't fully honor, respect, and take care of your Physical Body? Part of the lesson of the Four-Body System is to get all the bodies working for the same purpose, which is to grow Spiritually and to realize GOD. Many of us understand this with our Mental Body but haven't yet aligned the other bodies with this truth!

*   *   *

The Universal Law of Balancing and Integrating Your Four Minds

𝔍t's of utmost importance for us to learn to balance, integrate, and equally develop the four minds—subconscious mind, conscious mind, superconscious (Soul, Oversoul, Higher Self) mind, and monadic mind. Each mind is a level of mentation or thinking. The ideal is for the subconscious mind to become subservient to the conscious mind and for the conscious mind to become subservient to the superconscious mind, or Soul. At the third Initiation, this mind is merged with, and the monadic mind becomes each persons' teacher. At the seventh Initiation, one merges with the monadic mind. So these minds become linked like circles on a key chain. As one learns to become an Integrated Spiritual Master these circular links on a key chain become more and more merged and integrated until the four minds function as one mind. So, in other words, our conscious self is meant to become the Master of the subconscious mind, with the Soul or Higher Self acting as our Master Teacher or Guide. The conscious mind allows us to reason, whereas the subconscious mind operates at a more basic, instinctive level. The Soul/monadic mind is the all-knowing mind. A metaphor that illustrates how they work is to think of the conscious mind as a gardener. The gardener plants the seeds (thoughts), and the soil (the subconscious mind) grows whatever kind of seed is planted, be it a weed or a beautiful flower. The subconscious mind will follow orders whether they are rational or irrational. The subconscious mind doesn't care because it has absolutely no reasoning. It has no powers of reason on its own, yet it has an incredible number of abilities and intelligence factors. The best illustration for understanding this is the computer analogy. A computer is an astounding piece of equipment, capable of performing millions of computations per second, yet it doesn't care whether it's programmed to solve the problem of world hunger or to create a nuclear war. It has the capability to do either job efficiently, but it doesn't have the reasoning power not to want to create nuclear war. In the same vein, the subconscious mind does whatever it is programmed to do, no matter what. It has the intelligence to crate perfect health or cancer. It will create whatever it has been programmed to. Other functions of the subconscious mind include storing all of our thoughts, feelings, emotions, imaginings, habit patterns, impulses, and desires. From our infancy we have been programmed by our parents, grandparents, peers, teachers, ministers and extended family, not to mention television. All those exchanges of information have been stored in our subconscious. The key now is to consciously reprogram our subconscious mind! Methods of reprogramming our subconscious mind include doing affirmations and creative visualizations, journal writing, using affirmations cards, going on affirmation walks, using endless tapes, hypnosis and self-hypnosis, creating a picture of your desired reality, and acting as if, to name but a few tools to working with the subconscious mind! Well, let's continue with some other functions of the subconscious. Most dreams originate in the subconscious mind. See *The Universal Law of Dreams*. The subconscious mind can also be termed the habit mind for it stores all of our habits, both positive and negative ones. See *The Universal Law of Habits*. It further has the ability to sense the radiation of energy of any substance, not just water. It can be programmed to search for any Physical substance. The subconscious mind is also known to be the seat of our psychic abilities. The subconscious mind has five inner senses—clairvoyance, clairaudience, inner smell, inner taste and inner touch—that are the subtler counterparts of our five external senses. Now, the key function of the conscious mind is to be the programmer, protector, and Master of the subconscious mind. The subconscious mind is meant to be the servant of the conscious mind. Most people, not understanding how these Psychological laws operate, let their subconscious mind run them. When this happens, we become victims. The subconscious mind was never meant to direct our life. It will run us into oblivion if we let it, not because it is bad, but because it has no reasoning. In and of itself the subconscious mind is Divine; however, why would anyone let a nonreasoning mind run his or her life? Strangely enough, this is what most people do. The conscious mind can also be imagined as an inner gate or inner bubble that protects us from our own subconscious mind. When a thought or feeling or impulse arises, it is the conscious mind's task to use its powers of reasoning, discernment, and discrimination to check that thought at the gate. If the thought or impulse is positive, we let it into our mind. If it is negative, we push it out. Practicing this will ensure Psychological health. It is pretty much like Physical health. If we want to be Physically healthy, we put good, healthful food into our bodies. If we want to be Psychologically healthy, we put good, healthful thought into our minds. By pushing the negative thoughts out of our minds, we are refusing them energy. This is much like not watering a plant. The plant eventually withers and dies from lack of water (attention and focus). Once we have pushed the negative thought out, the second step is to affirm the opposite positive thought or Spiritual thought. This is called attitudinal healing. By continually disregarding the negative thought and affirming the positive thought, we can form a new habit in the subconscious mind within twenty-one days. The old habit dies because we are not giving it energy. *The Universal Law of Balancing and Integrating Your Four Minds* basically states that all four minds eventually need to merge and become one mind and function as one mind—the Soul and monadic mind guiding the conscious mind, and the conscious mind giving orders to the subconscious mind. It is of the highest importance in life to balance one's development in each of the four minds. If a person is developed in the conscious mind they will have a great deal of Personal Power, Self-Mastery, and will be very much the cause of their reality. If one is developed in the subconscious mind, the person will have a great deal of creative ability, access to their feelings and emotions, psychic abilities and artistic abilities. Many past life gifts resurface through the subconscious mind of abilities developed in ancient times. This is why a young girl could be a master painter without ever being trained. This is why a ten-year-old boy could have already graduated from college and have an IQ that is off the charts. Other abilities could be dowsing, working with a pendulum, healing abilities, and musical abilities. The list is endless. Most people do not realize that psychic abilities and clairvoyance, clairaudience, and inner taste stem from the subconscious mind and not the superconscious mind. Very often what happens is people tend to be either highly developed in their subconscious mind or superconscious/soul mind. The development of the conscious mind usually goes along with high Mental development. If a person is developed in the conscious mind but not the superconscious/soul and monadic mind, their consciousness and abilities might be very scientific, rational, and concrete in nature, but will not be attuned to the Higher Mind or abstract mind. If a person is developed on a subconscious level and not a superconscious/soul and monadic level, the person will be very developed artistically but the art will not have any Spiritual flavor. They may be highly developed psychically but they may not even believe in GOD. The superconscious/soul mind development deals with the higher senses and abilities that transcend the senses of the conscious and subconscious mind, like intuition, knowingness, higher comprehension, attunement to Higher Mind and abstract mind, to name but a few. It is only when these four minds are equally balanced that full GOD Realization can take place and full Integrated Ascension can take place! "Do not conform any longer to the pattern of this world but be transformed by the renewing of your mind. Then you will be able to test and approve what God's will is—his good, pleasing and perfect will." (Romans 12:2 NIV)

         *　　　　　 　　　　　 *　　　　　 　　　　　 *

The Universal Law of Balancing Selfishness and Selflessness

There is a time to be selfish and a time to be selfless. To be selfless is to direct your energies toward helping others. To be selfish is to take care of yourself. Balance is as always the key! We are not here to be martyrs and completely sacrifice ourselves for others. We must learn to be Spiritually selfish, not negative ego selfish. This may come into play in terms of having proper boundaries, or the need to be impersonally loving at times, or just taking care of the Physical Body so that we don't burn ourselves in doing service work. Being Spiritually selfish is an important quality in its place. Many Lightworkers get trampled on and then are filled with resentment because they don't understand this precept. The common belief is that it is egotistical to be selfish and Spiritual to be selfless! However, selfishness has a positive and negative component, as does self-lessness. People often are turned off to the idea of being saintly because of this misunderstanding. The true saint knows how to be Spiritually selfish when necessary. So, "the greatest among you is the servant of all", as Jesus said, but you have to take care of yourself also. "Do nothing out of self-ish ambition or vain conceit, but in humility consider others better than yourselves. Each of you should look not only to your own inter-ests, but also the interests of others." (Philippians 2:3-4 NIV) Sai Baba said, "Self is lovelessness; Love is selflessness." So take heed of those Biblical words and the wisdom of Sai Baba, but make sure you have it all in proper perspective. You are a child of GOD. You are a part of GOD. Not to be Spiritually selfish at times is to reject a part of GOD. If you are too selfless, you will probably be resentful. The lesson here is that when you are selfish, don't feel guilty, and when you are selfless, give and don't feel resentful. Be decisive in whatever choice you make! May the word of Lord Buddha seal this paragraph, "Only when envy and (*negative ego*) selfishness are rooted out of him may he grow in beauty."

*   *   *

The Universal Law of Being Spiritually Vigilant Against Limited Lens Seeing

It's very important for all of us to develop a "Full Spectrum Prism Consciousness"! Often people have disagreements, and it is not so much that they are coming from their negative egos as much as they are seeing things from different lenses. Some of these lenses are: race, religion, socioeconomic background, past lives, gender, age, country you grew up in, parental program, cultural programming, professional lens, type of education, to name but a few. It must be understood now that we don't just see with our Physical eyes, we see through our mind. Our thoughts create our reality. Our thoughts create our feelings and emotions! Thoughts are images in our mind! We see through our belief systems, through our perspective, through our perceptions and opinions! The mind is an amazing instrument! It can make you see whatever it wants you to see. Some people see out of power, some out of love, some out of wisdom. People see out of one of the Rays and don't see out of the others. People see out of some Chakras not others. People see Emotionally and Mentally. People see Spiritually and do not see with their five senses. Some people see out of the child, some out of the parent! People see out of one Sign of the Horoscope and are blind to the others. People see out of the negative ego and only see anger or fear! People see out of Spiritual/Christ/Buddha Consciousness and see only Love! One person sees a stranger and another sees the Christ. "Be not forgetful to entertain strangers: for thereby some have entertained angels unawares." (Hebrews 13:2) To one the glass of water is half empty, and to the other it is half full! Most people have no idea how limited their consciousness is by all these lenses! How many people have developed themselves in all Seven Rays, all Twelve Archetypes, all the Signs of the Zodiac, all Ten or Twelve Sephiroth of the Tree of Life? How many are balanced in all Seven Chakras? Any Chakra you overidentify with, or underidentify with, manifests as limited lens seeing. Some people only see out of survival, some people only see from sexuality! Why limit to one Chakra, why limit to one Ascended Master, why limit to one Spiritual teacher, why limit to one Sephiroth? When we integrate all paths, religions, Spiritual teachers, mystery schools, gurus, Ascended Masters, psychologies, philosophies, Spiritual teachings into unity and integration, what has happened is the infinite strands of GOD have become one Path! The Path of Synthesis Integration! All the strands, no matter how beautiful, are still lenses of GOD! Imagine seeing life from all strands and lenses of GOD, free from all imbalance, negative ego/fear based thinking and feeling, and free from all Earthly mass consciousness limited lens seeing! Now, let's say you have achieved Spiritual, Psychological, and Physical/Earthly Mastery, and you have fundamentally achieved all the balances and integrations brought forth in this book on the Universal Laws of GOD and this whole *Easy to Read Encyclopedia of the Spiritual Path*, and have learned to transcend negative ego/fear-based/separative thinking and feeling and have reprogrammed your conscious and subconscious thinking and feeling to the Spiritual/Christ/Buddha thinking and feeling, and so forth, even after all this is fundamentally achieved, it is so incredibly easy to fall back into limited lens seeing. Look what happened to Lucifer. He is a Fallen Archangel! Falling back into limited lens seeing can happen to anyone at anytime! Life, in truth, is a process of making constant adjustments—Spiritually, Mentally, Emotionally, Energetically, and Physically! All that is left to be said is: Kodoish, Kodoish, Kodoish, Adonai

'Tsabayoth! Holy, Holy, Holy is the "Full Spectrum Prism Consciousness of GOD!" Namaste!

*   *   *

The Universal Law of Building One's Antakarana

The Antakarana, or Rainbow Bridge, is the thread, and later the cord, which the disciple creates through meditation, understanding Spiritual practices, and specific, focalized Spiritual work. The disciple does receive help from the Soul and later the monad in this process, but the first part of the work must be done by the disciple. The Higher Self does not pay much attention to the unconscious Soul until it pays attention to the Higher Self! The monad has a thread or cord of energy, called Sutratma, Life Thread, or Silver Cord, that extends from it to the Heart Chakra of the disciple on Earth, and the Soul has a thread or cord that extends from it to the pineal gland of the disciple which is called Consciousness Cord. The Sutratma and Consciousness Cord work from above downwards, the Antakarana works from below upwards. Later, in the final stages of the building of this cord, at the fifth Initiation and Ascension, these three cords merge, integrate, and blend together, just as the personality, Soul, and later on, monad, merge. How does the building of one's Antakarana take place? It occurs in stages. The first stage deals with integrating the personality and the four bodies. The second stage is then building the bridge from the integrated personality and four bodies to the Soul. The third stage is building the bridge from the Soul to the Spiritual Triad and then the monad itself, the Spiritual Triad being the three interrelated aspects of Spiritual will, intuition, and the Higher

Mind, that make up the Three-Fold vehicle that the monad works through on Earth. The Antakarana in actuality does not just stop at the monad. It continues all the way back to the Godhead. Now, it's important to not only build the Antakarana up through the Soul and monad but also down through the Chakra Column to the base of the spine and then down into the Earth. This is called the Grounding Cord! How do you now actually build the Antakarana? Saying the Soul and monadic mantra (I am the monad/Soul, I am the Light Divine, I am Love, I am Will, I am Fixed Design) activates the monad, Soul, and Soul Star to do Spiritual work, the Soul Star being an instrument through which the Soul works through— an Etheric star of Light about six inches above the head. The Central Canal (Chakra Column, Sushumna) is the column of energy that extends from the base of the spine to the top of the head. It's important to widen the central canal and clear it of all Psychic debris. There are three meditations, given by Djwahl Khul, that are for the distinct purpose of widening and clearing the Central Canal and building the Antakarana. It is through the Antakarana and Central Canal that the Soul and Spiritual energies can flow! Those three meditations are The Triangulation Meditation (helps to clear your Central Canal and begins to build your Antakarana), The Spiritual Whirlwind Meditation (clears all unwanted material out of your auric fields), and The Corkscrew Meditation (to widen the central canal to the size of the circumference of your head). Please see *The Complete Ascension Manual* for detailed description. Make sure the Central Canal is built in a uniform manner from the Earth and feet to the crown, otherwise the energy can become dispersed and congested, causing Physical health problems. This issue speaks to the importance of proper grounding as well as attunement to the Soul and monad!

*   *   *

The Universal Law of Channeling

A great many people in this world think that if it is channeled, it is true. Nothing could be further from the truth. Not only is most channeling coming from the Mental or Astral Plane, but even when it is coming from the Ascended Masters and/or Spiritual Planes, because of the nature of channeling, it is filled with the belief systems, personality, philosophies, and personal agendas of the person who is doing the channeling. The development of one's consciousness enormously affects the channeling process, even within the finest channels on this planet. For a channel for GOD and/or the Ascended Masters is only as good as the development of one's consciousness in a holistic perspective. If a person's consciousness is not developed and balanced, the channelings and all psychic readings for that matter that come through that person will reflect that imbalance and ultimately be in danger of negative ego corruption, personal agendas, and contamination by the belief system of the person who gives the channeling or psychic reading! This is not a judgement upon channelers, it is just the nature of the process of channeling itself. To give an example here, a person who is developed in the First Ray of Power will bring through powerful, commanding, and charismatic channelings. If developed in the Second Ray of Love/Wisdom, the channeling will be filled with love and Spiritual wisdom. If developed in the Third Ray of Active Intelligence, the channelings will reflect keen intellectual knowledge and very practical information, whereas a person developed in the Fourth Ray of Harmony and Beauty will bring through very poetic and beautiful words. If, however, the channeler is not developed in the First Ray, the information will lack a certain power, and if undeveloped in the Second Ray, lack certain Unconditional Love and/or specific Spiritual Wisdom. A person developed in the Fifth Ray will bring forth incredible New Age science information, a person developed in the Sixth Ray will bring forth very devotional channelings, and if developed in the Seventh Ray, the channelings ill

come through in a very Divine order, with a certain pomp and circumstance. Now, let's have a look at the channeling process from the lens of
the Chakra system. We all know that we create our own reality by how we
think. This manifests within the Chakras as the Chakras being too open,
too closed, or balanced. The overstimulation or understimulation of the
Chakras is connected to our seven major glands. Improper thinking causes
the Chakras to be overactive or underactive, which causes the glands to be
overactive or underactive. Well, let's have a look at the channeling process
now. If developed in the First Chakra, the person will be very grounded
and their channelings will be very attuned to Mother Earth; if there is only
little energy in the First Chakra, the channeling will be very heavenly or
mentally oriented. If overactive in the Second Chakra, channelings will be
very emotional in nature and usually very creative and poetic; if undeveloped in this Chakra, the channelings will be dry and intellectual. If a person is overactive in the Third Chakra, the channeling will be powerful and
commanding, and timid, shy, and soft if underactive. Fourth Chakra:
channelings will either be extremely loving and flowery, or very scientific
and dry. Fifth Chakra: channelings are either highly communicative or
focused on silent meditation. Sixth Chakra: highly mental and filled with
visions and psychic experiences, or just very technical information. And if
the Crown Chakra is overactive, then there will be a lot of information
and light, but it will be very ungrounded and not integrated. It will be
Spiritually uplifting but the person receiving the channeling will not know
how to integrate it. If undeveloped in this Chakra, channeling will be
more earthly in nature. Every thought you think is reflected in the
Chakras. Every negative ego thought you allow in your mind will reflect
itself in the Chakras as being overactive or underactive. It is only when
you practice and realize the goal of becoming an Integrated
Melchizedek/Christ and Buddha that your Chakras can truly be balanced.
Perfectly balanced Chakras are a byproduct of becoming an Integrated
Melchizedek/Christ/Buddha. The ideal channel of information for the
Aquarian Age is to become as integrated and balanced as possible within

self, so the Love, Wisdom, Power that comes through your channel is integrated and balanced in nature. This means carrying a balance of the Seven Rays. This means carrying a balance of the Three-Fold Flame of GOD of Love, Wisdom, and Power. This means reflecting a balance of the Seven Chakras, as well as the Twelve Major Archetypes, and the Twelve Signs of the Zodiac. It is perfectly in Divine Order for everyone to reflect a certain Ray or theme of GOD for that is how GOD created us. So, the key understanding here is not that everyone should be exactly the same, or do channelings exactly the same way. The ideal is that every person strive to become an Integrated Melchizedek/Christ/Buddha in their practice of the Presence of GOD on Earth, and in doing so, even though your channelings may have a tinge or theme of your own monadic and Soul Ray, your channelings will also be reflective of being an Integrated Melchizedek/Christ/Buddha! One last thought on the issue of channeling: an enormous number of people and Lightworkers give their power to external channelings! Lightworkers are being asked by the Cosmic and Planetary Hierarchy to be much more discerning regardless of who the external channeled entity claims to be. Remember, in truth, there is no such thing as channeling. There are only people at different levels of Psychological and Spiritual development bringing through guidance that is being reinterpreted by all their filters, lenses, belief systems, subconscious programming, and level of Psychological vision. Take all external channeling with a grain of salt, and trust your own inner guidance above all else for the above mentioned reasons, and never give your power or your Spiritual discrimination and sword of discernment away ever again!

*   *   *

The Universal Law of Christ Consciousness

Christ Consciousness is not just for Christians. Christ Consciousness, Buddha Consciousness, Krishna Consciousness, God Consciousness, and the Consciousness of all religions are all the same thing. Just different words for one and the same thing. Swami Sivananda said, "Know well that the heart of the Vedas, the heart of the Bible, the Holy Koran, the Sacred Gathas, and all the world's scriptures are, in truth, one, and they sing in unison the sweet message of love and concord, goodness and kindness, service, and worship." In *A Course In Miracles*, the introduction says, "This is a course in miracles. It is a required course." What this means is not that everyone has to study the books, but rather that everyone has to learn the basic message contained therein which is to learn to undo the negative ego's thinking and to replace it with Christ Consciousness. There are only two ways of thinking or philosophies of life! Negative ego thinking and thinking with your Christ mind! You cannot go through your Spiritual Initiations and realize GOD without transcending the selfish, materialistic, fear-based mind of your ego. The core of *A Course in Miracles* instructs us that GOD created us, and our true identity is the Christ. Said another way, we are all Sons and Daughters of GOD, made in GOD's image. In the Old Testament the Jewish prophets said, "Ye are Gods and children of the Most High." David, in the Psalms, said, "Be still and know, I am God." Your true identity as the Christ cannot be changed. That is how GOD created you. You can think you are something other than this, but that does not change reality. You are the Christ, whether you like it or not. You have no choice in this because you didn't create yourself, GOD created you! The Spiritual Path is really not about trying to get any-place. It is just about reawakening to who you are. It is about demonstrating and being who you are! You are the Christ! So it's about demonstrating your true identity which is the Christ, the Buddha, the Eternal Self. So,

The Universal Law of Christ Consciousness is as simple as BEING a living Christ in your everyday life! Demonstrating Christ Consciousness in the marketplace and transcending negative ego, fear-based, separative thinking and feeling! What is the negative ego? If there had to be one word that describes negative ego more than any other, it is fear. And if there is one word that describes the Christ Consciousness more than any other, it is love. There are in truth only two emotions in life: love and fear. All other positive and negative emotions have these at their core. To understand fear is to see that it is projected attack. When we attack others we live in fear of *The Universal Law of Karma* operating in our own mind. This is why *A Course in Miracles* says to give up all our attack thoughts. Probably the greatest test of the Spiritual Path is to learn to release all core fear and to replace it with core love. When we have released all fear, we have released and transcended negative ego consciousness, and hence can live in Christ Consciousness. One of the great dispensations of the Twentieth Century given to us by the Ascended Masters has been the Core Fear Matrix Removal Program. With the Ascended Masters' help, this advanced technology can remove all the core fear programs from this life and all your past lives in a very short time. *A Course in Miracles* says there are no neutral thoughts. All thoughts are either fear-based or based on love. This is why it is of the utmost importance not to allow any thoughts that are not of GOD to enter your mind, and to affirm and visualize only thoughts of GOD and the Christ Consciousness. Be a living Christ! Transcend negative ego consciousness and live in Christ Consciousness. This is what *The Universal Law of Christ Consciousness* is all about. "Let this mind be in you that was in Christ Jesus!" Then said Jesus unto his disciples, "If any man will come after me, let him deny himself, and take up his cross, and follow me." (Matthew 16:24)

*   *   *

The Universal Law of Clearing Negative Psychic Energies

This law speaks of the importance of clearing negative psychic energies. There are two levels to Soul psychology: the psychological level and the psychic level. Both of these aspects are of equal importance to achieving Ascension and Self-Realization. The psychic level of Soul psychology deals with the principles of esoteric psychology that most people are not aware of. This arena is completely ignored by traditional psychology, and it is often ignored or deeply misunderstood in most Spiritual practices. That is why we will explain that issue of negative psychic energies in greater detail. It is crucial for you to pay attention to that aspect and clear yourself of all negative implants, negative elementals, Astral entities, Etheric mucus, parasites, negative imprints, toxic Astral energies, gray fields, and holes in the aura. The main point is to get rid of these unwanted negative aspects, and get purified and cleaned out. This is an area of work that is usually addressed by psychic healers, however, you don't need to be the least clairvoyant, clairaudient, or psychic to do that. Plus, you can do it yourself! You just need to ask the Inner Plane Ascended Masters! All Physical diseases and Psychological problems have negative implants, negative elementals, parasites, negative Astral energies, or Etheric damage connected to them. What might be interesting though is, that you can obtain mastery of your mind, emotions, and body and still be plagued by that negative kind of elementals, imprints, and so forth, in your auric field. So the question now is, where do these psychic entities originate? Much of this toxic psychic energy was implanted in childhood and in past lives. These negative implants exist in all your bodies—Physical, Etheric, Astral, and Mental—and are the result of past life traumas. For example, you may have been stabbed by a sword in a past life. On a psychic level that sword is still stuck in you and needs to be removed. This process can become quite complicated as you merge with your Soul and later with your monad, for you will begin to clear imprints from your Soul family of 12 Soul extensions' and your monadic family of 144 Soul extensions' parallel lives! Of course you will also have all the help you need from the higher realms. The Physical interface of all this Astral and Psychic debris appears as the core cause of many viruses and bacterial infections. Most medical doctors deal only with the material level. But the true origins of disease begin when we are implanted, usually during a traumatic event like an accident, depression, divorce, drug use, surgery—any Physical or Psychological imbalance. This period of weakness also allows the negative elementals, or parasites, to wreak more havoc in your system. The negative elementals are negative thought forms that attach themselves to different parts of our Physical or Metaphysical Bodies. They create pathways for viruses and bacteria to first enter the Etheric Body, and eventually the Physical Body. Isn't it that often a Physical illness is preceded by a downswing in your mood? The Physical Body has a natural defense mechanism that fights disease, but the Metaphysical Body does not! Everyone on Earth has those implants, and we have had them throughout all of our past lives. However, as we move upward on our Path of Initiation, it is important to clear them! It is also important to understand that even if you have cleared your implants and invaders, they can and do come back. So it is essential for you to have a tool and method for constantly reclearing yourself. So what can you do? First, make it a habit to place protection around yourself religiously three times a day. This will help a lot. Ask The Masters to remove all leaks, spots, holes in your aura, and to repair your Etheric Body. Yes, the Etheric Body, or Blueprint Body, can be damaged! This is why many people who have chronic illnesses never get better no matter what they do. If you are operating our of a cracked mold, so to speak, how can you possibly heal? Problems occur when we don't do our Psychological work of clearing the negative ego, and all negative emotions and qualities of judgement, anger, superiority or inferiority, and so on. These negative qualities, especially the Emotionally loaded ones, attract negative elementals, and this is why both the

Psychological and psychic Astral levels must be cleared simultaneously, or one will defeat the other. So what else can you do? Call forth the Seventh Ray of Saint Germain, the violet transmuting flame, and ask it to clear all Astral and Etheric debris! Or work with Ray number eight, the violet and green flame, which is especially used for cleansing purposes. Or you can call in the Core Fear Matrix Removal Program from Djwhal Khul and Vywamus. It will appear as a network of golden-white light strands that superimpose themselves over a person's light grid and through all the Chakras. The Matrix Removal Program not only removes the core fear from your Four-Body-system (not only from this life but from all your past lives and even your Soul extensions as well), it also removes negative implants and parasites, negative imprints, Etheric mucus, Etheric damage, Astral entities, gray fields, irritations, spot, and leaks from the Four-Body-system, and so on. What else can you do? Have your Etheric Body replaced by a new monadic Blueprint Body. It will assure you that you will be working with a perfect mold! Be vigilant about every thought you think, for it is your thoughts that create your reality, your feelings, emotions, behavior, and whatever you attract or repel in life. Lightworkers are not vigilant enough in this regard. They tend to go on automatic pilot too easily and forget that negative thoughts lead to negative feelings, and thus the attention of negative elementals, parasites, and lower Astral entities. Also, do not give Physical illness your power. Whatever you think programs your subconscious to create that thoughtform in your Physical Body! Remember, sickness is a defense against the truth! Christ can't be sick! One other very useful tool given to Djwhal Khul's Ashram by the Arcturians is the Prana Wind Clearing Device. It is like a fan anchored in your solar plexus that removes all the negative Etheric mucus gumming up your Psychic Body by blowing energy through all the meridians and nadis to clear our whole field. Those are some basic tools that you can use to clear negative psychic energies. For further information, please study

Soul Psychology, Revised Edition. The best thing you can possibly do is to LOVE THYSELF. Ponder on this!

*   *   *

The Universal Law of Co-Creation

There are a great many people who live their lives and do not call on GOD and/or the Masters for help on a regular basis, and they are missing out on unbelievable help and guidance from GOD and the entire GOD force. And on the other hand, there are people in life who are very heavenly oriented, who call upon GOD and the Inner Plane Ascended Masters or Angels for help, but they do not always do their part. GOD and the Masters help those who help themselves! The Spiritual Path is a team effort. GOD and the Masters will do their part, however, you must do you part by owning your Self-Mastery and Personal Power, and taking action where you need to. You must also take responsibility for programming your subconscious mind with positive thinking and visualization, so it may help the process of Co-Creation! So, the Spiritual Path is a 50/50 proposition. You must do your 50% and GOD and the Masters will do their 50%. There are many Lightworkers who call upon GOD and the Masters, but their lives are not working, or it seems that help is not forthcoming. This is not true, for every prayer is answered—in GOD's time and GOD's way. The Lord works in mysterious ways! Never forget this! A lot of the times the problem is really stemming from Lightworkers having too much negative thinking and negative emotions on a conscious and subconscious level, which is causing a great many blocks that even GOD and the Masters can't control if the Lightworker is not taking responsibility on that level. Another interesting concept of Co-Creation is in the realm of guidance and creativity. Often people pray to GOD and the

Masters for guidance which is good. It is also essential, however, to use your own co-creative powers of your intuition, mind, and creativity to create on the Earthly Plane. You are capable of coming up with your own answers and creativity to a great many of the issues and lessons of life. In the ideal relationship with GOD and the Masters, there is a Co-Creation that takes place and a sparking between the two levels! When both levels are operating at a 100% level, that is when true success, creativity, and manifestation will take place! The mind that GOD placed within us, as part of our creation, is unbelievably creative. It is an aspect of GOD's Mind. So, whenever you are working on any project or problem, definitely call on GOD and the Masters, but then sit down and brainstorm the answers yourself and see what you can come up with, with your own creative consciousness! The other extremely important point is the importance of taking not only Mental action on your own, but also taking Emotional action on your own, and Physical action on your own. Many Lightworkers are very naïve and really think that GOD and the Masters are going to do all for them, which, with no judgement intended, is a very naïve and childlike understanding. GOD and the Masters' help should be seen as a dessert! We are each Sons and Daughters of GOD, adults, and Masters in our own right! If GOD and the Masters did it for us, which they cannot anyway, but if they did, they would be taking away the very lessons we incarnated to learn. So, the key understanding here is to own your Love, Wisdom, and Power on all levels, not to just rely on one level! This is the true key to success! Co-creating with GOD and the Masters is the touchstone and key word for the Aquarian Age, the New Millennium, and the Seventh Golden Age. Working with the Cosmic and Planetary Ascended Maters on one's Spiritual Path could be called "The Rocketship to God."

*   *   *

The Universal Law of Compassion

One of the most important qualities to develop on the Spiritual Path is compassion. This is the recognition that since all is GOD, that other people's pain is our pain, and that other people's suffering is, in truth, our own suffering. Compassion does not mean, however, to be an empath where you take on the pain of others and make yourself Psychologically and Physically sick! So there is a fine balance to find between nonattachment and being an empath, which is compassion! Don't take on the suffering of others so that it is debilitating, but you can have the utmost compassion for their suffering. Compassion is one of the most important Buddha/Christ qualities a person can develop! As Lord Buddha said, "All beings long for happiness; therefore extend thy compassion to all." Heed those words of wisdom!

*　　　　　*　　　　　*

The Universal Law of Decisiveness and Making Decisions From an Integrated Perspective

One of the most important lessons on the Spiritual Path is to demonstrate "decisiveness and consistency" on all levels. This is really one of the great keys to God Realization and Integrated Ascension. If you are not decisive you will not be in your 100% Personal Power, and if you are not in your Personal Power 100%, you will not be in your 100% Self-Mastery. If you are not in your 100% Self-Mastery, you will not be consistent in all bodies and all aspects of self. In every choice you make in life you want to do it with all your being, not just part of your being! To be decisive means to do it with every part of your being, or don't do it at all. Whenever you do something, do it with all of you! Do it with all your heart, and soul, and mind, and might! Do it with your Spiritual Body, Mental Body, Emotional Body, Etheric Body, and your Physical Body! Do it with your superconscious, conscious, and subconscious mind! Do it in a Spiritual sense, Psychological sense, and a Physical/Earthly sense! Do it embodying all Seven Rays. Do it integrating all Seven Chakras. Do it considering all Houses in Astrology. Do it integrating all Sephiroth of the Tree of Life. Are you over or underidentified with one Sephiroth over another? Are you integrated and balanced and seeing life from the Full Cosmic Tree of Life? Are you making decisions from just a Planetary lens, or a Solar, Galactic, Universal, Multiuniversal and Cosmic perspective? Are you making decisions out of all Twelve Major Archetypes? Are you seeing life through all cards of the Tarot Deck? Own your 100% Personal Power! Keep a 100% positive mental attitude about it! Affirm and visualize it! Act as if it is already yours! Take 100% action in the earthly realm. Always be 100% decisive with full 100% Personal Power, 100% Unconditional Love, 100% Wisdom, 100% Active Intelligence and Physical Action, 100% Harmony and Beauty, 100% Precision and Detail, 100% Devotion to your ideal, and with 100% Adherence to the Divine order and structure you have set up for yourself! Again, if you are going to do something, then do it on all levels, or don't do it at all! It is better to not do something at all than to do it with half your being. Sometimes people are in their power, and sometimes they are not. It fluctuates. This is not consistency! They are not in their full unconditional love all the time! They do things Spiritually and Mentally, but not 100% Emotionally or Physically! They do not do things consistently with 100% power in all Seven Rays, which are the Personality Attributes of GOD. Others teach it, but don't demonstrate it. Some think it, but don't feel it. Some feel it, but don't think it! Some think it but don't speak it! Their conscious mind is doing one thing and their subconscious mind is doing another. One body is doing one thing and the other is doing another thing. They have personal power, but don't have faith. They have faith, but don't' have personal power. The combinations are endless! When you are consistent you become invulnerable and invincible on all levels because you cause your reality on all levels. The only level where that is not true is the Physical, and eventually at that level it is possible as well if you choose Physical Ascension. This is turning the Physical Body into light and being able to materialize and dematerialize the body! People don't pay their rent to GOD equally on all levels! Once you become an Integrated Spiritual Master you will be able to trust your intuition, heart, mind, feelings, instincts and Physical Body, for they will all be working in an integrated and balanced fashion, and they will give you instantaneous and accurate guidance. This will be true as long as you also have done your Spiritual and Psychological homework to release all negative ego/fear-based thinking and feeling and to only think and feel from your Spiritual/Christ/Buddha Mind and perspective. So, my friends, the ideal is to be decisive in all you do. Whatever you do in life, do it with 100 percent of your energies. It is better to be decisive and make the wrong decision than to be indecisive and make no decision at all, so as to not live in the "twilight zone". Ponder on this!

*   *   *

The Universal Law of Demonstrating and Practicing the Presence of GOD

If you want to be with GOD in Heaven, act like God on Earth. It's not enough just to think about GOD or just feel GOD. *Be* God in every moment of your life. This is the key to realizing GOD. "However many holy words you read, however many you speak, what good will they do you if you do not act upon them?" (Buddha) Sai Baba, the Cosmic Christ, said, "The fastest way to realize God is to see Him in everything and everyone, to see Him in our Brothers and Sisters because He *is* our Brothers and Sisters". Every person, animal, plant and mineral is GOD incarnate. Greet every person as if they were the Master Jesus or Buddha or Quan Yin—which in truth they are. "Do it unto the least of these my brethren, and you do it unto me," as Jesus said. Treat every animal as GOD. See in every mineral an embodiment of the Most High. Play the Ultimate Archetype. Play God! Be God! As Nike so perfectly put it, "Just do it" or maybe more accurate, "Just Be It"! Or as the Bibles states, "My little children, let us not love in word, neither in tongue; but in deed and in truth. (1 John 3:18) If ye know these things, happy are ye if ye do them. (John 13:17) But be ye doers of the word, and not hearers only, deceiving your own selves. (James 1:22) Those things, which ye have both learned, and received, and heard, and seen in me, do: and the God of peace shall be with you. (Phillipians 4:9) Be ye strong therefore, and let not your hands be weak: for your work shall be rewarded." (Chronicles 15:7) Or as Mother Teresa said, "We long for heaven where God is, but we have it in our power to be in heaven with Him at this very moment. But being happy with Him now means:

Loving as He loves,
Helping as He helps,
Giving as He gives,
Serving as He serves,
Rescuing as He rescues,
Being with Him twenty-four hours a day,
Touching Him in even His distressing disguises
Never despising, rejecting, or hiding our faces from him."

             *   *   *

The Universal Law of Developing a Flawless Character

Mahatma Karamchand Gandhi said, "All your scholarship, all your study of Shakespeare and Wordsworth would be in vain if at the same time you do not build your character and attain mastery over your thoughts and your actions." One of the premier qualities of an Integrated Ascended Master is a continual commitment to work on self and to correct character flaws. Sai Baba said, "The body will shine if the character is fine." If one makes an agreement then one should keep that agreement. If one sets a deadline and makes a promise to complete something then one should meet that deadline or at least have the courage to call and apologize for not being able to keep it. If one makes an appointment, they should not break it at the last second unless an emergency. If one makes a promise then they should keep that promise or not make it in the first place. If one makes a mistake they should admit their mistake and apologize. Another word for character development is developing Christ and Buddha Consciousness in one's Mental and Emotional Body. Once you have attained Master status and Spiritual leadership, and have lots of people coming to your workshops and lectures, you will be under a microscope of the highest order. Your every word, deed, action and written word will be microscopically examined. If there is the slightest bit of lack of integrity, inconsistency, character flaws, or lack of clarity on any level, your students and the general public will see it and throw it back at you. Remember the words of John Wooden, "Ability may get you to the top, but it takes character to keep you there." Abraham Lincoln said, "Nearly all men can stand adversity, but if you want to test a man's character, give him power." Many Spiritual leaders are not prepared for this and go through many hard lessons because of lack of integrity, inconsistency, and character flaws. Some of the feedback they get will be appropriate and some of it will be other people's negative ego looking for faults and criticizing to make themselves feel better because of their lack of self-worth and being caught in the negative ego. Not only will the public be an incredible mirror of your thoughts, words, and deeds on every level, but even if you remain in integrity and demonstrate a flawless character and clarity, you will still be attacked and criticized by people in the public who are run by their negative ego. Many people do not feel good about themselves and are totally run by the negative ego. This being the case, they are run by jealousy, competition, judgementalnesss, faultfinding, comparing, and the only way they can feel good about themselves is to attack others. So, even if you are perfect in all those qualities, you must be very firm in this within yourself. So when you have to deal with all these strange and eccentric people, you have developed a thick skin, so to speak. No time spent working on self is more valuable than proper character development. It may not be as glamorous as communing with celestial realms or other esoteric studies, however, this is the real key to making Integrated Ascension work. Without proper character development all other aspects of your Spiritual life will become poisoned by the contagion of negative ego. As the saying goes, "Your behavior while people are watching is important. However, your behavior while no one is watching is more important, for it reveals your true character." Your relationship to yourself is the foundation of your life. Take the time to build a Christed foundation and only Godliness will then be built upon this Spiritually integrated structure. As the Bible reminds us, "If you live by the sword, you shall die by the sword."

*   *   *

The Universal Law of Developing a Good Diet on a Spiritual, Mental, Emotional, Etheric, and Physical Level

We all recognize the importance of eating a good Physical diet, which is essential to keep the Physical chemistry of the blood in proper balance and provide the fuel we need for outputting energy. Well, in the same vein, we need to recognize the importance of nourishing our Etheric, Emotional, Mental, and Spiritual Bodies. People need to be much more conscious and vigilant over the thoughts they allow into their consciousness from within and without. This may be the single most important aspect of one's entire Spiritual Path, because it is our thoughts that create our reality, our feelings, emotions, behavior, and what we attract or magnetize. Every moment of our lives we are choosing either to think with our Spiritual Mind or our negative ego mind. If we do not control our mind we cannot have mastery over our emotions, and we will not be right with self, right with God, or right with any relationship in our lives. Far too many people live too much on automatic pilot and do not realize how incredibly powerful the mind is! Be joyously vigilant over the thoughts that come from within self, as well as over those thoughts that come from other people in the form of words, letters, books, magazines, and newspapers. To attain God Realization and inner peace it is imperative that you deny all negative thoughts from entering your consciousness from within and without. Every day first thing put on your semipermeable bubble of protection that allows in positive thoughts and feelings and keeps out negative thoughts and feelings. And be joyously vigilant! Every time you lose your vigilance and every time you fall into automatic pilot, you are in a state of hypnosis, and let other people hypnotize you! Now, in terms of your Emotional diet, the process is very similar. If you are listening to music, be more vigilant over the kind of songs and lyrics you allow yourself to listen to. Whenever we are in a receptive state we are in hypnosis, and the lyrics and the feeling tones will program your subconscious mind without you even realizing it. At all times we must strive to be the cause of our reality and not the effect! Also, be more discerning which people you spend time with. Emotionally negative people should be avoided if at all possible. If you do have to be with Emotionally negative people, keep your bubble of protection up. If you go to the movies, and you don't like how you feel watching it, don't just stay there because you spent six dollars, get up and leave. Watching violent and lower-self movies is not only an insult to your Emotional Body, it is an insult to your Soul and spirit, which, in truth, is what you are! Now, most people, when they are by themselves, let down their Mental and Emotional vigilance. Well, this is a 24 hour day and night job, even while you sleep! By the way, ninety-eight percent of our dreams are nothing more than a symbolic representation of our thinking and feeling during that day. So if you want to have good dreams at night, then think and feel positively during the day! This is actually the purpose of dreams, to give us feedback in visual form of how we have been thinking, feeling, and acting that day! Getting back to this point of being joyously vigilant while by yourself, do not get on automatic pilot when alone and give in to negative ego daydreaming. The second the mind starts going in a negative direction, stop it and direct it elsewhere. Constantly change the channel of your mind! This can be done just by stopping it or by choosing to think another thought. It can be done by doing an affirmation, a positive visualization, saying a prayer, or by repeating the name of God! Well, so far we have been discussing the importance of a good Emotional and Mental diet. Let's take a look now at the Psychic level. For example, you are by yourself and you are angry at someone, and you are playing out some angry confrontations in your mind and Emotional Body. This all seems to most people very innocent. Well, it is NOT! The anger that you are thinking about on the Psychic plane can be seen as arrows and darts shooting toward the subject of your thoughts. If their aura is not strong it will penetrate their fields and probably lodge in their liver or someplace else. The more evolved you are Spiritually, the more power your thoughts, images, and feelings will have on the inner plane. Also, realize that when you think of someone they telepathically receive it. We are all one. If people indulge in lower-self sexuality or fantasizing, this affects the other person. Our daydreams affect other people! Ponder on this! On an Etheric level, it is important to be joyously vigilant in terms of just energy. Again, this could be you walking into someone's house and not feeling comfortable with the energy in the room, or you coming home at night and feeling some strange energy in the house. Or you may feel some strange energies in your auric fields when waking up from sleep. If so, do not be passive and leave strange energy in your field. Immediately call forth the violet transmuting flame, a Platinum Net, or the Prana Wind Clearing Device from the Inner Plane Ascended Masters! Finally, on a Physical Body level, maintain your joyous vigilance. Don't eat when you are not hungry. "Too much food results in dullness of mind." (Sai Baba) Don't eat junk food just because you are tired! Get some Physical exercise, as well as some fresh air! There are hundreds of books that speak of the importance of eating a healthy diet on a Physical Body level, so we won't take that discussion any further! Heed those words! If you will do your part and keep joyous vigilance on all levels discussed in this paragraph, God and the Masters will do their part upon request and resurrect and rebuilt your Four-Body System, and 12-Body System into a well oiled, finely tuned Spiritual Vehicle and vessel for the "Integrated Christ" you are!

*　　　　　*　　　　　*

The Universal Law of Developing a Healthy Psychoepistemology

This law is of such importance that we decided to explain it in greater detail. The term Psychoepistemology (*epistemology* being the branch of philosophy that deals with the nature and origin of knowledge or knowing, and the prefix *psycho-* coming from the Greek word psyche, meaning "breath" or "spirit" or "mind") means the mind's or the spirit's knowing. What this means is that every person has an individual Psychological way of filtering their experience. Because your Psychoepistemology acts like a filter, you could also just use the term filter. Each of us has a philosophy or set of beliefs that serves as a filter or a lens for interpreting reality. The typical person who is not on a conscious Spiritual Path has a completely unconscious filter system. His or her view of the world is formed by the subconscious mind, which acts on the hodgepodge of beliefs from past lives, family upbringings, school, mass consciousness, mass media, and so on. A person with this type of filter does whatever flows unregulated into his or her consciousness from the subconscious mind. Fortunately, most people are more conscious than this. They have been exposed to various forms of philosophy and psychology and use these ideas to filter what enters the subconscious. These perception filters act like the filters a photographer puts on a camera's lens. Without the filter, the lens will allow the film to be exposed so that the colors in the photograph are a nearly perfect approximation of reality. None of us view reality in this way. We all have filters attached to our means of perception. As humans, we view reality through a lens with many filters attached. Among these filters are the balanced relationship of the Three Minds, Four Bodies, Feminine and Masculine balance, Heavenly and Earthly balance, Christ thinking versus negative ego thinking, Chakra relationships, society's lenses, personal power, self-love, attunement to the Soul or lack thereof. This phenomena with any of the above mentioned issues is known as "mind locks." A mind lock is when we get stuck in a certain aspect, lens, or belief system and don't realize it. We are, hence, locked in and only see life through a very small number of lenses. In truth, every belief system is a lens and potential mind lock. These principles and how they are integrated and balanced will determine how a person's experience is filtered. We will give here now some examples as to show how this filtration system operates.

Chakra System as a Filter: If a person is stuck in their first Chakra, he or she will filter reality through the lens of survival thinking. The filter will allow only survival-base thoughts to pass through to the film, and therefore, the picture this person sees will have those survival colors heightened. A person stuck in the second Chakra will filter all experience through sexuality. A person stuck in the third Chakra will filter all experience through the lens of emotions which is extremely common in our society. For people like this, all feelings and emotions are heightened, and they often base their decisions on how they feel rather than what they think. (Remember, it's our thoughts that create our feelings and emotions.) A person stuck in the fourth Chakra will see everything through the heart which may be a more evolved understanding, but nonetheless is still a lens. Someone who filters life through the throat Chakra—through will and communication—may interpret everything as a battle and a war. Being stuck in the Third Eye, there might be a focus on gaining wisdom and insight. Being overidentified with the crown Chakra, your sights are set on heaven, but you are not grounded and connected to the Earth. Balance and integration of all the Chakras is the most evolved and healthiest Psychoepistemology.

Feminine and Masculine Balance as a Filter: Those with the Feminine filter overidentify with feelings, emotions, and bodily desires. This type of person always goes through Emotional crises and lives on an Emotional roller coaster. Those with the Masculine filter overidentify with the Mental Body. They aren't comfortable embracing feelings, just as someone with an Emotional Psychoepistemology is less adept at embracing a logical approach. Also, the Feminine embraces the mystical and rejects the occult whereas those with a Masculine filter may not adequately embrace the mystical side of life.

Heaven and Earth as a Filter: The heavenly Psychoepistemology is very ungrounded and filters everything through an obsession with how to break the wheel of reincarnation and escape the Earth. And those with the Psychoepistemology of the materialist see through the filter of science and believe that the only thing that is real is what you can verify with your five senses.

Three Minds as a Filter: When overidentified with the conscious mind, the person is obsessed with control and power. The subconsciously identified types think the subconsciousness is the key to the Kingdom but don't truly understand the functioning of the conscious mind and often have no belief in God. They give too much power to the subconscious mind and don't realize the strongest force in their lives is the conscious mind that owns its will and personal power. And then there are people who see life through the filter of the conscious and superconscious mind while rejecting the subconscious mind. They have total overidentification with the Spiritual and heavenly things but lack a focus on Psychological and character development and making their life work on Earth. If stuck in the filter of traditional psychology, people accept only the existence of the conscious and subconscious minds and reject any belief in a superconscious mind or God at all. The most widespread imbalanced Psychoepistemology views life through the negative ego mind rather than the Buddha/Christ/Melchizedek Mind. In truth, it is the negative ego that causes imbalance and distorts our perception. All perception is in sense a dream, but the idea us to perceive and live God's dream, which is a mirror and/or window for the ultimate reality.

The Four-Body System as a Filter: Another way the Spiritual vision is limited is looking at the four types of people relating to their Four-Body system. There is the more Spiritual, Mental, Emotional or Physical type. Some people see life through their feelings and emotions. Other people are more intuitive and see life through that lens mainly. Other people still are mental and see life through their Mental Body and are not interested in intuition or feeling or their Physical Bodies. Other people see life through their five senses and are called sensation types. Others still are combinations like intuitive/feeling or intuitive/thinking or any combination you can think of. The ideal of course is to be integrated and to see through all four perceptual lenses in an integrated and balanced manner.

Astrology as a Filter: If you have a lot of "water" in your horoscope, you may have blind spots dealing with "air." If you have a lot of "fire," you may have blind spots with "earth" and vice versa.

False Holistic Theory as a Filter: It is true that you want to integrate your Rays, Chakras, Subpersonalities, Soul extensions, Four Bodies, and so on. However, the one thing you do NOT want to incorporate is your negative ego. You must disidentify with your negative ego and its faulty philosophy of life. You must reject your lower self and completely identify with your Higher Self to realize God. So, a common Psychoepistemology that Lightworkers commonly hold is the False Holistic Theory—the belief that everything in life must be balanced and integrated. Again, you want to balance everything except for one thing: lower self and Higher Self. You don't want to balance the negative ego way of thinking and the Christ way of thinking. If you believe in this theory, you will end up saying, "I am going to be loving have the time and attacking the other half. I am going to have high self-esteem half the time and low self-esteem the other half." So you want to get rid of all negative ego qualities and traits. You don't want to incorporate or balance them! Why would anyone want to balance the dark with the light? We are not here to incorporate darkness. Did not Jesus say to one of his disciples who started complaining, "Get thee behind me, Satan"! Jesus did not say, "Come integrate with me, Satan. Come integrate with me and let me love you and take thee into myself and into my bodies so I can turn thee into Light!" Master Jesus said, "Get thee behind me, Satan"! We are the light of the world, as *A Course in Miracles* says. Our true identity is light and God. All darkness is created by the negative ego, not by God. Darkness is just another word for negative ego. If you actually believe that you want to balance darkness and light, then your own mind will create darkness, for your thoughts create your reality. What you think doesn't create truth, but what you think is the reality you will live in. It is the mind that creates bondage or liberation. Mankind has not yet come to realize the incredible power of its own mind. At its best it will lead you to the sublime heights of God realization. At its worst, when not mastered, it will manifest psychosis and schizophrenia. Ponder on this!

Shadow Psychology as a Filter: Jungian psychology is responsible for another filter that often misguides people. "Owning your shadow" is a common Psychological concept. So many people believe that each person has to integrate his or her shadow. God is light. And we are light. There is no shadow within us. Any shadow we experience is created by the negative ego. God did not create the negative ego, man did. Therefore, we must not deny the negative ego, but need to recognize it, acknowledge it, take responsibility for it, and release it. The purpose of life is to transcend the negative ego, not to incorporate it. The idea here is to deny your shadow. Well, it's also essential to understand that we all have a negative ego potentiality, and we all have negative ego within us that we haven't cleared yet. There are some deluded Souls who go around thinking that the Dark Brotherhood or the negative ego do not exist, and this is very dangerous! In thinking this, they have been taken over by the dark side. We need to get clear on how both the negative ego and the Christ Mind work within ourselves. If we deny the existence of negative ego thinking as a potentiality, we are sure to be victimized by it. The ideal here is to make negative ego thinking, or the shadow, *unmanifest* potential. So the key lesson is not to incorporate our shadow, but to be on guard against releasing it for we all have the negative ego potentiality in us. It is just a matter of choice! And if you want to realize God you better not decide for the negative ego potentiality!

Traditional Psychology as a Filter: If the therapist is involved with Freudian Psychology, the client too will see everything through the lens of the second Chakra and the fight between the id, ego, and superego. In Humanistic Psychology everything will be seen through the lens of the Emotional Body and the expression of feelings. In Gestalt Theory everything is viewed through the lens of pro-existence and anti-intellectualism. In Adlerian Therapy, we have the lens of social psychology. In family systems counseling, it will be the lens of the family system and not the individual psyche. Someone involved with Behavioristic Psychology will see everything through the lens of positive and negative reinforcement, extinction of unwanted behaviors, and the effect of the environment upon behavior. Cognitive Psychology uses the lens of the effects of thinking upon behavior, and so on. To a nutritionist, everything is seen through the lens of nutrition. So, as you can see, it is important to remember that all of these filters will distort perception.

Philosophy as a Filter: Each philosophical viewpoint is a filter. There are literally thousands of philosophical filters, so we would like to give just one example here. The philosophy of Ayn Rand preaches selfishness as the answer to life's problems, which is certainly a soulless philosophy.

Profession as a Filter: Every profession trains its practitioners to have a filter. A comedian sees everything through the filter of humor. A lawyer sees things through the filter of an adversarial legal battle with a win/lose orientation. A businessman works through the filter of making money. An artist does so through the filter of beauty. A healer may look at everything in terms of energy, and a social worker through the filter of social implications, and an astrologer works through the astrological horoscope.

If your Psychoepistemology is imbalanced, your entire life and all your relationships will reflect this imbalance. If your Psychoepistemology is contaminated by the negative ego, your Four-Body system, all your relationships, and your entire life will be contaminated. Each one of these potentially imbalanced Psychoepistemologies causes the individual to see life from not only an imbalanced and slightly skewed state of consciousness, it also causes one to have a slightly imbalanced and skewed relationship to GOD and the Godforce. Being wrong with self will cause imbalance in every aspect of your life. Every time you buy into one of these potentially imbalanced psychoepistemologies, it limits your Full Spectrum Prism Consciousness that GOD would have you see from. Each time we buy into an imbalanced Psychoepistemology we see life from a smaller and smaller prism. Seek the highest possible truth within yourself. It will take great courage and discernment for many of you to free yourself from the viselike grip that the negative ego has held over you. The key to breaking free is examining your Psychoepistemology! The purpose of life is to wake up from the negative ego's nightmare and demonstrate our Christ Consciousness on Earth. The first step is to have this awakening. The second step is to see the Christ Consciousness in others. If you don't see it in others, you will lose it in yourself. Just as you are the Christ, so is your neighbor, no matter what their level or state of consciousness development. The third step then is to practice demonstrating this state of consciousness 24 hours a day, 7 days a week, and 365 days a year. It is by demonstrating this Psychoepistemology consistently that we pass our Initiations and will come to realize God! Everything, from the planet we live on to the religion we practice and our political inclinations, as well as our past lives, create filters that distort our perceptions. The mass media, schools, secular and Spiritual teachers all contribute to this accumulation of filters. We all like to feel that we see clearly, but the fact is that our view of reality is much more affected by these filters than we realize! So the ideal is to try to become crystal clear about which filters are affecting our consciousness, which means still being inclusive of accepting all filters as a part of the whole. The goal is to see through the lens of God! This is the clearing work we are all involved in, and this process requires great intro-spection, self-examination, and vigilance! "Your eye is the lamp of your body. When your eyes are good, your whole body is also full of light. But when they are bad, your body is also full of darkness." (Luke 11:34) Heed those Biblical Pearls of Wisdom!

*   *   *

The Universal Law of Developing an Attitude of Detachment and a Thick Skin

One of the most important qualities that all New Age Leaders must develop is an attitude of detachment, invulnerability, and thick skin. The ideal is to be like a rubber pillow that things gently bounce off of. The ideal is to let things slide off you like water off a duck's back. The ideal is to own that as a Master you are mentally and emotionally invulnerable because you cause your own emotions and thoughts. This quality necessitates cultivating a strong sense of self, a well-developed sense of self-love and self-worth, and unceasing mastery and personal power. It is essential that all leaders develop this quality, for no matter how clear you are, attacks will still come. And these attacks are really Spiritual tests to see how strong and ready for leadership you are. If you are truly immersed in your Mighty I Am Presence and Ascended Master Consciousness, they will have no effect! "Seek refuge in the attitude of detachment and you will amass the wealth of Spiritual awareness." (Bhagavad-Gita)

*   *   *

The Universal Law of Developing an Efficient Perception of Reality

One of the most important lessons of life is developing an efficient perception of reality. Our thoughts create our reality. Whatever we think seems totally real. When a person feel depressed, which of course is created by their thinking, it seems totally real. When a person feels anger, which is created by their mind, it seems totally real. The nature of the mind is that however you interpret yourself and life will be the dream you live in. Some people live in a self-created hell, and some live in a self-created heaven! The importance of learning to think properly about self and to see life with an efficient perception of reality cannot be underestimated. Every faulty thought about self and GOD will cause you to see the rest of life from an imbalanced perspective. Every imbalanced, negative ego, or faulty thought or belief will cause you to have a blind spot within self and in how you see your world. There are infinite numbers of faulty thoughts, for every Christ/Buddha thought has an opposite negative ego and/or fear-based separative thought. When people see life through the negative ego's eyes, everything they experience seems totally real and all their thoughts, emotions, and actions seem justified, even though they are living out complete illusion. When you dream at night, while you are in the dream everything seems real. You may be having a nightmare and it seems totally real. This is very much how life is. The only difference is that most people have not awakened to the fact that they are still in negative hypnosis and are still dreaming. This is because everything we think causes us to feel the way we do, and it seems and feels right. This is true from the negative ego's perspective, but it is completely illusionary when seen from a Christ/Buddha perspective. A person who feels righteously angry really feels justified in this response. However, in truth, they are just indulging their negative ego. If you believe in Humanistic Psychology then it is alright to express your emotions whenever and wherever you want, even if you attack and hurt people. If one has that philosophy then that person feels quite self-righteous in doing what they are doing. If you are a follower of Carl Jung you must own your shadow. If you are a Behaviorist then we have no free choice, and we are all rats in a maze receiving positive and/or negative reinforcement. People get stuck in philosophies an psychologies of all kinds and think they have the truth. What is truth? See *The Universal Law of Truth*. Developing an efficient perception of reality is a lifelong process. Deny any thought not of GOD to enter your mind. Be joyously vigilant at all times. Try to retain your GOD purity at all times. Be devastatingly honest with self, and examine your motivations for everything you do. Do your Psychological homework, not just your Spiritual homework. If so many people, Lightworkers, disciples, devotees, high-level initiates, masters, and even Archangels (Lucifer) have been taken over and don't even know it, don't think for a minute that it cannot happen to you. The second you think this, you have already fallen! So develop an efficient perception of reality so you may have the eyes to see and the ears to hear when the Biblical prophecy shall come true, "…no eyes have seen, no ears have heard, no mind has conceived what God had prepared for those who love him."

*   *   *

The Universal Law of Developing Appropriate Boundaries

The most important understanding is that appropriate boundaries have to begin within self, or it is impossible to have healthy boundaries with other people. Healthy self-boundaries begin with the understanding that there is the conscious mind, and then there is the content of consciousness from within and without. A person with healthy self-boundaries has disidentification or detachment from all of the content of consciousness and the outside world. The content of consciousness is all one's thoughts, feelings, emotions, impulses, desires, instincts, intuition, inner guidance, subpersonalities, appetites, inner child, and so on. To have self-mastery, one must have this detachment, disidentification, and self-boundary. It might be visualized as a golden bubble of light around one's self that serves almost like a gate or checkpoint for the conscious mind to Spiritually discern if that particular content of consciousness is positive or negative. "Deny any thought not of God to enter your Mind!" This is called healthy denial. A person with healthy self-boundaries first denies all thoughts and emotions of the negative ego and immediately affirms thoughts and emotions of the Melchizedek/Christ/Buddha Consciousness. This is how the subconscious mind within 21 days becomes reprogrammed. Most people on Earth allow themselves to become invaded by the content of consciousness. They are too run not only by the mind and feelings, but by desire, inappropriate belief systems, negative ego programming, inner child desires, the indolence of the subconscious mind, bad habits, and infinite numbers of subpersonalities from present and past life programming. This all stems, in truth, from improper self-boundaries. Without healthy self-boundaries one cannot choose one's life, for one's "programming" ends up choosing it for them. When one lets the subconscious mind and Emotional Body be the director, this is a direct invitation for the negative ego to be the commander in chief of your reality. If you do not develop healthy self-boundaries within self, it is impossible to develop healthy boundaries with other people. This is because one must be right with self before one can be right with GOD and right with others. If one is wrong with self or a victim within self, one will be off-kilter and a victim in relationship to others. This Platinum/Golden Bubble and self-boundaries also apply to protecting one's self from all energies coming from outside of self. If one does not have healthy self-boundaries in relationship to the content of consciousness coming from the outside world, one will be basically living in a state of hypnosis. Most of the people living in this world are living in hypnosis and don't realize it. Another word for hypnosis is hypersuggestibility. Without self-boundaries one is hypersuggestible to the programming and influence of the outside world upon your consciousness. This is also called being a victim. An integrated Spiritual Master chooses his or her reality on all levels from within and without. Once one has developed healthy self-boundaries within self where one can consistently cause and choose one's reality on all levels, then it is much easier to develop healthy self-boundaries with others. A Spiritual Master understands that there is a time to be selfish, and a time to be selfless. A time to take care of the self part of GOD and a time to take care of the other part of GOD, which are, in truth, one Eternal Self. A Spiritual Master understands that there is a time to say "No" and a time to say "Yes." Most people in the world say "Yes" way too much to themselves in relationship to self-boundaries and "Yes" too much to others. We must learn to deal with self and with others with firmness and with love. There is a time to be open and a time to be closed. There is a time to set up extra protection and a time to be more open and sensitive. Working with protection is one of the ways to develop healthy boundaries. People need protection from their own negative ego and inappropriate energies from the content of their own consciousness. Just as the negative ego thoughts and feelings exist within, they exist without in the form of other people in bodies and without Physical Bodies. People are being constantly victimized and hypnotized by other people's thoughts and emotions, as well as being influenced by people from the inner plane who are still run by the negative ego. These beings, of course, live on the Astral and Mental Plane. If you don't develop the understanding and ability to see and recognize the negative ego in all its insane forms and manifestations within self, you will not be able to see it in other people either. It will be like you have blinders on or you are under a negative hypnosis, which, in truth, you will be.

*   *   *

The Universal Law of Developing One's 38 Planetary and 11 Cosmic Senses of GOD

There are 38 Planetary Inner Senses and 11 Cosmic Inner Senses. GOD has built into us an extra sensory apparatus far beyond anything we once realized. Some of these higher senses in the Buddhic, Atmic, Monadic, and Logoic realms are far more refined than the standard extra sensory perception that most people think about when they use that term. Each of these Supersenses of GOD are connected to the different Planes of Consciousness of the Cosmic Physical Plane! It must be understood that everyone has all these Supersenses within them, however, because of how GOD created us, our Ray structure, Astrological Configuration, past life history, and so on, some of these Supersenses will be more developed than others! And this is how it should be! Not everyone is meant by GOD to develop all of these! GOD has created each person differently! And certain ones can, over time, be developed. Others may not be your Spiritual destiny, purpose, or puzzle piece to develop. Those of a more occult nature will be developed in certain ones, and those of a more mystic nature will be developed in other ones. This is why both the mystic and occult paths lead to the same place. To ideal, of course is to integrate both, the mystic and occult aspects of self within yourself! The foundation of all 38 Inner Senses is one's Psychological clarity and one's level of Integrated Ascension. If Integrated Ascension and Full Spectrum Prism Consciousness has not been achieved, then all the Inner Senses, both mystic and occult in nature, will be skewed, colored and in extreme cases corrupted and contaminated.

Physical Senses—Physical Plane: Smell, Taste, Sight, Touch, Hearing.

Astral Senses—Physical-Etheric Plane: Emotional Idealism and Imagination (deals with the concept of being able to formulate ideals and also engaging the Emotional Body and Desire Body by using Imagination; i.e. daydreaming), Clairvoyance, Clairaudience, Psychometry (ability to pick up an object and receive information about the person who owns it by following the psychic threads so to speak). Clairaudience, Clairvoyance, and Psychometry are restricted to the Astral Plane. All Clairaudience and Clairvoyance is brought through various filters. If a person's Psychological clarity is not developed, all channeling and Clairvoyance will be extremely corrupted and contaminated!

Lower Mental Senses—Lower Mental Plane: Discrimination (on the concrete mind level), Planetary Psychometry (on a Planetary level on the Lower Mental Plane), Higher Clairvoyance (on the Lower Mental Plane and no higher; person can see beings who exist on this plane of reality and no higher); and Higher Clairaudience (hearing on the Lower Mental Plane and no higher; person can channel entities from the Lower Mental Plane).

Higher Mental Senses—Higher Mental Plane: Spiritual Telepathy (ability to give and receive thought transference; automatic writing), Response to Group Vibration (deals with the tuning into one's group affiliation on Earth and/or even the group vibration of the Spiritual Hierarchy as a whole; the ideal is to maintain one's group identity, however, to also simultaneously remain in touch with one's group identity as well), Spiritual Discernment (higher level than in the previous category), Higher Clairvoyance/Clairaudience (restricted to the Higher Mental Plane).

Buddhic Senses—Buddhic Plane: Idealism (in the realm of pure thought on the Buddhic Plane; involves the ability to conceptualize and understand the Plan of GOD on the Buddhic Plane), Intuition (pure knowingness beyond rational thought), Divine Vision (having a higher sense of the Plan; involves clear seeing, intuiting, and knowing of the Ascended Masters' intent and of the Divine Plan as they conceive it on the Buddhic Plane; also, a more refined state of vision, seeing, and communicating with the Masters), Healing (ability to heal with light in an inner plane sense or in a type of laying on of hands using the pure radiance of GOD), Comprehension (ability to comprehend things from the Consciousness of the Buddhic Plane).

Atmic Senses—Atmic Plane: All Knowledge (ability to tap into all available knowledge at that level and to ascertain truth behind any situation; true knowingness), Perfection (pursuit of excellence; pursuit of a flawless character filled with Christ/Buddha attributes and a mind that transcends most negative ego qualities), Realization (full merger with monad; individual realizes their unity with the All and feels, intuits, knows, and demonstrates this on all levels as a reality of their being), Active Service (demonstration of GOD in daily life), Beatitude (deals with the sublime sense of beauty; it is beauty that carries the essence of GOD; Jesus Christ in his ministry exemplified beatitude),

Monadic Senses—Monadic Plane: Monadic Group Consciousness (greater feeling of unity with one's eleven other Soul extensions from one's Oversoul and 144 Soul extensions from one's monad), Full Monadic Merger (realization of achieving one's Ascension which is the same thing as saying one has merged with their monad), Monadic Comprehension (ability to comprehend things from the consciousness of the monad, and no longer the Higher Self), Monadic Vision (ability to see through the eyes of the monad and no longer through the eyes of the personality, Oversoul, negative ego, or lower-self desire) Monadic Realization (total feeling, intuition, and knowingness that you are the Mighty I Am Presence living in a Physical Body on Earth).

Logoic Senses—Logoic Plane: Synthesis (ability to see and function through a full spectrum prism rather than functioning through a fragmented lens of that prism upon the Logoic Level; it must be fully established and demonstrated as one is then a full representative of the Planetary Logos), Seeing with the Eye of GOD (Planetary vision which extends into Solar and Cosmic Realms as well), Divine Plan Comprehension (ability to comprehend the Divine Plan of the Planetary Logos, Lord Buddha, as He intends it to be manifested upon all levels of our Planetary System), Full Attunement with the Logos of the Planet (completion of your Seven Levels of Initiation; complete merger at the 99% level with your monad and with the Logos of our Planet, Lord Buddha), Logoic Realization (full realization of the Seventh Plane of Consciousness and the achievement of liberation from the Physical Wheel of Rebirth), Logoic Comprehension (level of comprehension that contains within it all Seven Planes of Consciousness; a level of comprehension where full Planetary Mastery is bestowed upon the initiate).

Cosmic Senses—Cosmic Plane: The eleven Cosmic Senses are: Cosmic Synthesis, Cosmic Knowledge, Cosmic Perfection, Cosmic Realization, Cosmic Service, Cosmic Beatitude, Cosmic Idealism, Cosmic Vision, Cosmic Comprehension, Cosmic Healing, Cosmic Intuition. These eleven senses are the Cosmic equivalents of the 38 Planetary Senses described above. The Planetary Senses were developed within the movement of the first Seven Levels of Initiation; the Cosmic Senses are developed within the 352 Levels of Initiation moving up the Cosmic Scale.

*　　　　　*　　　　　*

The Universal Law of Developing One's Conscience

Our conscience is the aspect of self that tells us right from wrong. It is our "moral compass," so to speak. There are many people who do not have a very developed conscience. How can that be? First, they are not connected to their Spiritual life. Without a Spiritual life their "moral code" is basically to do what they feel. Without a Spiritual life, one's feelings will be greatly run by the negative ego. They will be disconnected from their Higher Self and monad who do not pay much attention to the incarnated Soul until it begins to pay attention to Spirit. Spirit and your monad will let you know when you are doing something wrong. The problem is most people in this world including a great number of Lightworkers are extremely ego-defended. What does "ego-defended" mean? It means that the negative ego with its infinite number of voices, subpersonalities, belief systems, selfish motivations, narcissism, self-centeredness, separative thinking, attack thoughts, and negative ego ambitions has too much of a strangle hold on the personality. There are people that are so self-centered and run by the negative ego that they will say and do anything, and lie to your face over and over again and not even be bothered by it. They have almost zero integrity and clearly no conscience. How can that be? What causes this? It is caused by two things: lack of proper Psychological training and, hence, the individual being run by the negative ego. What is amazing is that if you would ask these people if they have a conscience, or are in integrity, and are being honest with themselves and others, every single one will say "yes" and think they are being in complete integrity. When the truth is, from the vision of Spirit, they are run by their self-centered emotions, negative ego, thirst for power, money, fame, and do not have a clue that their motives are selfish to the core. So we see, the development of conscience comes from two places. It comes directly from Spirit and it also comes directly from within one's

Psychological self. Most people are run by the negative ego, and this is why they have a hard time admitting mistakes, apologizing for mistakes, and seeing the infinite number of ways the negative ego causes one to be run by fear and self-centered motives. The development of conscience is blocked off when one allows oneself to be run by one's feelings and emotions. Believing that all negative feelings and emotions are real and come from outside of themselves causes people to do what they feel instead of being in integrity and listening to their conscience. Their conscience is, in a sense, drowned out by their overindulgence in their Emotional Body. Other people's conscience is drowned out by they letting their mind run them, and they are so run by all the thoughts in their mind that this, like the feelings and emotions, drowns out the voice of the Higher Self and the Holy Spirit, as well a the Psychological voice of the conscience. Other reasons why conscience becomes blocked are, just being run by the negative ego thought system, or not having the ability to see true motives. Many are wolves in sheep's clothing! Sometimes conscience is blocked out not because people are not trying on a conscious level, but because they are not in complete control of their subconscious mind. So their conscious mind is honestly trying, but their subconscious mind is running a different agenda. This is extremely common in this world, because people are not taught how to master the subconscious mind and how to make it subservient to the conscious and superconscious minds. This is why the development of "true conscience" and integrity depends upon enormous Spiritual and Psychological work that is done upon self so true Spiritual and Psychological Mastery can be achieved. By all means, listen to and develop your conscience to the highest level possible! The more you refine and purify your consciousness on all levels, the more subtle and refined your conscience becomes. As you become a full-fledged Ascended Master, your conscience will immediately speak to you if you start thinking the slightest negative thought, or if you indulge in the slightest negative feeling. It will notify you of even the subtlest forms of dishonesty within self or with others. Do not be victimized by your conscience, but do be in one hundred percent integrity and responsibility behind what you have caused and created, even on the subtlest levels. Now, one should not be a victim of one's conscience, for one has to always be the master of all one's energies, yet one should never deny one's conscience and suppress it, whether the lesson is some adjustment or correction that needs to be made within self or outside of self. In conclusion, one should not be overly sensitive, but not underly sensitive either. Appropriateness is also a key principle. Always remember the sacred words of Sai Baba, "The way to immortality is the removal of immorality." Ponder on this!

*   *   *

The Universal Law of Developing the Midas Touch

Midas was king of Phrygia, an ancient country in Asia Minor, whom the God Dionysus gave the power to turn everything he would touch into gold. Well, it lies within our power as well to turn everything we touch into gold. The formula for developing the Midas Touch is very simple. Stay in your power at all times. Remain unconditionally loving and forgiving at all times. Stay attuned to God, your own Mighty I Am Presence and the Ascended Masters at all times. Remain balanced in everything you do. Remain the cause of your own reality at all times. Most of all, strive to become completely free of ego. Never give into fear, separation, or self-centeredness. Take the vow of Bodhisattva and dedicate yourself completely to the service of humanity. Develop unchanging self-love and self-worth. Be attached to nothing and have only preferences. Pray and meditate constantly. Recognize that you are maintaining an individual body and a group body simultaneously, and nurture both. Purify your

Physical, Emotional, Mental, Etheric, and Spiritual Body of all Physical toxins, negative emotions, alien implants, negative elementals, Astral entities, negative thoughts, Etheric mucus, and imbalanced energies. Remain in the Spiritual Buddha/Christ/Melchizedek Consciousness at all times and never interpret reality from the negative ego or lower self mind. This is the key to developing the Midas Touch! It takes enormous commitment, self-mastery, self-discipline, great joy and great focus. You are here to achieve greatness and grandeur in God's Eyes. Do not waste this incarnation on lower-self, impermanent side roads. You were created for a much greater mission, purpose, destiny, and fate than this. Claim your empowerment, claim your leadership, claim your commitment to fully achieve and realize your Ascension, and let nothing in this universe stop you ever again, no matter how great the test. If you will now only strive to maintain these simple principles in your daily life, and hold on to them like a drowning man wants air, never giving in, no matter what the Spiritual test, you will have the Midas Touch, and everything you think, say, and do will turn to gold and to God! Namaste!

*   *   *

The Universal Law of Discipline

Life is a marathon, not a sprint! You need to set up a Spiritual regime and structure. It is just like going to the gym three times a week and working out. You don't exercise for three weeks and then stop. You must stay in shape. It is time to get back "the eye of the tiger", as they said in the *Rocky* movie. It is time to get back to the Spiritual gym, the Mental gym, the Emotional gym, and the Physical/Earthly gym! It is time to pay your rent to GOD on all levels! It is time to get Physically fit, Emotionally fit and Spiritually fit! You will never become a Master Manifestor with the

"Midas Touch" without having this attitude and demonstration! The negative ego will try and sabotage this. It will say, "I can't, I am too busy with the romantic relationship I am involved in. I am too tired! I will do it tomorrow! I will give in this one time! I give up!" Do not listen to the feeble negative ego excuses. Sai Baba said, "Discipline is the mark of intelligent living." You must ask yourself, do you want God Realization and God manifestation in every aspect of your life? If the answer is yes, then work your Spiritual program and do not stop your Spiritual practices! Don't be lazy and procrastinate! Unceasingly continue your Spiritual practices. The Upanishads teach us, "Not by the weak, not by the unearnest, not by those who practice wrong disciplines can the Self be realized. The Self reveals Himself as the Lord of Love to the one who practices right disciplines!" The negative ego has you work your program for a little while and then get distracted by side roads, temptations, Spiritual weariness, lack of self-discipline, lack of Spiritual structure, or giving up. The only way to manifest is to work your program. This is not a hundred-yard dash and then it is over and you are back to your regular life. This is a lifelong program. Being a Spiritual Master and a Master Manifestor with the "Midas Touch" is a full time job! "For God did not give us a spirit of timidity, but a spirit of power, of love, and of self-discipline." (2 Timothy 1:7 NIV)

*   *   *

The Universal Law of Divine Indifference

This law is truly a golden key! It is the cultivation of the quality of Divine Indifference. This is a quality of being the witness, objective, detached, yet still involved. It is the difference between sympathy and compassion. In sympathy you take on the other person's stuff. Compassion retains boundaries and a healthy Psychological immune system. An effective person and leader must have this quality. This allows one to respond to life instead of reacting. Ponder on this!

*   *   *

The Universal Law of Dreams

There are occasions when the superconsciousness creates dreams and occasions when they originate in the subconscious mind. For the most part, our dreams are created by our subconscious mind. A dream is basically a mirror of the way we think, feel, and act during our conscious daily life. A dream is like a newspaper we receive every night, depicting the organization and dynamics of our internal energies. A dream is an automatic process that the subconscious mind brings to us as feedback. This feedback is essential because very often we are all manifesting patterns in our lives that we are not consciously aware of. Our dreams are the main mirror we have to let us know that our conscious mind is a little bit out of tune with the superconscious mind and subconscious mind. Hence, every morning upon rising, each person should make attitudinal adjustments to make sure that their consciousness is in its proper state. This is one of the main ways that the superconscious, conscious and subconscious can work in perfect integration, harmony, and balance. The dreams also reflect, of course, all the positive patterns as well. If you are really Spiritually and Psychologically on target, this will be shown to you in your dreams. Dreams are in the universal language of symbols. By examining the relationship among the symbols, we can gain insight into and understanding of the thought patterns that are manifesting themselves in our lives through our actions. Now, the key question is, how do you find out what your personal symbols are? Examine every morning upon waking your dreams and your conscious thoughts, feelings, words, and actions from the previous day. By closely examining these things and your dream symbols, you will see repetitive symbols that keep arising. Keep a close record for these! Another key to finding your personal symbols is to just examine all the main symbols in your dreams. The subconscious, Higher Self, and Mighty I Am Presence will always give you symbols that really stand out and emphasize the point or lesson that is trying to be revealed. Just take each symbol and see what it represents. Sometimes dreams will either show a mistake or overreaction, or will point out disowned selves or subtle imbalances to adjust to be sure to get the whole picture. We are always dreaming about different people. Just examine the personality traits of that person and you will see that that aspect of yourself has been manifesting! Every aspect of your dream represents a part of yourself. Now, once in a while you will have a dream that is also depicting what is going on with another, or an outside situation. Sometimes it will be reflecting both, an inner and outer situation. It is always safer, however, to look at your dreams as reflecting parts of yourself. So the key to finding your personal symbols is to write your dreams down and keep track of them. Now, there is one thing you need to watch out for. When interpreting their dreams, people often do so from an imbalanced psychology and Spiritual philosophy. So they think they have gotten a confirmation on their belief system when in truth the negative ego is interpreting their dream and reinforcing its own philosophy. So, make sure to be totally 100% honest with self and never cease working on developing a Full Spectrum Prism Consciousness. As we proceed along the Ascension Path, it is common to have dreams of a more Spiritual nature. These dreams are not coming from the subconscious mind function of working things out via dreams, nor are they simply dreams of retelling the day's events so we can process these happenings. Working with these non-Spiritual dreams can reveal much that is going on with us and can greatly help our Psychological training. The dreams that come through the higher intuitive sense are often the actual recounting of inner-plane Spiritual encounters. People often recall attending classes of occult studies on the inner realms that are held at intervals by the Masters. There might be dreams of precognition that prepare us for events of a personal or planetary nature with which we will be involved. There might be dreams of actual encounters with specific Masters on the Inner Plane where the conversations might or might not be recollected by the conscious mind, but the knowingness of the meeting with the Master is brought forth in total clarity. Writing down your dreams can be of enormous value because you will then learn to understand both what the subconscious and the superconscious mind/higher intuition are trying to tell you, as well as from which place within the dream is truly originating. There are also dreams not to waste your time with. Sometimes dreams can be caused by eating a lot of food really late, planetary static, the Photon Belt, and a lot of other things, so the idea is to generally work with them but not be obsessive, to never give your personal power to them, and to also know when to let go of them. Always be the Master of your dreams and use them to fine tune yourself. Do not, however, let them master and use you! If you don't like the way any given dream has turned out, use a type of creative visualization to consciously recreate the dream the way you want it to go as a type of programming method. Always remember, the subconscious and dreams are not telling you what to do. The subconscious has no reasoning whatsoever! What the subconscious mind is doing is reflecting to you how you are manifesting your thinking, feelings, words, and behavior. They are not telling you what to do! They are just showing you what you are doing! By seeing this reflected and mirrored in symbols, you see it more clearly and hence can then make choices to adjust your consciousness if it is not reflecting your Spiritual and Psychological ideal. Working with your dreams can help you to really refine your Consciousness, develop a flawless character and hopefully be as GOD pure, refined, and immaculate as you can in your every thought, feeling, word, and deed!

*   *   *

The Universal Law of Empowerment

There are many levels to *The Universal Law of Empowerment*. First off, every person must own their "personal power" on a conscious mind level to achieve God Realization, Self-Mastery, and to become a full-fledged Ascended Master. Every person must own their personal power and become 100% in control of their mind, emotions, desires, Physical Body, energies, subconscious mind, negative ego, and inner child. Every person must also own their personal power, not give it to other people, outside situations, and even not give it to Spiritual teachers, gurus, the Ascended Masters, or GOD. Any true Spiritual teacher, and even GOD, is not interested in having your personal power, but in truth the opposite. They are interested in empowering you! The second level of empowerment is that once you become the Master of your subconscious mind you must give it loving commandments like a computer, to take advantage of its enormous abilities. Through utilizing affirmations, creative visualizations, and just doing Christ/Buddha thinking, you can program your subconscious mind to become your faithful servant! The third level of empowerment is calling on the incredible power of your superconscious mind, Higher Self, and/or Oversoul. The key understanding here is that it is not allowed to help you unless you ask for it. Call to your Higher Self any time you have a need or require assistance, and its power of guidance and manifestation will amaze you! The fourth level of empowerment has to do with also calling to and praying for help from your own Mighty I Am Presence or monad. This is the individualized Spirit or Spark of GOD within you. In truth, it is your real identity and what you are in the process of becoming once you become a full-fledged Ascended Master on Earth. The fifth level of empowerment is to call on the Trinity of GOD, Christ, and the Holy Spirit for help for your every Spiritual desire and need, and their infinite Love, Power, and Wisdom will supply your every need as long as your prayers are not motivated by the negative ego. The sixth level of empowerment is to call on the Planetary and Cosmic Ascended Masters, the Archangels and Angels of the Light of GOD, the Elohim Counsels and Masters, the Christed Extraterrestrials, Mother Earth, Pan, and the Nature Spirits, and the entire Godforce for your every need and desire! Ask and you shall receive the Infinite Love, Wisdom, and Power of GOD and the entire Godforce! And the seventh and last level of empowerment is centered in your Physical Body. Living within a Physical Body is the body elemental. It is a consciousness of the Physical that is filled with Love, Wisdom, and Physical Power to help you to fulfill your mission! The Physical Body has intelligence within it. Talk to your Physical Body and love it and make it part of your Spiritual team. It is very hard to fulfill your Spiritual mission if your Physical Body is not empowered! So do everything in your power to honor, respect, and take care of your Physical Vehicle so it can remain empowered and healthy and serve you well! This little paragraph sums up *The Universal Law of Empowerment*. As you see from these few lines, empowerment is not just First Ray power, but the empowerment of the Three-Fold Flame! If you try to empower yourself without unconditional love, this program will be ineffective. If you try to empower yourself without wisdom, it wont' work! So true empowerment must embody these three Divine qualities to truly call yourself empowered! This is true empowerment from GOD's perspective! Working with these Levels of Love, Wisdom, and Power in this balanced and integrated manner, free form negative ego and focused on   Christ/Buddha Consciousness, will unlock the infinite Three-Fold Power of Creation to be made available to you! GOD, the Godforce, and your own integrated balanced self are an unbeatable team!

*   *   *

The Universal Law of Equality

Lord Krishna revealed, "He who sees the supreme Lord abiding equally in all beings, the imperishable amidst perishable—he sees indeed!" There may be differences among men, in Physical strength, financial status, intellectual acumen, but all are equal in the Eye of GOD! "I look upon all creatures equally; none are less dear to me and none more dear!" (Bhagavad Gita) The negative ego tells us that we are superior to everyone else, inferior to everyone else, or both. Spirit tells us that we are all the Christ. People may be at different levels of demonstrating this truth, however, the "I" in you is the same as the "I" in me. The "I" is the God self, or the Christ. No matter what words we speak in any given sentence, the "I" is the same for everybody. God is incarnated as the Eternal "I" in everything and everyone! Heed the words of Master Jesus, "I leave you, hoping that the lamp of liberty will burn in your bosoms until there shall no longer be a doubt that all men are created free and equal! Be ye therefore perfect even as your father which is in heaven is perfect!" We leave you with the words of Dr. Martin Luther King, Jr., as spoken on the steps of the Lincoln Memorial in Washington, D.C. on August 28, 1963, "I have a dream that one day this nation will rise up and live out the true meaning of its creed, 'We hold these truths to be self-evident: that all men are created equal.'" Ponder on this!

*   *   *

The Universal Law of Everything in Life Being a Spiritual Lesson, Teaching, and Challenge

Everything that happens in life is a teaching, a lesson, a challenge and an opportunity to grow. Edgar Cayce referred to this when he said that everything that happens is a stepping stone for Soul growth. Everything that happens in life is a gift. It wouldn't be coming if we didn't have something to learn. Everything that comes to us is our own personal karma and is something that we have set in motion either in this lifetime or in a past lifetime. Each and every moment of our lives we are being Spiritually tested. Every thought we think is a Spiritual test. Every thought you think stems from love or fear. All day long, even when we sleep or dream, thoughts are coming to us from within and without. Every single moment of life is a Spiritual test to think only GOD thoughts. The same is true with every feeling and emotion you create. This is a Spiritual test. Your attitude, perception, interpretation, and belief system cause your feelings and emotions. This is an indisputable fact and law of the universe. If we think with our Christed Mind, we will create only Spiritualized feelings. If we think with our negative ego mind, we will create negative feelings and emotions. Every moment, even when you are by yourself, is a Spiritual test to see if you can keep your Emotional Body in a God Consciousness at all times. Every word you speak, every moment of your life, is a Spiritual test. Are your words coming from the negative ego or are they coming from the Heart of GOD? What is the mental motivation of your words? Are they sourced from the selfish, self-centered ego, or from true God Consciousness? What is the feeling tone of every word? Is there any attack energy, anger, or criticism, or do they carry the feeling tone of unconditional love and nonjudgmentalness? Every action you take, no matter how small, is a Spiritual test. Is that action coming from and motivated by GOD and God Consciousness, or by the negative ego and separative/fear-based consciousness? Every use of your energy, no matter how small, is a Spiritual test to see if you can use your energy to only serve GOD and not to serve the negative ego, fear, the lower-self desire, the carnal self, separative thinking, and victim consciousness. In every situation of life there is an appropriate response and an inappropriate response. Every moment of life is a Spiritual test to learn to respond appropriately the way GOD would have you respond. Every interaction with another person is a Spiritual test to see if we can remain in unconditional love, forgiveness, nonjudgementalnesss, patience, service, oneness, and egolessness at all times. Every interaction with an animal, plant, or mineral is a Spiritual test to stay in harmony with GOD and His three lower kingdoms. Every moment of life is a Spiritual test and Spiritual opportunity to realize GOD or not realize GOD. When you think a negative thought, you lose your realization of GOD on the Mental Plane in that moment. When you allow yourself to feel a negative emotion, you lose your realization of GOD in that moment on the Emotional Plane. When you behave inappropriately, you lose your realization of GOD in that moment on the Physical Plane. As Swami Nityananda put it, "There are various tests to which a devotee is subjected; they could be of the mind, of the intellect, of the body, and so on. A number of such tests are there. In fact, God is conducting tests all the time. Every occurrence in life is a test. Every thought that crops up in the mind is in itself a test to see what one's reaction will be. Hence, one must be always alert and aloof, conducting oneself with a spirit of detachment, viewing everything as an opportunity afforded to gain experience, to improve oneself and go on to a higher stage!" Now, what happens if we do not always pass these Spiritual tests? The answer is nothing, in the sense that everything is forgiven and everything always remains in unconditional love. Mistakes are positive not negative, and every mistake can be turned into a positive if you gain the "golden nugget of wisdom" from that mistake. Heed the wisdom of the Dalai Lama, "When you lose, don't lose the lesson." Sai Baba said, "Every experience is a lesson; every loss is a gain." Once God realization is achieved on a Spiritual, Psychological, and Physical/Earthly Level, one's only purpose to be on Earth is to serve. The most severe lessons of all come once a person moves into a position of leadership and/or Spiritual leadership over others. See *The Universal Law of Leadership and Self-Leadership*. Stay pure in GOD and always remember that everything that happens in life is a Spiritual test. Always listen to the small voice within you which shall be your inner guide. "In all thy ways acknowledge him, and he shall direct thy ways." (Proverbs 3:6) "For he shall give his angels charge over thee, to keep thee in all they ways." (Psalms) "A man's heart deviseth his way, but the Lord directeth his steps." (Proverbs 16:9) "And thine ears shall hear a word behind thee, saying, this is the way, walk ye in it, when ye turn to the right hand, and when ye turn to the left." (Isaiah 30:21) Heed the word of Lord Jesus: "He who follows me does not walk in darkness."

*   *   *

The Universal Law of Faith and Righteousness

The Bible says, "He that trusteth in his riches shall fall; but the righteous shall flourish as a branch." (Proverbs 11:28) This law is a loving reminder to stay righteous in God. In the Bible there is a wonderful story, the story of Job. Job was a righteous man of God who had a family and children, a big ranch, and material wealth. Satan came to God, saying that anyone can believe in and worship God when things are going well. But how about when things are not going well and all outer supports are being stripped away? Well, God had confidence in Job and so gave Satan permission to take away first Job's wealth, and then this wife and children.

Job remained righteous. Satan asked to try one more test—to take away
Job's health. Well, this was the straw that broke the camel's back for Job,
and he completely lost his righteousness. Later God came to Job and
shared with him that this had all been a test of character, virtue, and righteousness in God. It's easy to be righteous if everything goes right. The true
test lies in remaining righteous when things are not going so well. Job
heard the truth of what God was saying and then said, "Naked I came
from my mother's womb. Naked I shall leave. The Lord giveth and the
Lord taketh away. Blessed be the name of the Lord!" Job had regained his
righteousness, and his health, wife and children and wealth all returned.
Job went on to say, "Even if I should die, I will remain righteous in the
Lord." Everyone goes through this test at some point in their Spiritual
journey. It is really the ultimate test of our Spiritual faith and righteousness in God. No matter what your situation, keep your faith and righteousness, whether you face health challenges, monetary challenges, a
death, an end of a relationship, or problems of a Mental/Emotional
Nature. Hold on to your personal power and keep your faith for didn't
Jesus say, "Be thee faithful unto death and I will give you a crown of life"?
"The Lord openeth the eyes of the blind: the lord raiseth them that are
bowed down: the lord loveth the righteous." (Psalms 146:8) "A little that a
righteous man hath is better than the riches of many wicked."(Psalms
37:16) "The righteous cry, and the LORD heareth, and delivereth them
out of all their troubles." (Psalms 34:17)

                    *   *   *

The Universal Law of Faith, Trust, and Patience in GOD and GOD's Laws

One of the ways the negative ego sabotages is that it creates doubt, fear, and impatience. One of the keys to life is faith, trust, and patience. You must have faith in GOD, the Masters, and GOD's Laws some of which are being shared with you here in this book. How could you own your full personal power and positive thinking and feeling, with GOD's and the Masters' full love, wisdom, and power, and with the power of your subconscious mind, and with right action and applying all the insights and suggestions given in these pages not be successful in life? We are not dealing here with a whimsical thing. We are dealing with Cosmic and Universal Laws. If you apply them they work every time! For this reason have faith, trust, and patience in GOD and GOD's Laws. "But let him ask in faith, nothing wavering. For he that wavereth is like a wave of the sea driven by the wind and tossed." (James 1:6) Didn't the Bible say, "For we walk by faith, not by sight! (2 Corinthians 5:7) Now faith is the substance of things hoped for, the evidence of things not seen! (Hebrews 11:1) Therefore I tell you, whatever you ask for in prayer, believe that you will receive it, and it will be yours. (Mark 11:22-24 NIV) Be ye faithful unto death and I will give thee a crown of life!" Ask and you shall receive! That's law! You just need to have faith and trust in GOD and His Laws! Didn't Jesus say, "For verily, I say to you, If you have faith as a grain of mustard seed, you will say to the mountain move away to yonder place, and it will move, and nothing will be impossible for you! And they that know thy name will put their trust in thee: for thou, LORD, hast not forsaken them that seek thee. For ye have need of patience, that, after ye have done the will of God, ye might receive the promise. Be joyful in hope, patient in affliction, faithful in Prayer." (Romans 12:12 NIV) May the words of Master Jesus reverberate throughout your being forevermore, "If thou canst believe, all things are possible to him that believeth." (John 1:12) Those Biblical Pearls of Wisdom speak for themselves and don't need any further explanation! Ponder on them!

*   *   *

The Universal Law of Feedback

That which you cannot see within self you cannot see within others either. If you are not in control of the negative ego within yourself, you will not be able to discern the negative ego in others. If the Emotional Body within self runs you, you will not be able to see this happening within others. The same is true of the mind and/or Spirit. From this profound statement and understanding, you can see how important it is to develop one's self Spiritually, Psychologically and in a Physical/Earthly sense, otherwise you will not be able to see those same undeveloped aspects within others. What most people do is attract to them those people that have the same imbalances they have. This has a reinforcing effect of their imbalanced psychology and/or philosophy. Hence, the only people they get feedback from are people with the same imbalances! Ponder on this when you get or give feedback in the future!

*   *   *

The Universal Law of Feelings and Emotions

Course in Miracles says, "There are only two emotions, love and fear. Choose whom ye shall serve." In the Bible it says, "There is no fear in love; but perfect love casteth out fear; because fear hath torment. He that feareth is not made perfect in love." *The Universal Law of Feelings and Emotions* states that you have the ability to choose the way you feel because your thoughts and attitudes cause your feelings and emotions. Change your thoughts and you change your feelings and emotions. Change your thoughts and you change your whole reality. We want to refine, purify, and spiritualize our emotional self. There are many tools to healing our emotions, some of which are more yang and some of which are more yin. The six-step process for mastering emotions as described in *Soul Psychology* and the science of attitudinal healing both can be referred to as the yang method for dealing with one's emotions and feelings, whereas examples for a more yin approach to dealing with one's emotions would be the yin self-control method, yin acceptance method, yin cathar-sis method, yin indulgence method or yin secondary communication method as described as well in *Soul Psychology*. There is a concept called catharsis which is to give free expression and to identify and release your feelings through some expressive manner. This more feminine method is an essential tool to have, for by being given expression a lot of the negativ-ity can be released. This is important because a lot of people stuff these negative feelings and emotions but do not master them. In other words, it seems like self-mastery, but it is not. The negative feelings are controlled but are still manifesting in the subconscious mind. So in this case, it is bet-ter to give them some controlled creative expression (hitting a pillow, screaming) rather than hold all the negative energy inside oneself. We do not want to indulge our feelings and emotions, and we do not want to live in a state of repression and suppression. Self-mastery does not mean repression. It means self-mastery so one can properly integrate one's feelings and emotions. Now, there is the issue of the inner child. Our inner child is very connected to our feeling nature, and playful and fun side of ourselves. Many people do not properly integrate and parent the inner child, which causes the feeling nature to often suffer from low esteem, lack of self-love and/or the inner child acting out in inappropriate ways. The inner child is a very important aspect of self and should not be allowed to run one's life but definitely needs to be honored and integrated into a healthy, functioning psychospiritual system. If the inner child is denied or ignored, this tends to have a repressive effect on our feeling nature. If we let the inner child run us then that will cause our feelings and emotions to be out of control and run by the negative ego. Part of properly integrating one's feeling and emotional nature is to integrate, actualize, and realize one's Goddess nature. This applies equally to men as it does to women. This means honoring and sanctifying the proper integration of your feelings and emotions. It means learning to give expression to your feelings and emotions in multifaceted and creative ways. It means learning to use masculine and feminine methods of dealing with your negative feelings and emotions as is appropriate in any given moment. The next principle in properly integrating one's feeling nature is the issue of joy. Self-mastery, self-discipline, focused concentration, perseverance, and vigilance are all essential qualities and traits of a God Realized Being, however, it is also essential to integrate the feminine attributes of GOD which include joy, happiness, unconditional love, bliss, lightness of Spirit, humor, fun loving and playfulness, to name just a few. Do not just have vigilance against the negative ego thought system. Have "joyous vigilance." Enjoy your life. Stop to smell the roses. Life is not just a goal, it is also a process. Both must be honored. Part of understanding this law on feelings and emotions is also the understanding that it is not appropriate, as a great many people think, to do whatever one's feelings lead them to do. That would be irresponsible. Our feelings stem from our attitudes. And if our attitudes are egotistical, then all our emotions are going to be egotistical, based on fear and attack as well. Don't be seduced by this false philosophy. We can trust our feelings and emotions only once we disidentify from the ego and get the mind under control for again it is our thoughts that create our feelings. Think of something you did in the past that made you feel ashamed, and you will feel ashamed. Think of something funny that happened, and you will feel all joyous! Ponder on this! Now, there are some people who believe that it is Spiritually appropriate to have negative emotions and that they do not stem from the negative ego. It is okay to experience negative emotions as long as you take responsibility that it is your negative thinking that is causing it. We all fall into negative emotions at times and there is no judgement in this. The ideal, however, is to strive to think with your Melchizedek/Christ/Buddha Mind and hence create only emotions based on love, not fear. To create emotions based on oneness, rather than separation. To create emotions based on peace and harmony, rather than conflict. This is a process and does not happen in one day. The more self-mastery you attain over your mind, emotions, and negative ego, the more you will have Christ/Buddha feelings and emotions, rather than negative ego-based emotions. Never blame others for your emotions, for your own mind and interpretations of life create them. Feelings and emotions are not caused by outside situations and they are not caused by other people! No one has ever in the history of time caused you to feel anything! They may have attacked you or criticized you unfairly, but that did not cause you to feel anything. That is what is called the "catalyst"! The cause is your own choices, beliefs and thoughts! If you would have maintained your personal power, let it slid off your bubble, remained centered, not been attached, responded rather than reacted, and not given your power to control your feelings and emotions you would have been fine. It would have slid off your bubble and you would just respond back in a centered, powerful, calm, rational, unconditionally loving manner, setting a better example! The truth is, you are invulnerable Psychologically—Mentally and Emotionally. Children affirm their Psychological invulnerability when they say, "Sticks and stones can break my bones but names can never hurt me"! No one can make you think anything you don't want to. No one can make you feel anything you don't want to. You cause your own reality by how you think. You cause how you feel by how you think! Ponder on this!

*   *   *

The Universal Law of Focusing on One's Own Lessons Rather than Teaching Other People Theirs

Master Jesus said, "Do not try and take the speck out of your brother when you have a beam or log in your own eye!" This is one of the most classic statements of the entire Bible and sums up the whole lesson in a nutshell. People who are doing this do not have a clue that they have a "beam or log" in their own eye. The beam or log is their own negative ego and negative ego thought system. Being focused on teaching other people their lessons rather than learning their own is one of the most common pitfalls and traps of negative ego/fear-based/separative thinking. Part of the negative ego backward thinking is to stay focused "outside of self" rather than to "look within one's self!" The negative ego is "outer directed" rather than "inner directed." The person sees himself or herself as doing Spiritual service work helping others to see their lessons and pointing out all the lessons other people have. This keeps them "pointing the finger" at others and not looking at their own lessons! Leave teaching other people their lessons up to GOD. That is His job, not yours. So what that other people are not learning their lessons? That is their karma. It is always Spiritually safer and better to focus on your own lessons first. One of the first clues that you are caught in negative ego thinking on this issue is if you have any attachment or lack of inner peace if you don't say anything. That does not mean that you should not help people, however, make sure it is appropriate. It is a better policy to take the philosophy that if you don't have anything nice to say, don't say anything at all. Certainly never judge! "He that hath no sin, let him cast the first stone! Judge not that ye not be judged!" Be sure to give suggestions and advice only when asked or when it is appropriate. Be careful not to invade people's Spiritual, Psychological, Mental, Emotional, and Physical/Earthly boundaries in this regard. You are not here to teach anyone anything! You are here to demonstrate Godliness! Most often the best example is through actions and not by words! If you are right with self and right with GOD it should not matter in the slightest if other people learn their lessons or not! That is between them and GOD! Whether other people learn their lessons or not, is none of your business! The true test will come when you are in conflict with someone. The negative ego will want to teach that person a lesson. The negative ego cannot imagine not striking back and giving that person a piece of your mind. The negative ego cannot imagine being attacked and remaining silent. The negative ego cannot imagine turning the other cheek and just giving unconditional love! Well, the good news is, you are not negative ego, you are God! Choose who ye shall serve! You cannot serve two masters! Jesus said, "No man can serve two masters: for either he will hate the one, and love the other, or else he will hold to the one, and despise the other. Ye cannot serve God and mammon!" It is only when you are fully right with self and right with GOD in this manner that you then can truly be prepared to go out and teach in the proper manner! For you are hence going out to teach from a clear Psychological and Spiritual manner, and can truly be a clear mirror and reflection to your friends and students! None of your Psychological material, buttons, negative ego programming, and negative ego agendas in regard to this issue will be getting in the way! Only then as well will you be able to make the appropriate decision as to when to talk and when it is really best to be silent. It will also save you a lot of time and dealings with sometimes very negative and disturbed people by learning to have humility, turn the other cheek, and just be silent. Their attacks, criticisms, and negativity have no effect on you for you have your Golden Bubble of Light and all their negativity slides off your Golden Bubble like water off a ducks' back. It will ensure that when you do give advice or suggestions that you do it without a "beam or log in your own eye"! This is why it is so important to do your Spiritual and Psychological training, and practice and demonstrate all the information and tools that are being given to you. You are the hope of the world. It's incumbent upon you to integrate this training into your consciousness, and not just read about it but become it! Demonstrate it in your every thought, word, and deed! Then go out and teach it! It is up to those Spiritual Leaders and Lightworkers who are truly "pure of heart," who truly want only God Realization and God Purity with no negative ego deception or delusion, to go out into this world and raise consciousness! Ponder on this!

*   *   *

The Universal Law of Following a Path of Synthesis and Integration

The subject of synthesis and integration can be looked at from many different lenses and angles. The first and most important is to achieve synthesis and integration within self. Another angle, however, to look at synthesis is to look at all of the different Religions, Spiritual Paths, Mystery Schools, Spiritual teachers, Spiritual books and Gurus there are to follow. The value of a path of synthesis lies in the fact that no one path, except a path of synthesis, can give you the full truth. If you study Edgar Cayce, you get one slice of the pie. If you study the Bhagavad-Gita, you get another slice. The study of Hinduism, Buddhism, Christianity, the Islamic religion, each one gives you a different lens, so to speak. Each of these lenses is beautiful, but why limit oneself to just one slice of the pie, when you can explore GOD in all His Glory. Develop a "Full Spectrum Prism Consciousness"! If we are going to be like GOD, we must do the same in the development of our God Consciousness. If we identify with one lens only, we have blind spots. GOD sees through all lenses not just one or few. Ask at night to be taken to the Synthesis Ashram of Djwhal Khul who runs an Inner Plane Ashram that is specifically focused on the synthesis of all the Rays and all forms of understanding. Ask to be trained in developing a "Full Spectrum Prism Consciousness"! And when this is complete, call upon the Mahatma, also known as the Avatar of Synthesis, who is a vast Cosmic Group Consciousness Being who embodies all 352 Levels back to Source! Call upon the Mahatma, for both Cosmic and personal training in synthesis in all areas of your life, and He will help you! Everyone will have his or her own specific attunements and connections that are special, and this is wonderful and appropriate. Be open, however, to all the potentialities that come from seeing and understanding life from a "Full Spectrum Prism Consciousness" while following the path that you are choosing and this will enrich and accelerate your Spiritual Path in a most profound and beautiful way and manner!

*   *   *

The Universal Law of Forgiveness and Self-Forgiveness

In the Bible it says, "And the prayer of faith shall save the sick, and the Lord shall raise him up; and if he have committed sins, they shall be forgiven him." (James 5:15) *A Course in Miracles* states, "Forgiveness is the key to happiness." God has already forgiven everything. It is we who need to learn to forgive ourselves and our Brothers and Sisters. It is important to remember that no one has ever done anything to us, we have allowed it to be done to us. And if it happened, we attracted it or needed it for Soul growth. Earth life is a tough school, and in the movement of the very evolution of Earth it is inevitable that those evolving herein get caught in the lessons life must teach. The job of the Lightworker is to move through these lessons and in so doing, heal both him/herself and the world at large. This cannot be done if one is carrying around the ball and chain of guilt, judgment and nonforgiveness. As each of us moves forward into the exploration of certain major planetary issues, let's do so as a Son/Daughter of God, free from any guilt or shame. All inner and outer problems are being called to light so that they can be seen, cleansed, purified, and healed. They are not being called to light for either the judgment of self or others. Cast aside any blame, guilt, fear or shame that you might hold regarding these issues! By purifying yourself in the fire of divine forgiveness, you are likewise well on the way of purifying, clearing and healing humanity itself. In *A Course in Miracles* Jesus says that the Crucifixion was nothing more than an extreme lesson of love and forgiveness. He was not dying for our sins, because we do not have any sins. What he was demonstrating was that even in the most extreme lessons, in which a person is being beaten, tortured, crucified, and killed, it is possible to remain loving and forgiving. Jesus said, "Forgive them, Father, they know not what they do." He went through this most extreme challenge to prove to us that forgiveness is possible even under the most extreme circumstances. If Jesus could do it under these circumstances, then certainly we can forgive our-selves and others for all our lessons. That is why he demonstrated this example. So your negative ego could not say my lessons are worse! Now, the key to forgiveness is that we need to forgive both, ourselves and others. Remember the words of prophet Muhammad, "Forgive them who wrong you; join them who cut you off; do good to them who do evil to you; and speak the truth although it be against yourself." The outside world is really a projection screen for your own thoughts. To maintain unconditional self-love and worth over the long term you must forgive self and others for all of it is GOD, and you are God. "If we really want to learn how to love we must learn how to forgive," as Mother Teresa said. So, in forgiving oth-ers you are really forgiving yourself as well. Forgiveness is an essential key ingredient to maintain self-love, otherwise *The Universal Law of Karma* will bring those unforgiving thoughts towards others back to self, which will affect the personal level of self-love! In truth, you forgive others as well not as a charity to them, but as a charity to yourself! "And now abideth faith, hope, charity—these three; but the greatest of these is charity. " (2 Corinthians 9:7) Your forgiving them has nothing to do with them, it has to do with correcting faulty thinking within yourself. Many, however, on this Earthly Plane forgive others but do not forgive self. This is faulty thinking for everything is forgivable. This world is but a dream of GOD! And Earth is really just a Spiritual school to see if you can forgive self and others in all circumstances. By forgiving self for all mistakes, all guilt is relieved as well as regret. By learning from the experience and making a specific Spiritual vow to never let that mistake happen again, you can let go of all guilt and all regret. To not forgive self is to just make another mis-take that you will need to forgive yourself for! As *A Course In Miracles* says, "Forgiveness is the key to happiness"! There is no mistake in the history of the Earth and this infinite universe that is not 100% forgivable by GOD, and that is a fact. It is only the negative ego mind that holds grudges. As Jesus said, "You are forgiven, however, sin not more." Forgive yourself, make the appropriate adjustments and move on. The

Spiritual/Christ/Buddha Consciousness sees nothing in life to even for-give, for mistakes are positive and not negative. As we all know, perfection is not NOT making mistakes. Perfection is trying to not make conscious mistakes. As Paramahansa Yogananda said, "A saint is a sinner that never gave up!" "And be ye kind one to another, tenderhearted, forgiving one another, even as God for Christ's sake hath forgiven you." (Colossians 3:8)

                    *   *   *

The Universal Law of Fulfilling One's Puzzle Piece

ai Baba said, "Man will realize his mission on Earth when he knows himself as divine and reveres others as divine." Each person is cre-ated by God differently. Just like no two snowflakes are alike, neither are two people. Each person has a unique purpose and mission on Earth that they have come to fulfill. Some of this will depend on the skills and talents you have developed in this life and past lives and on the inner plane and all that you have done since your creation by God! "We have different gifts, according to the grace given us." (Romans 12:6 NIV) Leo Buscaglia is quoted as saying, "Your talent is God's gift to you. What you do with it is your gift back to God." As Jesus said, "Do not keep your good qualities hidden, but let them shine out like a candle lighting up a dark house. When a lamp is lit, it is not put under a bowl, but placed where it can brighten the whole room." Use your talents in service of God! Now, part of finding and fulfilling your puzzle piece also has to do with each person's Ray structure, for each person has a different set of Rays for their monad, Soul, personality, mind, emotions, and Physical Body. Having a particular Ray configuration will generally propel you into a specific line of work, but there are a number of contributing factors—environment, heredity, karma, astrological configuration, level of Initiation, and of course, freedom of choice—that will ultimately determine your particular profession. What the negative ego will do is tell a person that it wants them to live out someone else's puzzle piece. The negative ego feels that their puzzle piece is not glamorous enough. The negative ego may tell you to write a book, when it is not really your Dharma to do so. The negative ego may want you to be famous and a player on the world stage, when that is not your puzzle piece. Trying to live out someone else's puzzle piece is doomed to failure! True inner peace and fulfillment can only be found by living out the puzzle piece that is your true destiny, as GOD would have it be. This is also the puzzle piece that will bring you the greatest amount of success and the least amount of stress! The key is to become right with self and right with God and to become an integrated Spiritual Master to the best of your abilities, because there will be lots of Spiritual Tests along the way the higher you go. Also, be sure to physicalize and materialize your Spirituality so it is fully manifested, not just on the Spiritual plane and the Psychological plane, but also so it fully 100% manifests on the Physical/Earthly plane. In the final analysis, once you have found what is for you your right work, the true fulfilling of your puzzle piece lies within your ability to express your Spiritual nature within that work. Remember, it is not all up to God and the Masters, for, in truth, life is a Co-Creation. Since you are God, it is also up to you to help create your Spiritual mission. Trust your intuition! Do what Spiritually excites you. Do that which you do best and feel most skilled at. It must be understood that before you came into this world you wrote out a very detailed plan, blueprint, and contract for this lifetime. In this blueprint and contract you signed, you wrote out everything you wanted to accomplish this lifetime. This is all stored in deeper recesses of your subconscious mind and also by your Higher Self and monad. What you actually want to strive to do is to accomplish all you planned and then write out a new personal blueprint and contract for yourself that far surpasses anything you have previously

planned. The sky is the limit! One person on Earth can have an astronomical effect on the fate of the world. Be that person! Surprise God and the
Masters! The key to making the Masters notice you is to come up with
some form of service work to the world that is of value to them. Dedicate
yourself to being that person that will totally change this world in some
way special that only you can do with your style, gift, and grace. Show to
yourself, God and the Masters what you are made of. Show and prove to
yourself and to God, the Masters that you are one of those rare individuals that can manifest their Spirituality on all three levels—Physical,
Psychological, and Spiritual—and can fully manifest their Spirituality to
your fullest impact and potential on Earth. Leave a legacy. A legacy and
contribution to God is much different than worldly standards. The greatest contributors to the world are most often the ones no one knows about
and never will know about. Maybe the greatest contribution of all will be
the joy you spread. Your Christed example. Your kindness. Your egolessness and selflessness! Be relentless in your efforts and do not give up until
you succeed. It is only when all people fulfill their puzzle piece that the
Divine Plan can work. Ponder on this! Jesus saith unto them, "My meat is
to do the will of him that sent me, and to finish his work." (John 4:34)

*   *   *

The Universal Law of Geometric Codes and Their Effect on Your Chakras and Light Bodies

Geometric Coding is a divine mathematical process God and the
Masters use to create almost everything in the universe. Geometric
Coding has been used since the beginning of time and space and has no

boundaries in the creation of all things known and unknown to humanity at this time. It is a special mathematical coding for creation of light, electrons, neutrons, atoms, cells, amino acids, cellular structure, molecular structure, electromagnetic fields, epikinetic fields and all Light Bodies from here to eternity! Archangel Metatron, the creator of all light throughout God's infinite universes, and the Mahatma, a group Consciousness being of all Light Synthesis, work collectively as a team to create this miraculous miracle directly under God's leadership and command. Geometric Codes are the foundation of Creation. Everything in and of this Earth was created in part and parcel with Geometric Codes. Everything in Creation has a base structure of numerical coding. Numerology is founded on the basis of numbers having a direct relationship with all your emotions, personality traits, astrological placement, and your path in life, not only for the future, but for each day of your existence. Numerology is a good tool to understanding Geometric Codes but it is not the entire essence of the equation. Geometric Codes affect every level of existence from your blood, DNA, RNA, molecular structure, intellectual structure, cellular placement, Light Bodies, physics, and basically the evolution of your entire being on every level! Now, how do Geometric Codes affect your Light Bodies and Chakras? First, you must realize the importance of keeping your Chakras cleaned and balanced throughout your lives. If your Chakras are muddy or out of balance, this will create an overall imbalance throughout your entire system. Once you achieve a higher level of Spiritual/Christ/Buddha/God Consciousness your Chakras and Light Bodies will usually remain in balance aligning perfectly with your level of consciousness. Geometric coding has a direct relationship to this process of attunement to God and achieving the highest level of Spiritual/Christ/Buddha/God Consciousness. The higher your attunement and achievement of Spiritual/Christ/Buddha/God Consciousness, the more direct a relationship it will have to the re-coding of your Light Bodies. How does re-coding make a difference in your life and to your Light Bodies? As your level of consciousness increases, God dispenses his blessings of re-coding the geometries associated with the function and intellect of your Light Bodies. The geometric coding is re-calculated or re-configured so that the higher intelligence and higher divine light will be infused into all your Chakras and Light Bodies! You will reap the divine rewards of Geometric re-coding through the process of owning your personal power and creating this conscious reality for yourself. Geometric Codes affect every stage and level of your life experience, knowledge, intellect, psychology, Physical Bodies, the Earth, the list is endless! The key lesson is to learn to balance and integrate all of the Spiritual/Physical/Earthly/Psychological areas of your lives and remain in Spiritual/Christ/Buddha/God Consciousness throughout this school of life and experience!

*   *   *

The Universal Law of Giving

Mother Teresa said, "God loves a cheerful giver; she or he gives best who gives with a smile." There is a saying in *A Course in Miracles* that says, "To have all, give all to all!" What this means is that if you want to have GOD and everything on all levels, you must give everything on all levels. That which we hold back in giving to our Brothers and Sisters and the world is in truth that which we are holding back in giving to ourselves. This is true because we each are, in truth, an incarnation of GOD and the Eternal Self. We are not our Physical Bodies, living separate, unconnected lives to other people. In our true identity, as incarnations of GOD, every person and everything in GOD's Infinite Universe is a part of us. So when we hold back giving to another out of fear, competition, comparing, jealousy, envy, selfishness, or any other negative ego duality, we are in truth not giving to ourselves, for GOD and our Brothers and Sisters are literally part of ourselves. When we hold back giving, we think we are helping our-selves, when in truth we are not giving to our Self, in the larger context of who we really are. The negative ego will tell you that giving is losing. Spirit will tell you that giving is gaining. "Winning gives birth to hostility. Losing, one lies down in pain. The calmed lie down with ease, having set winning and losing aside." (Lord Buddha, Samyutta Nikaya III, 14) The only way to receive GOD and maintain GOD Realization is to give GOD every moment of your life. The second you stop giving GOD you have not lost GOD in truth, however, you have lost GOD in your Realization of His Holy Presence. So, no one can lose GOD in truth, however, you can lose your Realization of GOD by indulging in negative ego thinking and emotions. This is also why if you steal from your Brothers and Sisters on any level you are literally stealing from yourself. For you would be stealing from GOD, and stealing from your Brothers and Sisters who are God. All of Creation is part of you and you are part of all Creation. This does not mean that there is not a time in life to be Spiritually selfish, to take care of yourself, and to set proper boundaries where necessary. This is an essential lesson to learn in becoming an "Integrated Christ." What this does mean, however, is to not hold back giving on all levels for the reasons of selfishness, greed, narcissism, self-centeredness, competition, jealousy, envy, comparing, and any other negative ego motivation you can think of. "My conscience is clear, but that does not make me innocent. It is the Lord who judges me. Therefore, judge nothing before the appointed time; wait till the Lord comes. He will bring to light what is hidden in darkness and will expose the motives of men's hearts. At that time each will receive his praise from God." (1 Corinthians 4:4-5 NIV) You will only fully real-ize GOD and have everything when you are able to give GOD to every-one and everything. Be Spiritually selfish where GOD, the Holy Spirit, and your own Mighty I Am Presence guide you to be. Never, however, hold back giving on any level to your Brothers and Sisters because of neg-ative ego selfishness, which is the opposite of Spiritual selfishness, which is a good and needed thing at times. It takes a very pure heart and great

Spiritual discernment to know the difference. Jesus said in *A Course in Miracles*, "Helping my Brothers and Sisters is my true church." In reality, who is being helped the most is yourself. For in giving your all you are receiving all back from God. This is law! Here is one more "Biblical Nugget" from Master Jesus, "Take heed that you do not give alms making it a show; otherwise you will have no reward of your father in heaven!"

*   *   *

The Universal Law of Glamour, Illusion, and Maya

There is delusion on the Astral Plane, on the Mental Plane, and on the Etheric Plane. Each of these planes has a unique form of delusion specific to its level, and each of these delusions has its unique remedy. The form of delusion on the Astral Plane is called glamour, on the Mental Plane illusion, and on the Etheric Plane maya. The remedy for glamour is illumination, the remedy for the Mental-Plane illusion is called intuition, and the remedy for the Etheric-Plane maya is inspiration. "The dweller on the Threshold" is the sum total of all the delusion on all three levels. It is the sum total of the forces of the lower nature prior to illumination, intuition, inspiration, and initiation. Maya is experienced upon the Path only when one begins the Path of Probation (which is prior to the Path of Initiation), and deals with the world of vital forces where a person can be victimized by emotions, thoughts, and also just energy or vital force. Until one attains Self-Mastery, an aspirant can be swept around by all kinds of uncontrolled forces. It is for this reason that maya is predominately a difficulty of the Etheric Plane and Etheric Body. People are governed by maya when they are controlled by any force or forces other than those energies that come directly from the Soul. Inspiration of the Soul will devitalize and remove maya. The glamours that hold humanity are, the glamour of materiality (overidentification with materialism), the glamour of sentiment (pseudo-love based on attachment), the glamour of the pair of opposites (person swings back and forth between opposites without even-mindedness), the glamour of devotion (fanatically following a cause), and the glamours of the Path (working with the Ascended Masters from the negative ego's perspective). The remedy for dissipating glamour is illumination. Trying to dispel glamour with intuition or inspiration does not work. It is the illumined mind, or Buddha/Christ/Melchizedek thinking, that will get rid of glamour. Glamour is Astral in character; the Astral glamour needs the use of the illumined mind, just as the illusions of the Mental Plane need the next level above it which is intuition. The Astral glamour needs hard, straight, correct thinking in the service of the Soul's guidance. This is achieved through right analysis, discrimination, and right thought. Glamours of the First Ray would be: glamour of Physical strength, personal magnetism, and glamour of destruction. Glamours of the Second Ray would be: glamour of being loved, personal wisdom, and glamour of self-pity. Glamours of the Third Ray would be: glamour of being busy, "good" intentions which are basically selfish, and glamour of devious and continuous manipulation. Glamours of the Fourth Ray would be: glamour of harmony, psychic perception instead of intuition, and glamour of the pairs of opposites. Glamours of the Fifth Ray would be: glamour of materiality, the intellect, and glamour of knowledge and of definition. Glamours of the Sixth Ray would be: glamour of devotion, idealism, and glamour of World Saviors and Teachers. Glamours of the Seventh Ray would be: glamour of magic work, sex magic, and glamour of the mysterious and the secret! Illusion is the form of delusion on the Mental Plane, the remedy of which is called intuition. When a person lets his ego interpret reality rather than the Soul, he is lost in illusion. In the context of the Four-Body System, those people who are more intellectual than emotional in nature are more prone to illusion than

Gglamour. A person who is caught in glamour needs to learn how to become more polarized in the Mental Body. When a person is over-identified with the Emotional Body, he ends up being on an emotional roller coaster! Only intuition, and not illumination or inspiration, can dispel illusion. Intuition is inner knowingness that goes beyond logic and emanates from the Buddhic Plane of Consciousness and Higher Mind. One of the absolute keys to dispelling illusion is to learn to hold the mind steady in the light. Most people in the world let their minds wander willy nilly and do not keep them focused. People have not been trained to own their personal power and to retain Self-Mastery at all times. People let themselves operate on automatic pilot and lose their vigilance. When this happens, the ego or lower self becomes their director. "Let all bitterness, and wrath, and anger, and glamour, and evil speaking, be put away from you, with all malice." (Ephesians 4:32) Ponder on this!

*   *   *

The Universal Law of God Realization

God alone is the giver of life, the guardian of life, and the goal of life. (Sai Baba) The purpose of life is to realize God! This is not something GOD, however, will do for you! This is something you must do with your own personal power and free choice! All of Creation is going through this process. Even if we never ate of the Tree of Good and Evil or thought a negative go thought or feeling, we would still be going through the 352 Levels of Initiation! This was part of the Divine Plan of GOD, that all beings in GOD's Infinite Universe would not just be God because GOD created them, but would also go through this process of evolution to realize God with their free choice! "Who are you? God. Where did you come from? God. Where are you going? To God." "You have come from God, you are a spark of his glory; you are a wave of that ocean of bliss; you will get peace only when you again merge in him." (Sai Baba) The eating of the fruit from the Tree of Good and Evil, and the corresponding densification of matter made this process a little more complicated and a little more difficult, however this was in part our doing, for this was not part of The Plan! The good news is, that the Seventh Golden Age is at hand, and by the Grace of GOD and the Masters, and the effort of humanity itself, we are now waking up with Godspeed, and realizing from whence we came! To truly be a God Realized Being you must transcend all negative ego/fear-based/separative thinking and learn only to think with your Spiritual/Christ/Buddha Mind. You must integrate and balance the Seven Rays, Twelve Archetypes, Twelve Signs of the Zodiac, Twelve Sephiroth on the Tree of Life, all the cards in the Tarot Deck, Three Minds, Four Bodies, Four Faces of GOD, God/Goddess, Feminine and Masculine, Heaven and Earth. You must learn to properly parent your inner child. You must be able to totally ground your Spirituality on Earth and fulfill your Spiritual mission and puzzle piece on Earth. You must be able to do this in a totally balanced and integrated manner! You must also be able to develop all your talents on a Spiritual, Psychological and Physical/Earthly Level. This is where the confusion lies. Lightworkers develop their Spiritual talents and gifts in one area like channeling, Spiritual teaching, healing, science, and so on, which is wonderful, however, if they don't do it on all three levels (Spiritual, Psychological, Physical/Earthly) with no negative ego influence, and if they don't do it in a totally integrated and balanced manner, integrating the Seven Rays, Twelve Archetypes, balancing the vertical and horizontal planes of life, integrating and sanctifying the Four Faces of GOD (Spiritual, Mental, Emotional, and Material), balancing the Three Minds, Four Bodies, God/Goddess, Heaven and Earth, Feminine and Masculine, mastering the subconscious mind, mastering lower-self desire, mastering the feelings and emotions, mastering the

Physical Body, and one's energy, to name just a few, then disintegration and fragmentation will take place. Limited lens seeing will take place. Faulty thinking and negative feelings and emotions will slip in. Wrong motives, some bad habits and addictions will be prevalent. Health lessons will present themselves other than for reasons of just Spiritual mutation. The purpose of life is to try and retain God Consciousness at all times. The Spiritual Path is very simple. If you want to be with God in Heaven, you must act like God on Earth. A big part of this is holding to your Spiritual ideal, even if other people are doing everything in their power to stop you. When you let other people stop you from holding your Spiritual ideal and doing your Spiritual mission, you are putting other people before your relationship with self and GOD. The Spiritual ideal is to own your Personal Power, and be the Master and Cause of your own reality in service of GOD and Unconditional Love, and to stick to your Spiritual ideal and your Spiritual mission regardless of whether one single person supports you or not. When you are right with yourself and right with GOD, the Inner Plane Ascended Masters and the Angels, this is all you need. "If GOD be for you, who or what can be against you?" When you are right with self and right with GOD and learn to think with your Spiritual/Christ/Buddha Mind, it will not matter whether people praise you are criticize you. All you will care about is remaining in God Consciousness at all times, and serving regardless of the fruits of your service. Mahatma Gandhi said, "It's the action, not the fruit of the action, that's important. You have to do the right thing. It may not be in your power, may not be in your time, that there'll be any fruit. But that doesn't mean you stop doing the right thing. You may never know what results come from your action. But if you do nothing, there will be no result." Every moment of life is an opportunity to Realize GOD in that moment. You are already one with GOD, in truth, but we have incarnated into Physical Bodies and onto Earth to practice demonstrating and realizing this truth. All seeming setbacks will be welcomed as just another Spiritual lesson and test, and preparation for something even better to happen.

"Above all else to thine own self be true," will be your motto. To be true to yourself is to be true to GOD, for in truth they are one. You recognize that GOD and your Spiritual Path must come first, for that is the purpose of life. Your main purpose is to Realize GOD each moment, not to seek outward rewards or approval from others. The irony of life is, however, as the Bible states, "Seek ye the Kingdom of GOD and all things shall be added unto thee." Ponder on this!

*   *   *

The Universal Law of GOD's Laws

Everything in GOD's Infinite Universe is governed by laws. "Every cause has its effect; every effect has its cause; everything happens according to law; chance is but a name for law not recognized; there are many planes of causation, but nothing escapes the law." (The Kybalion) The key to becoming a Spiritual Master is studying and applying these laws and becoming obedient to them. There are laws of a Physical, Etheric, Emotional, and Mental nature! Whenever Souls get out of harmony with these laws, they cause their own suffering! The setting up of certain veils of limitation was to lovingly force Souls to become obedient to GOD's Laws! If there were no laws, then Souls would be unconscious for eternity and never change. What makes Souls wake up is that in being disobedient to the laws they bring suffering upon themselves, which forces them to seek truth as a means to alleviate suffering! Remember the Biblical words, "This Book of the law shall not depart out of thy mouth; but thou shalt meditate therein day and night, that thou mayest observe to do according to all that is written therein: for then thou shalt make thy way prosperous, and then thou shalt have good success." (Joshua 1:8) Living in harmony with God's Laws is the key to happiness and success!

It is possible to transcend all Physical laws! Sai Baba is a being who has transcended all Physical laws! Jesus demonstrated this by being able to walk on water, turn water into wine, and raise the dead! It is possible for all Souls on Earth to transcend all Physical laws through the process of God Realization and Integrated Ascension. So walk your path in harmony with God's Laws! "Therefore whoever hears these sayings of mine and follows them, I will compare him to a wise man, who has built his house upon a rock." (Jesus)

*   *   *

The Universal Law of Grace and Falling from Grace

Sai Baba teaches, "The grace of God is like insurance. It will help you in your time of need without any limit." At any level of Initiation, no matter how high you have gone, you can always fall from grace. Falling from grace means, you can become out of harmony with GOD, the Masters', and GOD's Divine Plan at any moment. Falling from grace does not occur in an instant. It is a prolonged series of choices that one makes to serve the negative ego rather than GOD and the Christ/Buddha Consciousness. Many Lightworkers once they achieve higher levels of Initiation become prideful, overconfident, and filled with self-aggrandizement, and have false feelings of invulnerability. "A man's pride shall bring him low; but honor shall uphold the humble in Spirit." (Proverbs 29:23) In truth, it is only by the Grace of GOD that we each are protected and live in grace each day. Many Lightworkers fall from grace, and the cause is always the same thing: they lost their Spiritual vigilance and allowed the negative ego to take over. This comes in many forms: self-aggrandizement, hunger for power, fame, and greed, to name but a few. The amazing thing is they do not even realize the negative ego has taken over. What happens often is that people who once had very pure motives, once they achieve personal and financial success and a modicum of power in their lives, they lose their Spiritual vigilance and their previous purity goes out the window and the negative ego comes back with a vengeance. It happened to Lucifer who was an Archangel and it can happen to any person on Earth even after achieving one's Ascension. Heed these words of guidance. Be aware of the negative ego within self and develop great Spiritual discernment in terms of seeing it within others. If you have blind spots to seeing the negative ego within self you also will not be able to see it in other people. This is an immutable and unchangeable Psychological law. Strive to be of the same character whether you have profit or loss, pleasure or pain, sickness or health, fame or infamy. Be ever vigilant no matter what level of success you have attained on any level, to maintain your attunement to GOD and His Kingdom! May these Biblical words reverberate throughout your being forevermore: "There but for the grace of GOD go I."

*   *   *

The Universal Law of Gratitude and Humbleness

The negative ego's attitude is to take people and life for granted. The Spiritual attitude is one of constant gratitude and thanksgiving. There is so much to be grateful for every day. And if you currently have handicaps and limitations, the Spiritual attitude is to focus on what you can do instead of what you can't do. "I can do all things through Christ, which strenghtens me." (Philippians 4:13) Look at Saint Francis, who apparently had terrible Physical health problems, and yet became one of the most revered Christian saints. Mother Teresa had terrible heart problems and yet she dedicated her life to serving and helping others. Remember, even the bad things that happen are really gifts and Spiritual tests—blessings in disguise. God will never give you more than you can handle! Be grateful for every moment in your life, for it is God who makes your heart beat every moment of your life! Prophet Muhammad taught, "A person will not enter hell who has faith equal to a single grain of mustard seed in their heart. A person will not enter paradise who has a single grain of false pride." And the Bible instructs us, "Humble yourselves before the Lord, and He will lift you up. (James 4:10) Better it is to be of a humble Spirit with the lowly, than to divide the spoil with the proud. (Proverbs 16:19) But he giveth more grace. Wherefore he saith, God resisteth the proud, but giveth grace unto the humble (James 4:6) Let another man praise thee, and not thine own mouth; a stranger, not thine own lips." (Proverbs 27:2) Or as Jesus so aptly put it, "For whosoever exalts himself shall be abased; and he that humbles himself shall be exalted."

*   *   *

The Universal Law of Grounding One's Spirituality

Many Lightworkers live in the Celestial realms and are not grounding their Spirituality on Earth. To fully realize God, one must do it on all three Levels—Spiritual, Psychological, and Physical/Earthly. We are here to be God on Earth. If we want to be with God in Heaven we must act like God on Earth. This is the Material Face of God. It must be honored, embodied, and sanctified. Our service must also take a Physical form so we are doing some good in this Earthly/Physical world, not just on the Spiritual, Mental or Emotional planes! Each person, in truth, is responsible for leaving a legacy in this world. Many Lightworkers are running away from their Earthly responsibilities. They are not manifesting their Spirituality in their Physical Bodies and in God's Physical Body! Some Lightworkers are arrogant and think they are too good to enter the Physical, which means grounding their particular gift and Spiritual mission onto the Earth. Whatever it is get it onto the Earth. Make a difference in people's lives Physically as well. Just having wonderful ideas, or visions, and never manifesting this in the Physical world means nothing! The purpose of life is not just to achieve liberation! We each have a Spiritual mission and contract as our way to make a difference in this Physical world. Remember, how much service work you do on the Earth does control how much the Spiritual powers that be will allow you to evolve! Those who do not serve will not be allowed to evolve, no matter what Spiritual practices you are doing! Now another insight in this regard has to do with the Seven Great Rays. The Major Rays are numbers one, two, and three. Ray one is Power! Ray two is Love/Wisdom! Most Lightworkers get stuck in the first two and do not properly integrate Ray Three of Active Intelligence. This means using your intelligence to manifest something in the Physical world. The lesson is to get our Spirituality out of the clouds and get it down to Earth. If you are not grounding your Spiritual mission you are not fully realizing God and this is a fact! We each have a responsibility to create Heaven on Earth. We are here to create a Utopian Society on Earth. Get your hands dirty a little and get involved! Do not use Spirituality as corruption to reject the Material Face of God and the Goddess Energies. As Sai Baba said, "Hands that help are holier than lips that pray!"

*   *   *

The Universal Law of Habits

Many people think habits are bad. This is not true. We want to get rid of only bad habits. Ideally we want to create good habits. It is the subconscious mind that stores all of our habits, both positive and negative ones. If we didn't have a subconscious mind to store our developed abilities, every activity would always take great focus and concentration. Let's take the example of learning how to drive a stick-shift car. When we first learn how, it takes a lot of conscious effort and willpower. After we learn how, it requires little conscious thought. It's stored in the subconscious. The subconscious mind's ability to store habits allows us to grow continually and develop new abilities without worrying about old ones. You can learn something in a day, but there is a basic Psychological or Metaphysical Law that states that it takes twenty-one days to cement a new habit into the subconscious mind. Remember, the subconscious mind is filled with all sorts of tapes that our parents and other people programmed into us when we were young. It is the job of the conscious mind to consciously make choices and break old habits and create new ones as to prevent that all this old programming from early childhood is controlling our present life. Let's remember the words of Aristotle, "We are what we repeatedly do. Excellence, therefore, is not an act but a habit."

*   *   *

The Universal Law of Having Preferences Rather Than Attachments

This law is about the importance of having preferences rather than attachments. "All suffering comes from one's attachments", as Lord Buddha stated in his four noble truths. With preferences you are happy whichever way a situation turns out, but with attachments you lose your inner peace if things don't go the way you had wanted. The negative ego causes us to be attached to everything. Spirit guides us to have preferences rather than attachments. An attachment is an attitude that causes us to get depressed or angry or upset if our expectations aren't met. A preference is an attitude that lets us be happy no matter the outcome. So what the Buddha basically is saying is that if we give up all our attachments, we no longer have to experience suffering at all. It isn't anything external that causes the suffering; it is our attachment to outside things that causes the suffering. Some people believe that they are not allowed to have preferences. It is very important in life that we have our preferences and that we go after them with all our heart, and Soul, and Mind, and might. However, if they don't come about, it is important to prepare to be happy anyway. By doing this, happiness becomes a state of mind rather than a condition outside of self. The happiness that so many are seeking lies in developing a certain perspective towards life. Always remember, a basic law of the universe states, "That which you are attached to you repel!" Ponder on this!

*   *   *

The Universal Laws of Healing

Following are the nine laws of healing according to Djwhal Khul as transcribed by Alice Bailey in her book called Esoteric Healing.

❖ All disease is the result of inhibited Soul life. This is true of all forms in all kingdoms. The art of the healer consists in releasing the Soul so that its life can flow through the aggregate of organisms, which constitute any particular form.

❖ Disease is the product of and subject to three influences: First, a man's past, wherein he pays the price of ancient error (reincarnational history); Second, his inheritance, wherein he shares with all mankind those tainted streams of energy which are of group origin (racial-cultural history); Third, he shares with all the natural forms that which the Lord of Life imposes on His Body. These three influences are called the "Ancient Law of Evil Sharing." This must give place some day to that new "Law of Ancient Dominating Good" which lies behind all that God has made. This law must be brought into activity by the Spiritual will of man.

❖ Disease is an effect of the basic centralization of a man's life energy. From the plane whereon those energies are focused proceed those determining conditions which produce ill health. These therefore work out as disease or as freedom from disease.

❖ Disease, both Physical and Psychological, has its roots in the good, the beautiful and the true. It is but a distorted reflection of Divine possibilities. The thwarted Soul, seeking full expression of some divine characteristic or inner Spiritual reality, produces within the substance of its sheaths, a point of friction. Upon this point, the eyes of the personality are focused and this leads to disease. The art of the healer is concerned with the lifting of the downward focused eyes into the Soul, the healer within the form. The Spiritual or third eye then directs the healing force and all is well.

❖ There is naught but energy, for God is Life. Two energies meet in man, but another five are present (Seven Rays—seven Chakras). For each is to be found a central point of contact. The conflict of these energies with forces and of forces twixt themselves, produce the bodily ills of men. The conflict of the first and second (the Soul and Personality) persists for ages until the mountaintop is reached—the first great mountaintop. The fight between the forces produces all disease, all ills and bodily pain which seek release in death. The two, the five and thus the seven, plus that which they produce, possess the secret. This is the Fifth Law of Healing within the world of form.

❖ When life or energy flows unimpeded and through right direction to its precipitation (the related gland), then the form responds and ill health disappears.

❖ Disease and death are the results of two active forces. One is the will of the Soul, which says to its instrument, "I draw the essence back." the other is the magnetic power of the planetary life, which says to the life within the atomic structure, "The hour of reabsorption has arrived. Return to me." Thus, under cyclic law, do all forms act.

❖ Perfection calls imperfection to the surface. Good drives evil from the form of man in time and space. The method used by the Perfect One and that employed by Good, is harmlessness. This is not lack of negativity but perfect poise, a completed point of view and Divine understanding.

❖ Harken, O Disciple, to the call which comes from the Son to the Mother (Soul to Body), and then obey. The Word goes forth that form has served its purpose. The principle of mind then organizes itself and then repeats that Word. The waiting form responds and drops away. The Soul stands free. Respond, O Rising One, to the call which comes within the sphere of obligation: recognize the call emerging for Ashram or the Council Chambers (heart center or head center) where waits the Lord of Life Himself. The Sound goes forth. Both Soul and form together must renounce the principle of life and thus permit the monad to stand free. The Soul responds. The form then shatters the connection. Life is now liberated, owning the quality of conscious knowledge and the fruit of all experience. These are the gifts of Soul and form combined. This last law is the enunciation of a new law which is substituted for the Law of Death, and which has reference only to those upon the latter stages of the Path of Discipleship and the stages upon the Path of Initiation."

Djwhal Khul said that, "Ill health is basically misdirected thinking." Ill health then is the physicalization of negative ego thoughtforms. Health is the physicalization of Christ/Buddha Consciousness and thinking. Lack of health is not a bad thing, but a good thing, being nothing more than a neutral indicator of an imbalance or misdirected thought in the psyche. If we didn't have health lessons, we would never learn. It is our ultimate teacher to help us align our minds and emotions with God's Laws. Instead of cursing your body for getting sick, bless your body for being your neutral and objective guide, which does nothing more than mirror your state of consciousness. If our bodies never gave us these signals, we would never achieve liberation and true God Realization. Our bodies in essence force us to remain on our Spiritual Path. God is balance, and it is our bodies that force us to hold to this ideal. God's Sons and Daughters can often be quite rebellious and disobedient, like little children. It is through suffering and health lessons that most of us have found God and our Spiritual Paths. Let the Physical Body teach you to remain balanced, integrated, and attuned to the Mighty I Am Presence at all times! Now, it must be understood that many people are suffering from Physical health problems, and misdirected thinking is definitely a reason for Physical challenges, but not the only one! A great many Lightworkers suffer from a great many Spiritual mutational symptoms! A great deal of these health lessons are from accelerated Ascension processes! This is an absolute fact and must be clearly understood! It also needs to be understood, however, that there are a small number of cases where the negative ego can use

Spiritual mutation as a catch all or as a defense mechanism for not learning one's lessons! There are some individuals who think what they are going through is all Spiritual mutation and Ascension, however, in truth, some of it is Psychological unclarity and lack of mental, emotional and negative ego mastery, and a lack of being Physically grounded and integrated in one's bodies and living on Earth! For example they may not like the Earth, so their consciousness and soul does not stay in the Physical Body. Their consciousness is in the clouds and stays their as does an aspect of their soul! This disintegration and fragmentation takes a great toll on the Physical Body! There is not enough energy in the lower Chakras! These individuals get totally activated and expanded Spiritually in their quest for Ascension, however, are not often integrated Psychologically, or in a Physical/Earthly level, or both! Hence the Physical Body symptoms are indeed Spiritual mutation symptoms, but are also a manifestation of improper Psychological and Physical/Earthly grounding! Such individuals often seek Ascension as a type of escape from the Earth instead of embracing Earth life and being integrated into it in the proper way and learning their Spiritual lessons and tests! So as you see, Spiritual mutation can be misused by the negative ego, to make one think all Physical health lessons are Spiritual mutations, when some may have consciousness causes, or have their roots in not being properly grounded, and some may even be Physical health lessons that need to be addressed by a homeopathic doctor, naturopath, herbalist, or even medical doctor! So it is important to always have an efficient perception of reality and to be clear on where the causes of Physical health lessons are coming from and to see that some come from Spiritual mutation, some from one's consciousness and psychology, some from one's diet, sleep patterns, Physical exercise or lack thereof, some from lack of Spiritual Groundedness and balance! Ponder on this!

*   *   *

The Universal Laws of Hermes Trismegistus

"The Principles of truth are seven; he who knows these, understandingly, possesses the magic key before whose touch all the doors of the temple fly open."—The Kybalion

1. The principle of Mentalism
2. The principle of Correspondence
3. The principle of Vibration
4. The principle of Polarity
5. The principle of Rhythm
6. The principle of Cause and Effect
7. The principle of Gender

These seven Hermetic principles are the basis for the entire Body of Hermetic philosophy. Below is an in-depth explanation of them.

The Principle of Mentalism

"The all is mind; the universe is mental." This principle embodies the understanding that everything in the universe is created by thought. There is nothing that exists in the material universe in which this is not the case. Edgar Cayce, in his channelings of the Universal Mind, said over and over again, "Thoughts are things." The entire universe was created by the thought of God. As God's sons and daughters, humans create reality both metaphysically and physically by the power of mind. The great law of Spiritual psychology is that thought creates reality. Everything that exists is spirit: matter is just densified spirit; spirit is just refined matter. All is simply energy.

The Principle of Correspondence

"As above, so below; as below, so above." This famous aphorism was created by Hermes. What this law means is that the thoughts and images you hold in your conscious and subconscious minds will manifest their mirror likenesses in your external circumstances. The outer world is a mirror of your inner world. If you hold thoughts of poverty, you will have no money. If you hold images of ill health, that will manifest in your Physical Body. This law works unceasingly for the good or the bad. By understanding this law, you can use it for your benefit instead of your detriment. The most profound application of this law is seen in the life of Sathya Sai Baba. Whatever He thinks instantly manifest on a Material Level. He creates Physical objects with a wave of his hand, and he says he does it by just thinking and imaging what he wants to create. This is the same law but here it is speeded up. Earth is a school for practicing these laws of mind control. Imagine what would happen if the average person on the street were manifesting his thoughts instantly, as Sai Baba does. If he had a negative thought about someone at this level of vibration it might actually Physically kill the person. Imagine what all your negative thoughts and emotions would instantly do to your health. For most people, it is a good thing that thoughts don't manifest that quickly yet, or they would be in a lot of trouble. The higher the level of your Initiation and the higher your vibration, the more quickly your thoughts will manifest. That is why the Spiritual Path at the higher levels has been called the straight and narrow path and why it is visualized as a pyramid that gets narrower as you move toward the apex.

The Principle of Vibration

"Nothing rests; everything moves; everything vibrates." This principle explains the difference among the various manifestations of matter and spirit. From pure spirit all the way down to the grossest level of matter, there is a continuum of vibrations. Every atom and molecule is vibrating with a certain motion, speed, and frequency. It is the combination of these factors that determines the form of any given object, be it of a physical or metaphysical nature. Everything is in motion and is vibrating, and nothing is at rest. Even a Physical object, a chair, for example, is actually in a state of motion. The atoms and molecules are vibrating, and there is space between the atoms and molecules. This is true of the atoms as it is true of the solar system, galaxy, universe, and omniverse, for the omniverse is nothing more than a large atom. The microcosm is like the macrocosm. Sai Baba can take a Physical object and transform it into a new object just by changing that motion. You do the same thing using your thoughts. The entire universe is in a state of motion revolving about the Great Central Sun. Every atom is a mini-universe within every molecule of your Physical Body. How you think manifests in your emotions, actions, health, and what you attract to yourself because energy follows thought. The ideal is to create a motion that is determined by your Higher Self, rather than by your lower self, or negative ego. Each of the seven Initiations is a higher level of vibration and motion. God is the highest pinnacle of vibrational frequency. That must be your goal.

The Principle of Polarity

"Everything is dual; everything has poles, everything has its pair of opposites; like and unlike are the same; opposites are identical in nature, but different in degree; extremes meet; all truths are but half-truths; all paradoxes may be reconciled." This is a fascinating principle. Take, for example, heat and cold. Although they are opposites, they are really the same thing; it is merely a matter of different degrees. The same could be said of spirit and matter. They could be likened to water: freeze water and it becomes ice, or matter; boil water and it evaporates and becomes a gas, or spirit. They are identical in nature but different in degree. If you look at a thermometer, where does heat terminate and cold begin? In actuality, it is totally relative to body type and individual preference. The same principle applies to all pairs of opposites—light and dark, large and small, hard and soft, positive and negative. The principle also applies to the Mental Plane. Take, for example, love and hate. They are the same but different in degree. The importance of this law lies in understanding your ability to transmute vibrations from one extreme to the other. This, in reality, is the study of alchemy. The alchemists of the Middle Ages were preoccupied with changing base metals into gold. This is possible, as Sai Baba demonstrates so clearly and instantly. However, the real meaning of alchemy is that you can change your base thoughts and emotions into Spiritual gold, or Soul-realized energies. Hate can be transformed by the power of your mind into love. Your lower self can be transformed into your Higher Self. Separation can be turned into oneness. Guidance by your negative ego can be turned into guidance by your Soul. An empty bank account can be transformed in a full bank account. All this can be achieved by using the art of polarization. To accomplish all that, you simply need to polarize your Consciousness differently. If you are run by your Emotional Body, you need to become polarized in your Mental Body. If you are identified with your Mental Body or intellectual self, you might need to become polarized in your Soul. If you are merged with your Soul, you will need to become polarized in your monad. If you are merged with your monad, you need to become polarized in God. All are degrees of the same thing. The science of attitudinal healing involves working with this art of polarization. That is why Psychics were predicting a shift of the Physical Poles of Earth—the poles of humanity's consciousness were not shifting from fear to love.

The Principle of Rhythm

"Everything flows, out and in; everything has its tides; all things rise and fall; the pendulum-swing manifests in everything; the measure of the swing to the right is the measure of the swing to the left; rhythm compensates." You can see this law manifesting in every aspect of life: in the tides of the oceans, in your need for sleep after a day of work, in the creation of a star and its eventual collapse, in the rise and fall of nations, and even in the operation of the omniverse. For every action there is an equal and opposite reaction. You see it in your breathing; you see it in God's breath as He breathes creation out and then breathes creation in. You see it in the movement of stars and in the science of astrology as the Earth moves through the signs of the Zodiac. You can also see the law of rhythm operating in human mental states, where the Hermetic practitioner finds its greatest and most useful application. Hermetists cannot annul this principle or cause it to cease operating; however, they have learned to escape its effects upon themselves to a certain degree by applying the mental law of neutralization. The degree to which they are able to do so is determined by their application of this law and their level of Initiation. Hermetists have learned how to use the law instead of being used by it. The Hermetist's understanding of the law of polarity polarizes him at the point at which he desires to rest and then neutralizes the rhythmic swing of the pendulum which would tend to carry him to the opposite Mental and Emotional Pole. The Master does this by using will and detachment to create a state of consciousness that is not swung back and forth like a pendulum. Whereas the masses of humanity live on mental and emotional roller coasters, the ideal is to attain a state of consciousness of divine indifference, evenmindedness, equanimity, inner peace, joy, unceasing happiness, and bliss. Krishna explains the very same teaching in the *Bhagavad-Gita* when he says that the goal is to remain evenminded in the face of profit or loss, pleasure of pain, sickness or health, victory or defeat, rejection or praise. There is a point of neutrality or objectivity or divine detachment that is not caught up in the pendulum-swing between polarities. There is a state called God-Consciousness in which you don't have to have a bad day. In the highest application of this principle of neutrality, it is even applied to the Physical Body; for example, Sai Baba never sleeps, never needs food, never gets tired. He can bilocate and be in two places at the same time. This is the Ascended Master State of Consciousness in which the monad, or Spirit, merges completely with the Physical Vehicle, and the Physical Body is turned into Light. Duality is transcended. Whether you are on an emotional roller coaster or are evenminded and have unceasing equanimity and joy is determined by the polarization of your mind. That is why the understanding of these principles is so important. In his later life as Buddha, Hermes expounded on this point further when he said, "All suffering comes from one's attachments and wrong points of view." Part of the purpose of writing this book is to show how the principles are the same in all religions—whether you study the Egyptian teachings, Hawaiian Huna, Buddhism, Christianity, Hinduism, Taoism, the Koran, or another—even though they might be expressed in slightly different ways.

The Principle of Cause and Effect

"Every cause has its effect; every effect has its cause; everything happens according to law; chance is but a name for law not recognized; there are many planes of causation, but nothing escapes the law." There are no accidents. Everything in the universe is governed by Laws: there are Physical Laws, Emotional Laws, Mental Laws, and Spiritual Laws. By understanding these Univeral Laws you can learn to operate in grace instead of accumulating karma. Many times it is difficult to know why things happen. That is because there are many dimensions of realty in which causations can occur. As Edgar Cayce said over and over again in his readings from the Universal Mind, "Every jot and tittle of the law is fulfilled." No one escapes anything, even though it might sometimes appear that some people are going unpunished. In truth, they are not. The Hermetists understand the art of rising above the ordinary plane of cause and effect by moving onto a high plane of consciousness and, hence, becoming masters instead of victims, and causes instead of effects. The average person on the street is an effect, not a cause. He is a victim of thoughts, moods, emotions, desire, appetites, his lower self, other people, biorhythms, his Physical Body, past lives, subconscious programming,

heredity, the weather, astrological influences, vital forces, discarnate spirits, glamour, maya, illusion, and the environment, to name a few. The
Master rises above such elements and masters them. By the time of the
sixth Initiation and Ascension, all of them have been transcended. The
Masters obey the causation of the Higher Planes, but they help to rule
them on their own planes. At each level of Initiation a Master rises to
another Plane of Consciousness, hence becoming a greater cause. The key
for most people on the Earth Plane is to gain mastery over the mind,
which leads to mastery over the emotions and desires and also to mastery
over the Physical Body and appetites. Djwhal Khul has called this mastery
over your three lower Vehicles—the Physical, Astral, and Mental Bodies.
The basic causes of the details of your life are the thoughts and images you
hold in your conscious and subconscious minds. By learning to be
absolutely vigilant and allowing into your mind only thoughts of God,
love, perfection, perfect health, prosperity, joy, oneness, and equanimity,
you will create those qualities both inwardly and outwardly. Your thinking
must be subservient to your Soul and monad (Spirit), instead of to your
lower self and negative ego. When these lessons are mastered then there is
no longer any reason to attend this school called Earth life, except for
service to your Brothers and Sisters who have not yet mastered them. Be
the cause, be the Master, be the Co-Creator with God that you truly are.
Then you are using this principle instead of allowing it to use you. If you
are not a master, you are a victim; that is the law of polarity. Change your
polarization with the power of your mind and the power of your God-
given free choice.

The Principle of Gender

"Gender is in everything; everything has its masculine and feminine principles; gender manifest on all planes." Everything has a yin and yang. On
the Physical Plane each person has a male or a female Physical Body, however androgynous he or she might be in terms of thoughts and feelings. In

Chinese philosophy, foods are divined into yin and yang. This law applies not only on the Physical Plane, but also on the Emotional, Mental, and Spiritual Planes. Father God and Mother Earth; yang emotions and yin emotions; yang thoughts and yin thoughts. The key point here is that the Spiritual Path is the path of balance and integration. Buddha called it the Middle Way. He demonstrated that the path to God was not the path of either self-indulgence or asceticism but was the path of balancing the male and female aspects within the self and also of balancing the Heavenly and Earthly aspects within the self. The Spiritual Path also includes the balancing of the Four Minds, the Four Bodies, and the Seven Chakras. It also means proper balance between the Soul and the ego. This is achieved by transcending negative ego, hence keeping the ego in its proper relationship to Soul, allowing it to take care of the Physical Body but not to interpret your life. As mastery is achieved this balanced state becomes more habitual and doesn't require as much time and energy. Balance is achieved by "knowing thyself" and understanding the universal laws that govern your being. To know God, you must understand God's Laws.

*　　　　　*　　　　　*

The Universal Law of Higher Self and Lower Self Desire

Aristotle is known as having said, "I count him braver who conquers his (lower self) desires than him who conquers his enemies, for the hardest victory is the victory over self." In Buddhist and all Eastern Philosophy it is taught that one must transcend or get rid of all desire. The Buddha said, "With desire the world is tied down. With the subduing of desire it's freed. With the abandoning of desire all bonds are cut through."

(Samyutta Nikaya II, 69) This teaching of the need to transcend and get rid of desire has created a lot of confusion. It has also created a rejection and disownment of the feeling nature. This is not because the statement is untrue, but is because this statement is misunderstood. Lord Buddha also said, "The master never gives in to desire. He meditates. And in the strength of his resolve he discovers true happiness! When your light shines without impurity or desire, you will come into the boundless country! The master cuts all ties. He gives up all his desires. He resists all temptations. And he rises!" It is essential to transcend desire, but what is meant here is "lower self desire," not "Higher Self desire." Sri Anandamayi Ma said, "You will have peace only if you rise above desires." It is the desires of the negative ego and the carnal, hedonistic, lower-self that needs to be transcended and gotten rid of, not Spiritual desire. The desire body is integrally connected to the Emotional Body and/or Astral Body. The cutting-off of desire is the complete blocking of one's feelings, emotions, and subconscious energy. It is essential in life to have Spiritual desire. A desire to achieve God Realization. A desire to be of Spiritual service. "Set your mind on things above, not on earthly things." (Colossians 3:2 NIV) Without Spiritual desire you will have no enthusiasm and/or Spiritual passion. It is not passion we want to get rid of; it is lower-self passion, not Higher Self passion. Passion is connected with enthusiasm. When we engage the Emotional Body in everything we do, we also engage the subconscious mind, which is the real powerhouse and magnetic force that magnetizes and attracts things into our life. "Life by the Spirit and you will not gratify the desires of your sinful nature." (Galatians 5:16 NIV) The Eastern religions talk about giving up desire. The ideal of life isn't to give up desire, but rather to only have Higher Self desire. Ideally, your all-consuming desire in life is to attain God Realization, liberation and Ascension, and to be of service. As Paramahansa Yogananda said, "To realize God you must want Him as much as a drowning man wants air." "Delight thyself also in the Lord and he shall give thee the desires of thine heart." (Psalm 37:4)

*   *   *

The Universal Law of Holding One's Frequency

It is quite interesting that in every real cyclone that hits the Earth, if you are in the very center of it, everything is totally still. This truth reigns supreme in a Spiritual and Psychological sense as well. For the Spiritual Path and life itself is often like a cyclone. From God's perspective, everything that happens in life is a Spiritual test and lesson to see if you can stay centered, calm, balanced, unconditionally loving and remain in your Christ Consciousness at all times. The key lesson of life to be able to do this is to learn to be a master on a Spiritual/Psychological and Physical/Earthly Level, and then to balance and integrate these three levels as well. The other key is to transcend all negative ego/fear-based/separative thinking and feeling and to only think with one's Spiritual/Christ/Buddha Mind and Feelings! Being able to do this along with being balanced and integrated is the key! The other key is that you must learn to own your personal power and self-mastery at all times and be the cause of your reality at all times and not the effect or victim on any level. The other key is you must be the absolute master of your mind, emotions, subconscious mind, inner child, lower-self desire, and negative ego! We have all heard the quote that he who masters self is greater than he who masters the whole world! The other key is to always remain right with self and right with God as your two most important relationships. If you are right in those two, then all relationships to people and things and life remain right. It is the ability to maintain absolute self-mastery over your mind. By mastering the mind, you can master and choose your feelings, emotions, behavior, and master your Physical health and what you attract and magnetize into your life! By mastering your mind and recognizing happiness and inner peace is a state of mind and/or perspective that is not based on anything outside of self, this is how one learns to live at all times in the Center of the Cyclone or Eye of the Hurricane! Now in Spiritual terminology this is called "learning to master and hold your frequency"! This is one of the most important Spiritual abilities that a Spiritual leader, teacher, channel, disciple, initiate or Spiritual master needs to develop! For if you cannot master and hold your frequency, how can God and the Masters rely on you to hold Spiritual Leadership, Global World Service, advanced Spiritual assignments, allow you to move into Cosmic Levels of Ascension, and give you increased levels of Spiritual current and Cosmic frequencies? If you cannot master and hold your frequency on all levels in a balanced and integrated fashion then the inner and outer forces of life will be continuing to knock you off balance! This is why the purpose of life is to become an "integrated and balanced" Spiritual Master! Earth is a school to practice this. When you learn these lessons, then you remain on Earth to be of service and help others achieve these things! Then you ascend Spiritually and/or Physically and graduate, so to speak, to continue your integrated Spiritual service work at a higher level of existence on the Inner Plane in a more expansive arena! Thus, moving slowly but surely through the 352 Levels of GOD and the Mahatma, back to Source where eventually we will all serve as Cosmic Ascended Masters serving all of Creation! One of the premiere lessons of the Spiritual path, to be able to walk this path, is to learn to live at all times in the Center of the Cyclone, the Eye of the Hurricane, and to be able to master and hold your frequency Spiritually, Psychologically, and in a Physical/Earthly manner at all times in a balanced and integrated way!

*   *   *

The Universal Law of Honoring and Sanctifying the Material Face of God

In the study of esoteric thought, it is understood that there are Four Faces of GOD. There is the Spiritual Face, the Mental Face, the Emotional Face, and the Material/Physical Face. No one face is better than another. They are just different aspects of the Creator. There is often a conscious or unconscious belief that the higher dimensions are more Spiritual or sanctified than the third dimension of Earth or the third dimension of the Universe. There are many Heavens of GOD and the Material Universe is one of GOD's Heavens. The Divine Plan is not to escape the Material Universe and Earth, but rather, to bring Heaven to Earth, to create a Christed/Buddha society on Earth. The work towards the achievement of such a society is based first on each individual attaining their own personal Ascension. The term "Ascension" is really a misnomer. When we ascend, we do not leave the Earth, we are grounding our Higher Self and monad into our Physical Bodies on Earth. So, Ascension is really descension. The purpose of life is to become a walking embodiment of the Mighty I Am Presence or Christ/Buddha on Earth. The Earth is Holy Ground. Never forget this! Didn't God say to Moses, "Put off they shoes from off thy feet; for the place wheron thou standest, is holy ground." (Exodus 3:5) Ponder on this!

*   *   *

The Universal Law of Huna Prayers

The Huna method of prayer as taught by the Kahunas of Hawaii is to write out on paper in very clear and precise language exactly what you want to manifest. Address the prayer to exactly the being or beings you are asking to respond to it. Then say your prayer three times out loud. Then command your subconscious mind to take the prayer to your soul or monad with all the mana, or vital force, that is needed and necessary to manifest your prayer. Wait about fifteen seconds to allow time for the subconscious mind to do that. Finally, to complete the prayer process, say the phrase, "Lord, let the rain of blessings fall!" Before performing the prayer, it is recommended that you do some deep breathing or physical exercise to build your vital force and that you forgive anyone who needs your forgiveness, so that the path to the Higher Self is clear. Huna belief also recommends praying from full personal power and not from weakness or lack of self-worth. The Universal Mind through Paul Solomon said that the clearest form of psychology and religion on the planet was the Huna teachings of Hawaii. You can use Huna Prayers for any area of your life. The power and effectiveness of this particular technique will amaze you! Never forget, you create your own reality. The Godforce responds to your free will choice and to the power of your spoken word. You are God, and your word is law! These prayers are sacred, so make sure that it is your Higher Self writing them and not your negative ego. As the Shinto saying goes, "A single sincere prayer moves heaven. You will surely realize the divine presence through sincere prayer." Your soul or monad will not respond to any prayer that would hurt another person or yourself. "Prayer must emanate from the heart, where God resides, and not from the head where doctrines and doubts clash." (Sai Baba)

*   *   *

The Universal Law of Hypnosis

Hypnosis is actually a very common phenomenon that happens to all of you throughout your day. Every time you are feeling like a victim or are on automatic pilot, you are in a state of hypnosis. Every time you let your subconscious mind run you, you are hypnotized. Every time another person's thoughts or feelings affect you, you are in a subtle state of hypnosis. When you read a book, watch television, or drive your car, you go into a state of hypnosis. If you are a person who is a victim instead of a master of your life, you are living most of your life in a state of hypnosis. Hypnosis is a form of relaxation. It is suggestibility. It is much like meditation. They are both altered states of consciousness, the difference being, that the intention of hypnosis is to give suggestions to the subconscious mind while the intention of meditation is to quiet the mind and/or approach the Spiritual world! But the actual states are not unlike each other. Now, hypnosis occurs when the subconscious mind is running the conscious mind—when you are doing things by habit, daydreaming, fantasizing, or on automatic pilot! Hypnosis is not bad. It's just widely misunderstood in this society. To the ordinary person, hypnosis as well as self-hypnosis are tainted with negativity caused by a misuse of the tool by stage hypnotist and misinformation spread by the media! It becomes dangerous only when you are not consciously choosing, controlling, or in some way monitoring and directing the process. The hypnotherapist cannot force suggestions into your mind. The only effect they could have is the effect you would let them have! Ponder on this! The only effect they could have is the effect you would let them have! You cannot be hypnotized against your personal power or will! You cause your own reality! If someone criticizes you and you feel hurt and rejected, you have been negatively hypnotized. You have let another person be the programmer of your emotions! Actually, there are three basic depths of hypnosis: the Beta Level is full consciousness, the Alpha Level is the state between waking and sleeping, and the Theta Level is the early stage of sleep, deep hypnosis or deep meditation. The Delta Level is deep sleep! The deeper the level of hypnosis, the more suggestible a person becomes. If a suggestion is given to a person in a conscious state, the reasoning or critical faculty either rejects or accepts it. In hypnosis it goes immediately into the subconscious mind. This is the reason for giving yourself suggestions while in an altered state of consciousness. So how can this information now help us in our every day life? Since our childhood, our subconscious mind has been programmed by our parents, peers, television and so on. As a result, we need to clean out and reprogram our subconscious mind! Hypnosis or self-hypnosis is a wonderful tool to accomplishing this task. An ideal time for programming is during meditation or when you are waking up or falling asleep! That way the suggestions/affirmations go right into the subconscious mind! Programming with suggestions and affirmations still works when you are in a conscious state, but it requires more repetition. Reprogramming our subconscious mind is one of the most important things one can do, for it is the subconscious mind that runs our Physical Body! In the future, hypnosis, self-hypnosis, and the understanding of programming and suggestion will be a basic part of every aspect of our society! It can be used as a replacement for anesthesia, to cure insomnia, headaches, phobias, for physical healing, past life recollection, in the realms of dentistry, surgery, weight control, smoking, constipation, stage fright, for pain alleviation, childbirth, habit removal, emotional healing, crime and law enforcement, sports, the learning of languages, amnesia, and the finding of lost objects, to name but a few! The subconscious is the seat of memory and it picks up everything that is going on, even though the conscious reasoning mind does not! While in a waking state witnesses may remember nothing about a bank robbery, whereas under hypnosis they can recall even the license number of the car the robbers were driving! Are you starting to see the profundity of hypnosis? Under hypnosis, a person can be given suggestions to hallucinate in all five senses and they will experience whatever suggestions the hypnotist gives them to experience.

98% of the world lives in a subtle form of hypnosis all the time. Automatic pilot is hypnosis. Day dreaming is hypnosis. Not owning your 100% personal power all the time is a subtle form of hypnosis. Being run by the subconscious mind is a subtle form of hypnosis. Being over emotional is a subtle form of hypnosis. Being run by the inner child is hypnosis! People meet others and the other person tells them they don't look well physically. They felt fine before they met that person on the street or wherever. Later they feel sick because that person has hypnotized them without necessarily meaning to. It occurs because the individual is a victim and hypersuggestible. The person is now sick and it is a massive hallucination. Not that they are not sick, but the sickness came from allowing that negative thought to be implanted into the person's subconscious mind and now the subconscious mind has made the person's Physical Body sick. This is why doctors in Japan often do not tell the patient of a serious illness so they do not create a self-fulfilling prophecy! Now there is one statement, attributed to Emile Coue, a famous French hypnotist who coined the famous affirmation, "Every day, in every way, I am getting better and better." He said, "When the will and the imagination are in conflict, the imagination will win out." Talking about the Law(s) of Hypnosis, it seems very important to make this statement part of this discourse! The imagination is the seat of the subconscious mind, so what this statement is saying is that the subconscious mind is more powerful than the conscious mind. Nothing could be farther from the truth! The most powerful force in this universe is human will and personal power! If this were not true, nobody could ever achieve Self-Mastery! The subconscious is definitely more powerful if you are under hypnosis, but is not if you are not under hypnosis! The subconscious mind is an amazing tool! And it is only through mastering the subconscious mind and aligning it with the conscious and superconscious mind that we shall realize God in all His Glory!

*   *   *

The Universal Law of Inner and Outer Organization

If you want your outer life to be together you have to keep your mind and emotions organized and together. One of the absolute keys to Spiritual and worldly success is to pay attention to every thought, every word, every feeling, every piece of energy, and every deed! As the great Hermetic Law states, "As within, so without. As above, so below"! If you want your outer life to be successful you must make your inner life immaculate on every level. You must make sure your every thought only serves GOD and Christ/Buddha Consciousness. You must make sure your every feeling and emotion only serves GOD and Christ/Buddha Consciousness. You must make sure every use of your energy only serves GOD and Christ/Buddha Consciousness. You must make sure every physical action you make only serves GOD and Christ/Buddha Consciousness! You must make sure that every word you speak only serves GOD and Christ/Buddha Consciousness! To maintain a flawless character and immaculate nature Spiritually and Psychologically takes enormous attention to detail in an inner and outer sense. Since our thoughts create our reality, if our mind is disorganized we are going to have disorganized feelings and emotions. If our mind is disorganized our energies are going to be a little chaotic. If our mind is disorganized our behavior is going to be a little chaotic. If our mind is disorganized our life is going to be chaotic. So, the key is to keep your consciousness all organized! If you are disorganized you are never going to be able to manifest effectively. If you are disorganized then what will manifest in your life is disorganization and chaos! Part of wisdom is having the smarts to start your day by getting organized first. Many people run around like chickens with their heads cut off! They are like a mouse on a wheel, putting out a lot of energy but not going anyplace. Get organized first! A clear mind and heart will help to create a clear manifestation! So, one of the keys to inner peace is the ability to compartmentalize or organize certain things in your mind! Learn how to file things away in your own mind and to keep your consciousness organized, which is essential to do, otherwise one cannot maintain a constant state of inner peace. Make Spiritual Lists! The advantage of writing things down on lists is that you do not have to try and remember anything, so your consciousness stays free and clear to be creative and receive inspiration, guidance, and direction. It allows your consciousness to sparkle with creative ideas and sparkling potentialities. It also allows you to really keep track of details. Nothing is lost. It allows you to "Pursue Excellence" at a very refined level. Another advantage of writing things down and keeping lists is that you don't forget. Creative and channeled ideas are constantly flowing through you, and if you don't write them down you will forget them. This attention to detail is to take advantage of every little nuance of creative and sparkling potentiality. This attention to detail and striving to be "immaculate" in everything that one does establishes an integrity in your person. You do not fudge. You hold to your Spiritual and Psychological ideals! That greatly helps in manifestation, for your entire being becomes this incredible magnet of attraction for this "Immaculate Spiritual/GOD/Christ/Buddha ideal! So strive for immaculate organization within your own consciousness, and your outer life shall reflect this perfected state! Namaste!

*　　　　　*　　　　　*

The Universal Law of Inner and Outer Spiritual Parenting

To begin with, we must understand that from a Spiritual perspective there is no such thing as children! There are only adults Souls who incarnate into children's bodies! There is no such thing as a child Soul.

They have usually had hundreds of past lives, and hundreds of sets of parents! Secondly, each person chooses their parents! That's a fact! A person's karma does dictate this to a certain extent, and of course, the availability of parents on Earth, however, you do have a choice in the matter! Thirdly, contrary to popular opinion, the Soul does not live in the womb. This is illusion. It has a very deep connection to the fetus, however the Soul does not incarnate into the Physical Body until just right before birth or just after birth! The body is not the Soul! Also, the belief that some people have that children are a blank slate and it is only the parents and environment that cause it to have the personality it has is ludicrous! This is called Tabula Rasa! This is illusion. Each Soul coming in has had hundreds of past lives so they have totally formed personalities, however this of course is not to say that parents and environment do not affect the child, for it has a very profound effect! Now, in truth, children when they are born are total victims, and they remain victims most of their childhood. Children do not know how to cause their reality by how they think! They do not know how to cause their emotions and feelings by how they think! They do not know how to protect and shield themselves from the negative thoughts, words, and behaviors of other children or adults for that matter. So in truth, they are at the mercy of their parents, extended family, teachers, peers, and so on, who program them! They are programmed into personality level thinking because our education is completely devoid of any Psychological and/or Spiritual education. They are taught to think with their negative ego mind which is called normal. But it is not! Children as they are growing up need parents to be in control and to provide parenting, structure, guidance, and direction. The parents should be the child's Spiritual teachers! Some parents think children should be allowed to do what they want. This is called spoiling, and will teach the child not to have self-control and Self-Mastery with self! In truth, parents are the conscious minds that children don't have! By proper parenting with firmness and love, and the parents being in charge, the child begins to develop and learns how to achieve a healthy conscious mind! A conscious mind which knows how to have some degree of Self-Mastery over their thoughts, feelings, emotions, subconscious, inner child, desire body, and negative ego! Then there are some parents who believe children and parents should be equals. This would be poisonous to the child! Children need parents to guide them, teach them! To let the child be an equal is to let the negative ego, Emotional Body, nonreasoning subconscious mind, personality, and desire body run the child's life! A child needs Spiritual, and Psychological and Physical/Earthly training and education! Some parents try to live through their children or try to shape their children to be totally like them. This is wrong! Children need guidance but need to be allowed to follow their Soul inclinations as well! There is a balance to be found! In the Hawaiian teachings the Higher Self is called the Aumakua or "utterly trustworthy parental self". Just as our Higher Self is our "utterly trustworthy parental self", we are meant to become the "utterly trustworthy parental self" for our real children and inner child! Our job is to teach our outer children to become the "utterly trustworthy parental self" for themselves! Which brings us to the subject of inner parenting! We all have a relationship to ourselves! What is this self? Another name for this self is the inner child or child consciousness. Each person must learn to parent their child, and this applies, as we have learned, inwardly and outwardly! There are two ways of parenting either ourselves or a real external child—the Spiritual way or the egotistical way. The Spiritual way of parenting is to be firm but loving, so yin and yang are balanced. The wrong way to parent is to be too firm or too permissive. A parent who is too firm is excessively critical which translates into the child both inner and outer feeling unworthy or unloved, and having low self-esteem. When a parent is too lenient the child can become spoiled or rebellious. Both are products of negative ego and imbalanced thinking! A firm and loving parent helps the child become balanced and well adjusted. So tough love is the key! The child consciousness is a psychic reality. Learning to raise the child within you properly, you will also be a much better parent to your real children. Your inner child really just wants your unconditional love, just as a real child does. Down deep, your inner child wants firmness, just as a real child does. If you are firm and loving, then both the child within you and your flesh-and-blood children will develop self-control, personal power, and self-love. Be firm and loving with your inner child and self, just as God is firm and unconditionally loving with us as a parent. For just as God is, of course, unconditional, He is firm in the sense that he does have Universal Laws He expects us to learn and to follow, and if we don't follow them and become obedient to them, we cause suffering upon our self. The suffering is not a punishment, it is just a reminder or a signal to seek truth and understand God's Universal Laws on a Spiritual, Mental, Emotional, Etheric, Physical, and Earthly Level! Ponder on this! This law is an absolute key to becoming right with self!

*   *   *

The Universal Law of Integrated Meditation

Just as prayer is talking to God, meditation is listening to God. Very often Lightworkers are better at talking than meditating. The reason for this is that the lack of proper Psychological training has caused most people to be run by the mind. The negative ego causes the mind to be overactive. In the Bhagavad-Gita, Krishna instructs Arjuna, "It is true that the mind is restless and difficult to control. But it can be conquered, Arjuna, through regular practice and detachment. Those who lack self-control will find it difficult to progress in meditation; but those who are self-controlled, striving earnestly through the right means, will attain the goal!" The combination of lack of mastery over the mind and feelings, and the negative ego's control over the mind makes it hard to sit still. The key to appreciating meditation and having effective meditations is to have meditation first in the right perspective and second to use effective meditations. There are more active and more quiet types of meditation. There are hundreds of forms of meditation, each with a different purpose and use. To become an "Integrated Spiritual Master" and to Realize God in a full spectrum prism manner, which is to see and experience God through many lenses not just one, it is good to practice many different forms of meditation. Different types of meditation achieve different things: "Ascension Activation Meditations" with Spirit and the Masters will accelerate your Ascension Process like nothing else. (*Ascension Activation Meditations of the Spiritual Hierarchy: A Compilation*; 15 Ascension Activation Meditation Tapes) "Breathing Meditations" take you out of your mind and immediately quiet your whole system. The "So Ham Meditation", the meditation most recommended in the Eastern world, where you repeat the word "So" on the in-breath, and the word "Ham" on the out-breath, will bring you deep inner peace. Practicing the "Om or Sound Meditation", where you chant the word "Om" or "Aum" over and over in your mind at a slow but steady pace, it is possible to hear the Music of the Spheres on each of the different dimensions. "Channeling and Automatic Writing Meditation" will bring you an enormous amount of love and light into your consciousness and energy fields! "Soul Travel and Bi-Location to the Ascension Seats of God" is a way of running the Spiritual Current of God and the Masters at the various levels and dimensions of reality. "Chanting the Mantras, Names of God, and Words of Power" will keep your mind and heart always steady in the Light and Love of God, and serve as an impenetrable shield of armor against anything and everything that is not of God. "Meditating with Nature" allows you to experience, commune, and merge with nature. Doing "Creative Visualization Meditations," the visualizations will imprint and impress themselves upon your subconscious mind like a video camera, and if meditated upon on a continual basis, will outpicture those images into your outer reality. "Self-Hypnosis Meditation" can be used for the purpose of

God attunement or self-programming. (Self-hypnosis, hypnosis, and meditation are all extremely similar; they are all states of consciousness, the only difference being the purpose which you are using them for.) And "Meditating in Silence," in the silent sanctuary of your own heart where the Presence of God resides, and you completely quiet your mind, feelings, Physical Body, and outside concerns, will bring you peace that passeth understanding! It is "Integrated Meditation" in the sense of working with your Three Minds, and integrated in the sense of using those different types of meditation as outlined in these pages that will help you become a more well rounded and integrated God being. In truth, every moment of life is a meditation. Every moment of life is going to church! Every moment of life you are on your Spiritual Path and you are either causing and creating Godliness or you are not. Use everything in life to practice meditation and Godliness! It is all in your perspective. You can make life a most wondrous meditation or live a life of automatic pilot, hedonism, lower-self desire, anger, and upset! The choice is yours! "Choose once again," as *A Course In Miracles* says.

*				*				*

The Universal Law of Integrated Prayer

One of the most important Spiritual practices of the Spiritual Path is prayer. It was the Universal Mind through Edgar Cayce the "Sleeping Prophet", who said, "Why worry when you can pray?" It is such a simply understanding, but so easy to forget! Why try and do everything on your own when you have the help of GOD, Christ, the Holy Spirit, your Mighty I Am Presence, your Higher Self, and the entire Godforce to help? The reason that prayer is so important is that GOD and the Godforce are not allowed to help unless you ask! We have been given free choice, and GOD and the Godforce are not allowed to enter unless asked! The infinite Power/Love/Wisdom of GOD and the Godforce is literally available for everyone! You just need to ask! "The righteous cry, and the LORD heareth, and delivereth them out of all their troubles. (Psalms 34:17) Then shall ye call upon me, and ye shall go and pray unto me, and I will hearken unto you. (Jeremiah 29:12) And it shall come to pass, that before they call, I will answer; and while they are yet speaking, I will hear. (Isaiah 65:24) The LORD is nigh unto all them that call upon him, to all that call upon him in truth. (Psalms 145:18) Call unto me, and I will answer thee, and show thee great and mighty things, which thou knowest not." (Jeremiah 33:3) It must also be understood that in the highest and most complete integrated understanding of prayer, it is not just enough to say the prayer! To have its most beneficial effect after you pray, you first off need to have total faith that it will be done! Many people pray but then give in to self-doubt right afterwards, which does not completely sabotage the prayer, however, the results will be quicker if faith is maintained! Sai Baba is quoted as saying, "Have faith in yourself. When you have no faith in the wave, how can you get faith in the ocean?" God answers all prayers! Let's remember what is written in the Holy Bible, "For I was an hungred, and ye gave me meat: I was thirsty, and ye gave me drink: I was a stranger and ye took me in: Naked, and ye clothed me: I was sick, and ye visited me: I was in prison, and ye came unto me." (Matthew 25: 35-36) Prayer in its fullest sense of the term is an "Integrated Process and a Co-Creative Process" with every aspect of self doing its part. After faith has been established, then one's attitude should go forward in life with 100% personal power and positive attitude as if the prayer were already accomplished! In truth, it is already accomplished, and the prayer is a reality on the Plane of GOD, and we are now just waiting for it to manifest back down on Earth! So, not only should you walk around with 100% faith, personal power, and a positive attitude after praying, you should also completely Mentally,

Emotionally, and Physically "act as if it is already accomplished!" You should even experience this truth with all five senses. See it being real, hear it, touch it, smell it, and taste it! You should live your life on every level of your being as if the prayer has been answered! And if ever you start to slip from this "immaculate conception" in your own mind, you should immediately do an affirmation and positive creative visualization to reaffirm the "Truth of GOD" back into your reality! So in other words, to pray properly and in an integrated manner, the Mental Body, Emotional Body, Energy Body, Physical Body, and five senses must all do their part! That way there will be consistency on all levels of your being! Praying in this integrated manner is called "Miracle Mindedness". It is this state of consciousness that causes miracles to happen in your life! Many people often pray, however it is not done from 100% personal power, owning the fact that you are a Son and Daughter of GOD! It is not done from the state of consciousness that you are One with which you are praying for! It is done from lack of self-love and self-worth, and so the negative ego is telling the person they are not deserving of the prayer! On the other hand, the person is holding some guilt and subconsciously believes they should not receive it! The person prays but does not have faith! Then they pray but do not keep a positive Mental and Emotional attitude and feeling! Then they do not act as if, they act as if it wasn't, not believing that which they have just prayed for! If you are going to pray, then fully believe and know that what you are asking for is going to come about. Otherwise, why do it? The lesson is for you to be 100% decisive! If you are going to make the effort to do the prayer and call forth the Love, Wisdom, and Power of GOD and the Godforce, then stand behind that decision and believe in what you are doing! Go even one step beyond belief, and just know it! Know that GOD and the Godforce will come to answer your Prayer! "He will regard the prayer of the destitute, and not despise their prayer. (Psalms 102:17) Be not ye therefore like unto them: for your Father knoweth what things ye have need of, before ye ask him. (Matthew 6:8) If ye then, being evil, know how to give good gifts unto your children, how much more shall your Father which is in heaven give good things to them that ask him?" Make sure to have not only faith, but also trust and patience! This has to do with trusting not only GOD, but also trusting GOD's Laws! "O Lord of hosts, blessed is the man that trusteth in thee *(and thy laws)*." (Psalms 84:12) The law is " Ask and you shall receive! Knock and the door shall be opened!" Trust in GOD and GOD's Laws. Then one must also be patient, for we are living in a physical reality and matter vibrates at a much slower level than the mind, feelings, or energy! That must be taken into account! Many people lose their faith and trust because they become impatient! "For ye have need of patience, that, after ye have done the will of God, ye might receive the promise." (Hebrews 10:36) Have patience, and receive the promise! So, Lightworkers often pray but don't keep their faith, trust, patience, don't own their power 100%, don't have 100% self-love and self-worth, don't keep negative ego thoughts out of their mind, don't act as if but act as if not, don't affirm and visualize, and go back to worry, which are negative affirmations! They do not accept GOD's reality as the truth, don't see it coming to pass with all five inner and outer senses, don't live their life like their prayer has already been accomplished, and don't pray again when their attitude and emotions start slipping back into lack of faith and knowingness on all levels! Therefore, what we have is not "integrated prayer", no, we have "fragmented prayer"! The person prays, but then sabotages the prayer by not doing their part! Prayer is not just about GOD, and the Masters doing everything! True prayer is a co-creation between GOD and the Sons and Daughters of GOD who are Spiritual Masters and Co-Creators within themselves! Mother Teresa said, "Prayer is not asking. Prayer is putting oneself in the hands of God, at his disposition, and listening to his voice in the depths of our hearts." When you own all aspects of self at the 100% level, this is when the true co-creation of GOD can take place, and by the Grace of GOD and the Masters true miracles can take place! We leave you with the words of Jesus, "If ye abide in me, and my words abide in you, ye shall ask what ye will, and it shall be done unto you. (John 15:7) All things, whatsoever you ask in prayer, believing, you will receive!" (Matthew 21:22)

*   *   *

The Universal Law of Integrated Spiritual Growth on All Three Levels: Spiritual, Psychological, and Physical/Earthly

There are three levels of integrated Spiritual growth that each person on Earth must master to truly achieve God Realization. These three levels are the Spiritual, Psychological, and Physical/Earthly Level. The Spiritual Level of God Realization deals with building one's Light Quotient and Light Body, Love Quotient and Love Body, and Power Quotient and Power Body. With the anchoring, activation, and actualization of your Higher Chakras eight through three hundred thirty. With the anchoring and activation of your Higher Bodies, like The Annointed Christ Overself Body, The Zohar Body of Light, The Higher Adam Kadmon Body, to name just a few. The Spiritual Level of growth also deals with one's ability to channel, pray, meditate, and co-create with GOD and the Godforce, with the creation and establishment of one's Antakarana back to one's monad and Source, as well as with other forms of Spiritual practice such as chanting, repeating the names of GOD, and reciting mantras. It also deals with the process of completing your Twelve Levels of Initiation, and the cleansing and integration of all your Soul Extensions from your Higher Self and monad. The Psychological Level of Spiritual Growth is a totally unique level and must be mastered in its own right.

Spiritual practices will not help you achieve Psychological Mastery. Most Lighworkers are much more developed in their Spiritual Body than they are in their Psychological Body. This often leads to massive corruption of the Spiritual Body later on the path it is not corrected. The Psychological Level is the foundation of your entire Spiritual house. The reason for this is that your thoughts create your reality, and hence this level of Spiritual growth enormously affects the Spiritual and Physical/Earthly Levels. The Psychological Level deals with key core issues such as: owning your personal power, self-love, self-worth, your bubble of protection, Christ/Buddha thinking rather than negative ego/fear-based thinking, balance, integration, transcending lower-self desire, proper parenting of the inner child, reprogramming the subconscious mind, mastering the subconscious mind, mastering and properly integrating your feelings and emotions, developing your inner Spiritual higher senses, letting go of attachments and replacing them with preferences, balancing your Three-Fold Flame of Love, Wisdom and Power, becoming a cause of your reality instead of an effect, balancing your Four-Body System, balancing and integrating your conscious/subconscious/superconscious minds, integrating and balancing the Seven Rays, Twelve Major Archetypes, Twelve Signs of the Zodiac, removing implants and negative elementals, learning to make appropriate choices at all times, and developing your psychic abilities, to name but a few. The development of a healthy and balanced Psychoepistemology is one of the most importance aspects of the Psychological Level. See *The Universal Law of Developing a Healthy Psychoepistemology.* One interesting insight into these three levels of growth is that the Physical Body grows automatically. If an adolescent drinks and smokes too much, and never Psychologically matures, they will still Physically grow, although their Physical growth could be slightly stunned. Spiritually, if a person focuses on the light and continues to do Spiritual activations they will continue to Spiritually grow, even if they have chronic health problems and are undeveloped Psychologically. The Psychological Level is slightly different however, because it does not grow automatically as the Physical Body does. Just because a person Physically grows into an adult, it doesn't mean that they are Psychologically one. Just because the Spiritual Body achieves Ascension and/or the Seven Levels of Initiation, doesn't mean the Psychological self is evolved in the slightest. So just because the Physical Body grows and the Spiritual Body may be growing, this says absolutely nothing about the Psychological Level of development. The Physical and Spiritual Body, once you get tapped in, can grow and evolve almost automatically. This is not true of the Psychological Body. Always remember that for every thought the negative ego has, the Buddha/Christ/Melchizedek Consciousness has an opposite thought and attitude. Whatever the problem, Christ Consciousness can help you find a way out. GOD did not create the negative ego, people did. It is the misuse of free choice. So the key point here is that GOD and the Masters cannot help you develop Psychologically, and your Physical Body cannot help you. They cannot create a healthy Psychoepistemology for you, for this is a by-produce of your own thinking, and GOD and the Masters cannot control your mind, your feelings and emotions. This is your job. So being an adult Psychologically, and becoming a master Psychologically, will only happen when a person takes responsibility for being the cause of their reality, and becomes the Master of their thoughts and emotions, and develops a healthy Psychoepistemology and/or Spiritual philosophy on all levels. Building Light Quotient is easy, it is just a matter of calling it in from the Celestial realms. Physically feeding the Physical Body is easy, and the Physical Body will grow even when we abuse it and feed it junk food. The real nuts and bolts of the Spiritual Path is the Psychological Level. It again is the foundation of your Spiritual house. If you do not address this level properly it will totally corrupt the Spiritual work you have done and it will make the Physical Body ill over time. Now, the third and final level of Spiritual growth now deals with the Physical/Earthly Level. Again, the Physical Body will grow Physically into adulthood no matter how evolved or unevolved one is Spiritually, Psychologically, or Physically. What a lot of Lightworkers do not realize is that there is an evolutionary process for the Physical Body as well. One aspect of this is having a healthy Physical Body, eating a good diet, setting Physical exercise, fresh air, and sunshine, drinking lots of pure water, getting enough sleep, and so on. Besides the health of one's Physical Body there is also the issue of bringing Light Quotient, Love Quotient, and Power Quotient into the Physical Vehicle itself. Ascension is descension, in truth. For the ideal is to fully ground one's Mighty I Am Presence and Light/Love/Power Bodies fully into the Four-Body System, which includes the Physical Body. We are meant to become embodiments of GOD in our Physical Bodies on Earth. We are meant to Physically ground all the Higher Bodies into the Four-Body System, to anchor all of our 330 Chakras into the Physical Body. Another aspect of evolving the Physical Vehicle is building one's immune system Spiritually, Psychologically, and Physically. Part of the evolution of the Physical Body is to remove all negative thoughts, feelings, emotions, energy, and physical toxins from its physical and etheric cells, organs, glands, tissues, and blood stream. The highest level of evolution of the Physical Vehicle is the process of bringing down and anchoring so much of GOD's and your own Mighty I Am Presence's Light, Love and Power into the Physical Vehicle, that a process of etherealization takes place in the Physical Body itself. The highest level and form of this evolutionary process is where at death, translation, or Ascension, an individual can choose if they want to ascend the Physical Body as well. The final aspect of evolving the Material Face of GOD deals with the evolution of not only the Physical Body of yourself, but also the Physical Body of GOD. In our case, this is the Earth Mother, our worldly civilization, and our solar system. Paying attention to the Earth Mother, worldly civilization, politics, social issues, changing the world, and current events; developing a relationship to the many Kingdoms of the Earth Mother. Grounding your physical service mission on Earth. Caring about all the problems and inequities going on in the world, such as hunger, homeless people, child abuse. Saving the rainforests, endangered species. And on and on. It is our job to create Heaven on Earth, a utopian society.

Jesus taught and set an example of living in the marketplace. As it is written in the Bible, "But be ye doers of the word, and not hearers only, deceiving your own selves." (James 1:22) "My little children, let us not love in word, neither in tongue; but in deed and in truth." (1 John 3:18) Heeding those words of wisdom, we shall create a fifth-dimensional society and a New Jerusalem. And it shall come to pass what is written in *The Book Of Revelation*: Then John saw a new Heaven and a new Earth. He heard a voice proclaiming: "I am the beginning and the end. I will make everything new once more so that God and the people shall live together. There shall be no more pain, nor sorrow, nor death, for all such things will have passed away." Then an angel took John to the top of a high mountain, and showed him the holy city, the new Jerusalem, whose walls were of jasper and whose streets were made of gold. Through the city ran the River of Life, whose waters were as clear as crystal. Here there was no need of sun by day nor of moon by night, for in the city dwelled God and his Son, and all who came there walked in the light of their glory! Let us all individually and collectively walk in the light of our glory and fulfill and embody God's Revelation as revealed to John!

*　　　　　　　　　*　　　　　　　　　*

The Universal Law of Integrating and Cleansing One's Soul Extensions

Each person has twelve Oversouls. Each Oversoul has twelve Soul extensions, or twelve personalities, that incarnate into material existence, although not necessarily just on this planet. The twelve Soul extension of one's Oversoul work for the development of the monad or Mighty

I Am Presence. Each of your Soul extensions is a person (just like you) who is either incarnated on another planet in this galaxy or universe or working on the inner plane. These twelve people make up your Soul family—just like on a larger level each of your twelve Oversouls has twelve Soul extensions, so you have 144 in your monadic family. In taking on the responsibility for Ascension you are taking on the responsibility for being a teacher for and helping your eleven and 144 other Soul extensions from your "greater body," so to speak. After first getting yourself Psychologically integrated and cleansed in terms of all your subpersonalities, Archetypes, past-life aspects, thoughtforms, feelings, emotions, intuition, instincts and so on, the next step is to integrate and help cleanse your other Soul extensions. All your subpersonalities, Archetypes, past-life aspects, thoughtforms, feelings, emotions, intuition and instincts are also like a family. They are your subconscious, superconscious and Four-Body-System family. This inner family must first be integrated and cleansed before you are really in a position to be truly helpful to your other Soul extensions from your Oversoul. It also must be remembered that your Soul extensions have free choice and you cannot order them around or you will create karma for yourself. To integrate a Soul extension means to unify or blend Spiritually with its Energy Body. This creates a greater electrical circuiting in your field and Energy Body, helping to build your Light Quotient. It also makes you more expansive in terms of your auric field, and allows you to incorporate the knowledge, wisdom, and abilities of these other people in your Soul family. Not all Soul extensions are necessarily developed. Some can be unconscious and unevolved. The goal is for you to become like an Oversoul teacher for first, your Soul family, and second, your monadic family. One of the biggest effects of integrating and cleansing your Soul extensions is the balancing of your karma. You must balance 51% of the karma from your Soul family of twelve to achieve Ascension. It is possible to do this process without actually knowing you are doing it. Often this is done through one's own Psychological and subpersonality clearing work. It is happening Spiritually and is then filtering through the subconscious mind for cleansing. In merging with a Soul extension you are in a sense absorbing its karma and cleansing it. Its karma is your karma because you come from the same Oversoul and monad. You must stop thinking of yourself as a separate Soul extension, but rather understand that you are an Oversoul and monad made up of many aspects. You are not working for yourself but for the Oversoul and monad, just as your fingers work for your Physical Body. If you try to go too fast you might burden yourself with karmic lessons that could debilitate your Physical, Emotional, Mental, and Spiritual Bodies beyond your ability to cope effectively. The stronger you are in all your bodies, and the clearer you are Psychologically, the less the karmic repercussions in your Four-Body-System. Always ask not only for the integration but also for the cleansing of your twelve, or 144, Soul extensions. In requesting the cleansing, much of the karmic implications can be short-circuited. In integrating Soul extensions there is an electrical charge that is put in place and a greater electrical wiring that is added to one's field. There is definitely a need to have integration time after a Soul extension is added to one's field. The fact is that certain Soul extensions will be easier to assimilate than others. After one has integrated and cleansed the 144 Soul extensions from one's monad, the process continues. In the first seven dimensional levels one is working for monadic Ascension, which is the Ascension of all twelve Oversouls into your monad. One has to achieve planetary Ascension in all twelve Oversouls, not just your own Oversoul. As you move past your seven levels of Initiation, you will begin to form groups of Souls and monads, which then merge together in unity consciousness. This must be done to realize the eighth- and nine-dimensional Level, Bodies, and Chakras. So, the next step is working with the eighth level which means the six monads of one's group-monadic vehicle. This entails integrating the twelve Oversoul leaders of the six monads. The ninth level is the integration and cleansing of one's Soul extensions of the entire six-monad configuration (which means 864 Soul extensions). The tenth Level involves the integration and cleansing of Soul extensions from the solar-monadic grouping, the eleventh level is the integration and cleansing of the galactic-Soul-extension monadic grouping, and the twelfth level is the universal-monadic grouping. (See *Cosmic Ascension* for further information.) So, one does this incorporating through a group-monadic module, which is very important to understand. For example, on the solar level one does not have to integrate all the Soul extensions in the entire Solar System, just a certain number that make up the group-monadic module to which one is connected. One integrates the Solar System this way through just six monads. On the Solar Level the number of monads is much larger. As one moves to the Galactic Level, the principle is the same and this is also how one incorporates Solar Systems into one's being. At the Universal Level this is how one incorporates Galaxies into one's being. The same thing happens at the Multi-Universal Level. At the actual Source Level one is incorporating multi-Source Levels into one's being through this same massive group-monadic module concept. The key point is that we each, in truth, are not an individual consciousness. This separation is illusion. We are each a group consciousness and individual identity simultaneously.

*   *   *

The Universal Law of Integrating One's Twelve Levels of Initiation Into One's Four-Body System

There are 352 Initiations to achieve full God Realization. Seven levels of Initiation to achieve liberation from the physical wheel of rebirth, and nine levels of Initiation to complete Planetary Ascension! The Tenth

Initiation marks the first Initiation on a Solar Level, the Eleventh Initiation the first on a Galactic Level, and the Twelfth Initiation the first Initiation on a Universal Level. To become a fully realized Melchizedek, you must fully complete your 12 major Initiations. The First Initiation has to do with basic mastery of the Physical Body, the Second Initiation with basic mastery of the Emotional Body, the Third Initiation with basic mastery of the Mind and hence over the Threefold Personality (Physical, Emotional, Mental Body)! The Third Initiation is also referred to as the Soul Merge. Initiations basically have to do with the amount of light quotient you are holding in your auric field. The completion of your Initiations is more a sign of the development of your Spiritual Body, but not necessarily the development of your Mental, Emotional, Etheric, or Physical Body! It used to be a more integrated process, however. because of this unique period of history at the beginning of a New Millennium, the end of the Mayan Calendar, the period in Earth's history called mass ascension, Lightworkers have been given the Divine Dispensation to Spiritually complete their first seven Initiations, even though their four lower bodies have not necessarily been integrated! On the taking of your Sixth Initiation, and merging with your monad, you could call yourself a Spiritual Master, but not an integrated Master, unless you have integrated your Initiations into your Four-Body System. To achieve liberation from the wheel of "physical" rebirth on Earth you must at least achieve the beginning of your seventh Initiation. So, you can achieve physical liberation from the wheel of rebirth, however, if you don't integrate these Initiations into your four lower bodies properly you will have to reincarnate on the Astral or Mental Plane. If you don't do your Psychological work, you will not be allowed to pass any more Initiations, no matter how much work you do. The seventh Initiation is the "ring-pass-not" for avoiding accountability on a Mental, Emotional, Etheric, and Physical Level. Now, what does it mean to integrate your Initiations into your four lower bodies? To continue this discussion, it must be understood that there are three levels to the Spiritual Path: the Spiritual, Psychological, and Physical/Earthly Level. All three must be mastered!

Most people are way more developed in their Spiritual Body than their Psychological Body, or Physical/Earthly Body! To be developed in your Spiritual Body may mean that you have a high Level of light quotient, you may be a channel for the Masters, and/or you may have enormous amounts of Spiritual information in your information banks. This is great, however, to become a full-fledged Ascended Master you must also be a Master of the Psychological Level and Physical/Earthly Level. A person may have a highly developed Spiritual Body, however, they may function in their life like a child, be run by their Emotional Body, lower-self desire, Inner Child, Mental Body, subconscious mind, negative ego, and may be filled with all kinds of emotions. This is fragmented ascension! Only one third has been mastered! So let's have a look at the other two thirds, and let's see what it means to integrate your Initiations into your Mental, Emotional, Etheric, and Physical Bodies! Integrating your 12 Levels of Initiation into your Mental Body means that the mind becomes a servant of the Godself, that you are the Master of the mind and not vice versa; it means getting rid of all negative ego thoughts and learning to think only with your Melchizedek/Christ/Buddha Mind, and developing a healthy, balanced Spiritual philosophy! The Emotional Level of integrating your 12 Levels of Initiation deals with the understanding that your thinking causes your feelings and emotions. All negative feelings and emotions are caused by the negative ego philosophy of life, and all positive feelings and emotions are caused by the Melchizedek/Christ/Buddha philosophy of life. When you can live in a state of basic unconditional love, forgiveness, non-judgementalness, compassion, joy, happiness, inner peace, and equanimity all the time, no matter what is going on outside of self, you have integrated your higher levels of Initiation into your Emotional Body! Your 12 Levels of Initiation get integrated into your Etheric Body, or Energy Body, when you learn to run very high frequency Spiritual currents through it at all times, and keep your Energy Body filled with Love/Light and Power. Also, to completely repair your Etheric Body, which is the Blueprint Body for the Physical, from past life or present life damage that has occurred to it! If you do not repair the Etheric Body, it is hard for the Physical Body to recover from illness because it is working from a damaged blueprint! In terms of integrating your Initiations into your Physical Body, and raising its vibration and frequency, eating a very refined Physical diet is important, as well as keeping the Physical Body fit. Breathing. Sleeping. Grounding your mission. Integrity and consistency between the superconscious, conscious, and subconscious mind, and Physical Body. Mastering sexuality. Mastering money. Anchoring your Mighty I Am Presence into Earth Life! Loving Earth and Earth Life! Demonstrating integration on these three major levels is also a major key to raising the frequency of the Physical Vehicle! Your thoughts and emotions greatly affect the frequency of your Physical Body. By following these precepts, you will not only become a Spiritual Master, you will also become a Psychological Master! It is when these three levels are mastered and your full 12 Levels of Initiation are complete, that you will become a full-fledged Ascended Master and full-fledged integrated Melchizedek/Christ/Buddha. One last thought: if you thought that once you passed your Seven or Twelve Levels of Initiation and Ascension that everything would get easier, be aware that in some ways this is true, but in other ways, the Spiritual Path actually becomes much more difficult. The key lesson here is that in becoming a Spiritual Master and moving into Spiritual Leadership and Planetary World Service which you will eventually, you will be tested by GOD and the Masters unmercifully. If you are not an "Integrated Melchizedek/Christ/Buddha on all levels and at all times, even under the most extreme tests and lessons, the universe will quickly show you this! Ponder on this!

*   *   *

The Universal Law of Integrity

Integrity could be seen as consistency between the Mighty I Am Presence, Higher Self, conscious mind, subconscious mind, Emotional Body and Physical Body. What happens often is that the conscious mind thinks and responds one way and the subconscious mind thinks and feels something else. The conscious mind says that it wants to do something, but the Physical Body doesn't end up doing it. People say they are going to do something and they don't. What if God did not keep His Commitments? Prophet Muhammad said, "When you speak, speak the truth; perform when you promise." Learn from the Biblical words, "He who walks with integrity walks securely." (Psalms 10:9) Grace erases karma! Don't say you are going to do something if you won't. And don't use the excuse of being human for a possible lack of integrity. This is just a ploy of the negative ego and a misconception of what it means to be human, for human at its highest is hu-man or God-man. Identify yourself as God living in a Physical Body! Remember, everything in the infinite universe is a part of GOD. So if you are not in integrity, or are dishonest or negatively selfish in your business, you are stealing from God, which is yourself! Even if you have no money, maintain your integrity, honesty, egolessness, and selflessness. Strive to always maintain the highest integrity. Strive to maintain your Melchizedek/Christ/Buddha Consciousness in your every thought, even when alone. Strive to keep it in the feelings and emotions you choose to create. Keep it in every action you take and every behavior you demonstrate. Certainly keep it in every verbal interaction. If you don't have your word, what else do you have? Jesus said, "Heaven and Earth will pass away, but my words will not pass away!" Words to live by! For remember, "We have not received the spirit of the world but the Spirit who is from God, that we may understand what God has freely given to us. This is what we speak, not in words taught us by human wisdom but in words taught by the Spirit, expressing Spiritual truths in Spiritual words." (1 Corinthians 2:12-14 NIV) Do not allow yourself to be lazy and procrastinate, to be hedonistic, to give into fatigue or to use your Physical Body and its elements as an excuse to break your integrity and striving for a flawless character. Carl Gustav Jung, the Swiss psychologist, said, "Man's greatest sin is his indolence." This is laziness; this is giving too much into the Emotional Body and the line of least resistance in the subconscious mind. Your word is law and your word is God. Integrity pays off! "For the LORD God is a sun and shield: the LORD will give grace and glory: no good thing will he withhold from them that walk uprightly." (Psalms 84:11) The key words are integrity and consistency at all times between your thoughts, words, and actions. This is the behavior of a true Ascended Master. Ponder on this!

*   *   *

The Universal Laws of Karma

" **F**or verily I say unto you, till heaven and earth pass, one jot or one tittle shall in no wise pass from the law, till all be fulfilled. (Matthew 5:18) And it is easier for heaven and earth to pass, than one tittle of the law to fail. (Luke 16:17) And let us not be weary in well doing: for in due season we shall reap, if we faint not. (Galatians 6:9) Say ye to the righteous, that it shall be well with him: for they shall eat the fruit of their doings." (Isaiah 3:10)

The basic law of karma states that you sow what you reap; what you put out comes back to you. This is *The Universal Law of Cause and Effect.* You might think that there are a lot of people living in this world who get away with too much, but no one gets away with anything. As the Bible says, "Every jot and tittle of the law is fulfilled." "Every cause has its effect; every effect has its cause; everything happens according to law; chance is but a name for law not recognized; there are many planes of causation, but nothing escapes the law." (Kybalion)

The Universal Law of Karma extends over many lives. Even if it appears that someone has unfairly taken advantage of another and escaped unscathed, it is really not so. The Soul continues even if you have reincarnated into another Physical Body. The Edgar Cayce files are filled with examples of this point. Jesus provided an excellent understanding of *The Universal Law of Karma* when He said, "Do unto others as you would have others do unto you." This is more literal than we realize.

There are different levels of karma. Personal karma would be what we have set into motion with the power of our consciousness. When we incarnate into this world, we are born into groups based on our skin color, our religious affiliation, and so on. This would be called group karma. When a person is born into a black body in the United States, he or she has to deal with racism and prejudice—not because a black body is inferior to a white body, but because of the low level of Spiritual Consciousness of so many Souls on this plane. A person in a black body, or in the body of any other minority, takes on the karmic lessons of that group. Another type of karma is national karma. We are born into a certain country and are then indoctrinated with its egotistical identifications. If, for example, there was a nuclear war between Communist China and the United States, we would get caught up in this national karmic lesson. No man is an island unto itself. Then there is planetary karma. This particular school called Earth has certain unique lessons that are quite different from those on other planets in this galaxy or universe. We must deal with the planetary karma and the phase or history we are born into. It could be said that all karma is personal in that we, as Souls, choose our skin color, our families, our religion, and the country we are going to grow up in before incarnating. In that sense, one could say that all karma is personal karma because we choose it.

The word *karma* has often been associated with "bad" karma, the idea that we must experience some form of suffering because of a lesson not learned. This is distinguished from the state of grace. The truth is that everything in this universe is governed by laws. There are Physical Laws, Emotional Laws, Mental Laws, and Spiritual Laws. When we fall out of harmony with these Universal Laws, we suffer. Thus karma is not a punishment but a gift—a sign that we are out of balance.

The proper attitude toward everything that happens in life is "Not my will but thine. Thank you for the lesson." Buddhism calls this non-resistance. The idea is to work and learn from the universe instead of fighting it. This does not mean to give up our power—just the opposite, in fact. It means owning our power and viewing what has happened as a teaching, lesson, challenge, and opportunity to grow. Look at karma as a stepping stone for Soul growth.

There is no need to suffer. Suffering is not God's design, it is our own. It is a sign that we are letting our negative ego or separated, fear-based self be our guide, rather than the Soul or spirit.

There is no such thing as sin. A sin is like some indelible stain on our character that cannot be removed. Sin is an egotistical concept, not a Spiritual one. There are no sins, only mistakes. The true meaning of sin is "missing the mark." Mistakes are actually positive, not negative. The idea is to learn from them and, most of all, forgive ourselves. Perfection is not never making a mistake. True perfection is the state of always forgiving oneself for one's mistakes and then trying to learn from that experience.

Another very important point in respect to karma is that all lessons are learned within self. In other words, if you are having a vicious fight with a former friend but choose to forgive and unconditionally love that person, letting go of your animosity, you are freed from karma, even if the other person chooses to hold on to a grudge for the rest of his or her incarnation,. This is a very liberating concept.

Karma comes back to us on all levels: Physically, Emotionally, Mentally, and Spiritually. How we take care of our Physical Body in this lifetime will determine how healthy a Physical Body we have in the next lifetime (if we are destined to return). If we master our emotions in this lifetime and become peaceful, calm, joyous, and happy, then when we incarnate again in our next lifetime, as babies we will be peaceful, calm, and joyous. Some people believe in the idea of the Tabula Rasa, or blank state. This is obviously absurd. We are not blank slates when we are born. As a matter of fact, there is really no such thing as a child. There are only adult Souls living in babies' bodies. The average person has 200 to 250 past lives. The Soul with all twelve of its extensions has an average of 2,400 to 3,000 past lives.

Another very interesting point in respect to karma is the understanding that there really is no such thing as linear time in the Spiritual world. Time is simultaneous. Our past and future incarnations are happening now, for the now is ultimately all that exists. It is possible to have karmic bleed-through from any of the eleven other Soul extensions still in incarnation. This bleed-through can come from the past or the future. This is a very difficult concept to understand on this plane. Try to grasp this concept with your right brain rather than your left brain. For example, karmic bleed-through can manifest as physical symptoms you are experiencing but which in reality aren't your own. Let's say one of your fellow Soul extensions is close to death in his or her incarnation. You may be experiencing this or running some of their karma through your Physical Body.

There are three permanent atoms in the Physical, Mental, and Emotional Bodies. These permanent atoms are recording devices for personal karma. They also dispense karmic pictures into the bloodstream; this has an enormous effect on the glandular system. This is part of God's system for implementing *The Universal Law of Karma* fairly. With respect to how karma relates to blood transfusions, organ transplants, and animal organ transplants, all three are definitely not recommended and should be avoided if at all possible. Take, for example, blood transfusions. Let's say that you are a third-degree initiate and have just taken your Soul Merge Initiation. Then you go into a hospital and get a blood transfusion from a person who hasn't stepped onto his or her Spiritual Path yet. The blood, physically and Spiritually speaking, would be totally dissonant to your vibration. You would be, in essence, running another person's karma through your bloodstream. An organ transplant would be even worse, especially from an animal donor.

Nothing happens by chance. The working of karma is quite an intricate process, bringing into play a multiplicity of unseen and subtle forces. There are, therefore, great Spiritual beings whose Divine job it is to help this law work out in the most efficient and productive way possible. One of the main groups of beings is called the Lords of Karma. They guide and oversee the playing out of the continuous stream of deed and intent from humanity, interpenetrating Physical/Etheric, Astral, and Mental Bodies and worlds. There is also what is known in occult literature as the Karmic Board, which functions as the governing board of the Lords of Karma. It is set up as a review board where beings who have reached a certain high degree of Initiation can on the inner planes come to speak, confer, and file complaints and commendations. All is noted by the board, and no one should go lightly or casually before it. To do so also involves an act of karma upon the being who ask for a special hearing. If, however, your motives about a given situation, are pure, the Karmic Board is available for consultation, as their entire jurisdication lies within the realm of karma per se, and they are only too willing to be of service. The forces that determine the actual working out of karma take into account all that humanity does, desire and acts upon, as well as the interplay of Astrological influences, Ray influences, and collective karma. These factors are so intricate that many Spiritual beings hold office relating to this issue alone.

Another important point about karma is that you are only given as much as you can handle. This is controlled by your Soul and monad. If all your karma was dumped on you at once, you obviously couldn't handle it. It is possible to slow down the karma coming your way if you are feeling overwhelmed, and it is also possible to speed up your karmic lessons if you want to grow faster. You can do this by praying for it to your Soul or God. It is their joy to work with you in the way in which you feel most comfortable.

All good karma from past lives and this one is stored in the Causal Body, or Soul Body. The building of this Causal Body is one of the main requirements for achieving liberation from the wheel of rebirth. To achieve Ascension, you need to balance only 51 percent of the karma of all your past lives (that is, the karma of your personal lives, not the karma of your eleven other Soul extensions). Much of the karma you experience in life is not necessarily from past lives, but has been created in this life. For example, let's say you fall asleep at the wheel while driving and get into a serious car accident. The lesson may be as simple as being foolish enough to drive when one is overtired. All karma from past lives is basically just programming in your subconscious mind and in your three permanent atoms. It can all be transformed in this life if you learn to be the Master of your three lower vehicles—the Physical, Emotional, and Mental Bodies—in service of spirit and unconditional love. It is possible to completely clear the subconscious mind and the three permanent atoms of all negative programming and to replace it with positive programming.

The Universal Laws of Karma even extend to the type of Soul you attract during intercourse and the conception of a child. The kind of Soul that is attracted is greatly determined by the quality of feeling and love that is shared and being made manifest during the lovemaking experience.

The basic law of the universe is that our thoughts create our reality. All karma has its antecedent in some ancient thought that led to a feeling or action. It is sometimes helpful to do hypnotic regression work to release karmic blocks form past lives or early childhood. Under hypnosis you can reexperience a past trauma, thus gaining insight as to the cause of particular karmic results. Very often you can then release that program from your subconscious mind.

Another understanding about karma has to do with a Master taking on the karma of one of his or her disciples. Sai Baba, the great Master from India, has done this frequently with devotees. In one instance he took on the heart attack, stroke, and ruptured appendix of a devotee who otherwise would have died for sure. Sai Baba became very ill for ten days. Over twenty-five of the finest doctors in India were at his bedside on the tenth day. He had turned completely black, and the consensus of the twenty-five doctors was that the had only minutes to live. Sai Baba would not take medication and said, "At four o'clock today I will be giving a lecture." The doctors thought he was crazy. At the appointed hour he apparently sprinkled some water on himself and was instantly cured. The twenty-five doctors began praying to Sai Baba for help before treating any patient.

Grace erases karma. King David in the Bible, who was "Beloved of GOD", lusted over another man's wife and had her husband sent to the front lines of thew war so he would more likely be killed and David could have her. David repented for his sins, and became one of the greatest kings of Israel. GOD always welcomes his prodigal Sons and Daughters home no matter what they have done! It is true that all karma must be balanced. Karma can be balanced by grace, by learning, and by service! Even Hitler is forgiven and, in truth, is an incarnation of GOD! He will have to achieve Spiritual/Christ/Buddha Consciousness first and balance all his karma though before he will be allowed to return to his Spiritual home. This will happen, for the Divine Plan will not be complete until all Souls return home. There is absolutely nothing in the history of the infinite universe that is not 100% forgivable! It is only the negative ego that thinks not. However, the definition of GOD is "GOD equals man minus ego!"

Examples of Karma as it extends over past lives and/or future lives:

The following examples are from the Edgar Cayce files:

The first example is that of a man who lived in Rome in a past life. He was a very handsome man, and he used to go around criticizing other people for being fat and not handsome like himself. In his present life he had an underactive pituitary and was obese. This is one very good example of how the three permanent atoms often release karma into the bloodstream, adversely affecting the glandular system.

In another of Cayce's readings a man had knifed and killed someone in a past life. In this life he was suffering from leukemia.

In another reading a woman had an overpowering fear of animals. This fear came from an experience in ancient Rome when this entity's husband had been made to fight wild beasts in one of the arenas.

While here are given a number of examples of bad karma carrying over to this life, karma can also be positive in nature. For example, how did Mozart create piano concertos when he was only five years old? The answer is that he had four or five lifetimes as famous musicians precious to this life.

If you are a healthy American, how did you receive a healthy body, and why is it that you grew up in the United States? You could have been a starving Somali, or you could have grown up in Communist China or a thousand other places that wouldn't have allowed you the freedoms and opportunities you have here. Too often we focus on the bad things that have happened to us and blame our karma instead of looking at the good things and being grateful for our positive karma.

Djwhal Khul on The Universal Law of Karma and Rebirth:

The following 13 statements by the Ascended Master Djwhal Khul are from the Alice Bailey Book *The Reappearance of the Christ,* and provide a good summation of the entire process.

❖ *The Universal Law of Rebirth* is a great natural law upon our planet.

❖ It is a process instituted and carried forward under *The Universal Law of Evolution.*

❖ It is closely related to and conditioned by *The Universal Law of Cause and Effect.*

❖ It is a process of progressive development, enabling men to move forward from the grossest forms of unthinking materialism to a Spiritual perfection and an intelligent perception that will enable a man to become a member of the Kingdom of God.

❖ It accounts for the differences among men, and in connection with *The Universal Law of Cause and Effect* (called *The Universal Law of Karma* in the East) it accounts for differences in circumstances and attitudes toward life.

❖ It is the expression of the will aspect of the Soul and is not the result of any form decision; it is the Soul in all forms that reincarnates, choosing and building suitable Physical, Emotional, and Mental Vehicles through which to learn the next needed lessons.

❖ *The Universal Law of Rebirth* (as far as humanity is concerned) comes into activity upon the Soul Plane. Incarnation is motivated and directed from the Soul Level upon the Mental Plane.

❖ Souls incarnate in groups, cyclically, under law and in order to achieve right relations with God and with their fellow men.

❖ Progressive unfolding, under *The Universal Law of Rebirth*, is largely conditioned by the mental principle "As a man thinks in his heart, so is he." These few brief words need most careful consideration.

❖ Under *The Universal Law of Rebirth*, man slowly develops mind; then mind begins to control the feeling and emotional nature; finally it reveals to man the Soul and its nature and environment.

❖ At that point in his development, a man begins to tread the Path of Return and orients himself gradually (after many lives) to the Kingdom of God.

❖ When, through a developed mentality, wisdom, practical service, and understanding, a man has learned to ask nothing for the separated self, he then renounces desire for life in the three worlds and is freed from *The Universal Law of Rebirth*.

❖ He is now group-consciousness, is aware of his Soul group and of the Soul in all forms, and has attained—as Christ had requested—a stage of Christ-like perfection, reaching unto the "measure of the stature of the fullness of the Christ."

*   *   *

The Universal Law of Keeping One's Mind Steady in the Light

We will see what we look for. When we see fault and judgment, we are in reality faulting and judging ourselves, for what we see in another is just a mirror of our own state of mind. When we see only God, love, and blessing, that is what we give to ourselves. Whether we see it or not, that is what is there, for that is what God created. Faulty perception doesn't create truth; it just creates the reality we live in. We can see the glory of what God would have us see. If we see fault, then we are creating separation from ourselves, from God, and our Brothers and Sisters. Spirit would guide us to remain in a state of oneness at all times, for all is God. All forms of perception, according to *A Course in Miracles*, are a type of dream. God would guide us, however, to live and experience the happy dream of the Christ Consciousness, which is a perfect mirror of the state that Jesus calls knowledge. By living the Christ dream or perception, Jesus says, a translation into pure knowledge will inevitably take place. So keep the mind steady in the light. "The mind of sinful man is death, but the mind controlled by the Spirit is life and peace, because the sinful mind is hostile to God. It does not submit to God's law, nor can it do so. Those controlled by their sinful nature cannot please God." (Romans 8:6-8 NIV) What manifests in life is where you put your attention. Keep your attention only on GOD, only on Love, only on Light. When temptation or negativity arise, one of the many tools you can use is to inwardly or outwardly chant one of the many names or mantras of GOD which will keep the mind where it needs to be. An idle mind is the devil's workshop! "The name of the Lord is a strong tower: the righteous runneth into it, and is safe." (Proverbs 18:10)

*   *   *

The Universal Law of Leadership and Self-Leadership

One of the prerequisites to becoming a leader among people is to become a leader within your own self. Each of us is the president of our inner constituency which is comprised of our Mental, Emotional, and Physical Bodies, Personality, Chakras desires, instincts, feelings, thoughts, intuition, sensations, subpersonalities, past-life aspects, inner child and subconscious mind. If one does not know how to govern oneself, it is not possible to effectively govern another. If you are not a strong leader over yourself, your inner constituency is victimizing you! The first key quality to becoming an effective inner and outer leader is the quality of personal power. Without personal power you will become completely victimized by your energies. Personal power translates into self-mastery, self-discipline, and the ability to remain focused and committed at all times and being the cause rather than the effect of your reality. It translates into being a master of your self and your life rather than a victim. Never give your personal power away to anyone or any aspect within yourself—ever! The key is to always remain in your power which takes great mental discipline and training! You do not want to give your power to your thoughts, feelings, emotions, desires, Physical Body appetites, sexuality, instincts, imagination, dreams subpersonalities or any other inner qualities! And you also do not want to give it away to other people! True leaders maintain their personal power at all times, no matter what the situation! Now, the second key leadership quality is love. Love and personal power are the two most important ingredients to psychospiritual health! The ideal leader has what might be called tough love. He/she is tough as nails in his focus and discipline but loving and harmless as the Virgin Mary. A true leader never attacks and is never negatively angry. He might have positive anger, an expression of the Spiritual Warrior Archetype, or great First Ray destructive energy used in a positive sense to destroy outdated form, but he is never negatively angry. True Spiritual leaders in whatever field always use their power in a loving way. Hitler, Stalin and Mussolini all had personal power, but they obviously didn't have love. One of the great tests of the Spiritual Path as disciples and initiates move into leadership is the test of power. Will the power go to their heads and will it become abused? It will if they have not done their Spiritual homework on learning how to control their negative egos within themselves. When run by the negative ego, leadership is used for self-centered, selfish, misguided purposes. Instead of using this position of power to help and serve others, the position is used to help and serve one's own selfish goals and aims. It needs great wisdom (Third Ray) to find the perfect balance between power (First Ray) and love (Second Ray)! See *The Universal Law of Balancing and Integrating the Threefold Flame.* Another key quality of true leadership is selflessness. A true Spiritual leader is the servant of all and totally without ego in focus. As Master Jesus so beautifully said, "The greatest among you is the servant of all." So as you see, the key to effective leadership lies in your level of Psychological or psychospiriutal clarity. If you are not in control of your negative ego, Emotional Body, subconscious mind and Desire Body and you have not learned how to parent your inner child, you will not be qualified to lead anything, for you have not learned how to lead yourself! Stay in your power, be loving and wise, and selfless, and get the negative ego under control and Psychologically clear, and you will be recognized as a leader by yourself, God and The Masters because you are right with self, with God, and with your Brothers and Sisters. True leadership must be earned! By continually demonstrating the Christed qualities of leadership rather than negative-ego leadership, you will earn the admiration and respect of those you lead! Never forget that the Psychological Level is the foundation of your entire Spiritual life! It is absolutely essential that all Lightworkers attain mastery on the Spiritual Level, the Psychological Level and the Physical/Earthly Level. All three levels are separate and require a different level of mastery! So, as has been stated, one of the most important qualities of leadership is to practice what you preach. Anyone

can give a good lecture or channeling. The real test is, can you demonstrate your message? Once you are put into a leadership position, there are
many tests awaiting you, some of which are power, money, fame, attachment, sexuality, desire, anger, fear, selfishness, false pride, greed, duality,
jealousy, vanity, and egotism, to name but a few. Other qualities to practice and develop in terms of leadership are, the ability to sell self which is
one of the most important archetypes to develop (the Seducer Archetype
in its higher expression), then social skills, and a good balance between the
right and left sides of the brain which, in other words, is a good balance
between intuition and common sense. Also, learning from mistakes and
failures and making appropriate adjustments, the ability to receive feedback in a non-egosensitive manner and also to offer feedback in an uplifting manner. Good leadership also requires organization and attention to
detail. When details are not paid attention to, they come back to haunt
you. To be outwardly organized, one's mind and emotions must be properly organized. It is really the little things on the Spiritual Path that are the
most important ones! Other qualities of true leadership include clear
vision, seeing the big picture and not getting lost in the little picture, the
pursuit of excellence in everything you do without being a perfectionist or
overcritical but with the understanding that mistakes are okay, and well,
true leadership also includes qualities such as cooperation and communication. Effective communication often begins with good communication
with yourself, your Four-Body System, your Three Minds, your Chakras
and your Mighty I Am Presence. This integrated communication within
self then translates to effective communication with others in alignment
with the Soul. So, all of us as we progress on our path will be put into
positions of power and leadership over others and, in truth, all of us are in
that position right now. How do you treat the person who cleans your
house, or pumps your gas? Do you walk your talk? All of us rule over our
thoughts, emotions, body, subpersonalities, archetypes, instincts, sensations, and intuition. We each are the president or ruler. How does a man
of military back ground rule his personality? Probably in the same way he

rules his troops. How does a housewife who has been dependent on her husband most of her life and not learned to own her masculine side rule her energies? She doesn't, she is victimized by them. We all must become the divine ruler first over ourselves. Only then will we truly have the ability to rule over others! Another aspect of leadership has to do with becoming a leader for your own Soul extensions. Each person has twelve Soul extensions that comprise their Oversoul and 144 Soul extensions, or personalities, that comprise their monad or Mighty I Am Presence. The ideal here is to become a leader and teacher, somewhat like an Oversoul, for your own twelve Soul extensions, which is your Soul family, so to speak. Becoming a leader for your Soul family is one of the beginning steps to becoming a leader in the world. After achieving your personal Ascension and taking your sixth Initiation, the next step is then also to become a leader for all 144 Soul extensions from your twelve Oversouls, which are connected to your monad and Mighty I Am Presence. Then you have become a true leader within yourself, and this then allows you to be a natural-born leader among humanity! The true purpose of all our Spiritual Paths is not to hide in a cave, or a monastery. It is to attune to these higher energies and then ground them properly into the mind, emotions, Etheric Body, Physical Body, and, finally, into the third-dimensional Earth life and society. The purpose of the Divine Plan is to bring Heaven to Earth, not just to achieve liberation from the wheel of rebirth and then escape Earth existence. True Ascension, as has been stated many times, is *descension*. It is being the Mighty I Am Presence on Earth, helping others to become their Mighty I Am Presence, and eventually, helping to create a Mighty I Am Presence Society. The true Spiritual leader is willing to become totally and completely involved in Earth life and in all society's institutions, serving as a leader and a Spiritual warrior in an attempt to enact change. "You must be the change you want to see in the world," Gandhi said. You must lead by example! "Teachers must be examples of Love and Truth," as Sai Baba put it. How can you expect someone to be compassionate with you if you do not show compassion to others? How do you expect someone to give you unconditional love if you are not willing to give your love unconditionally? How do you expect someone to be understanding of your mistakes if you are not understanding of theirs? How can you expect someone to not judge you if you are always judging others? Your thoughts are real living things, and as you think, so you are! So stay in your power, be loving, wise, selfless, and Spiritualize your ego! That is the ticket to true leadership. Look at Lord Buddha, our Planetary Logos, or Lord Maitreya, the Planetary Christ. They wield awesome powers the likes of which we can only dream about, and yet their love, respect, admiration, compassion, harmlessness, and support knows no boundaries. Melchizedek is the ruler in our entire universe. God is the ultimate ruler in the infinite universe. They rule with complete egolessness, the perfect blending of feminine and masculine, the perfect blending of the Threefold Flame of Love, Wisdom and Power, the perfect blending of all the Rays, all the Archetypes, all the Sephiroth of the Tree of Life, all the Signs of the Zodiac. Let us aspire to rule and lead with inclusiveness, rather than exclusiveness, with oneness and group consciousness rather than elitism, with love and innocent perception, seeing the divine in all regardless of the appearance, wealth or status. Let us not be swayed by impermanent materialistic values but rather set our sights high on those values and ideals that are permanent and eternal and treasured by our Higher Self and Mighty I Am Presence! "If you will not rise above the things of the world, they will rise above you. Be in the world, but let not the world be in you." (Sai Baba) To close this paragraph, let's have a final look at some of the ideal qualities of an effective leader: stable, tactful, patient, tenacious, trustworthy, tolerant, understanding, upbeat, flexible, precise, professional, impersonal and personal, punctual, quick-thinking, reliable, resilient, resourceful, reputable, responsible, self-starting, self-assured, self-confident, self-mastered, self-disciplined, service-minded, sincere, friendly, honest, industrious, innovative, intelligent, harmless, kind, knowledgeable, likable, logical, intuitive, mature, motivated, open-minded, organized, poised, polite, positive, assertive, articulate, attentive to detail, calm, cheerful, conscientious, consistent, courteous, dependable, determined, dynamic, efficient, compassionate, extroverted when needed, discerning, forgiving, joyful, detached yet involved, even-minded, self-loving, centered, balanced, inner-directed, faithful, trusting, successful, accepting, nonjudgmental, nonaggressive, group-oriented. The true leader is a leader yet not superior, competitive or self-righteous. Is authoritative, tolerant, assertive yet never aggressive or intimidating, harmless, discreet, honest, and has integrity. Heed that law, for remember, everybody will be put into a position of leadership at some point, and in truth, everybody is in that position right now! "If one student is bad, only that student is affected. But if one teacher is bad, hundreds of students get spoiled." (Sai Baba)

*   *   *

The Universal Law of Learning to Live in the Tao

There is a state of consciousness known as the Tao where one is in a state of balance! To remain in this balance, which might also be termed being centered, one has to constantly make infinite numbers of minor adjustments in all aspects of oneself and one's bodies! We constantly have to adjust our thinking and have to guide it away from negative ego thoughts and back to Christ/Buddha thoughts. We constantly have to make adjustments in our thinking and feeling to prevent our Emotional Body from veering into negative ego feelings and emotions. We constantly have to make adjustments in our Physical Body in terms of our posture, movement, body language, sleep habits, breathing, and diet, to keep our Physical Body in balance. When we sleep at night and have dreams, this is feedback from the subconscious like an imaginary newspaper of how we are manifesting our thoughts, feelings, and behaviors. By reading this newspaper, and learning this language, we can gain valuable information as to adjustments we need to make in our thinking, feeling, behavior, and perhaps certain blind spots we may be unaware of. Negative perfectionism is when one listens to the negative ego who says that mistakes should not ever happen and when they do it judges you and others for making them. Everybody makes mistakes! That's how we learn! The key lesson is that when you do make a mistake, the idea is to learn from that mistake and gain the golden nugget of wisdom, learn the lesson, forgive self, and try not to let it happen again. As the Dalai Lama said, "When you lose, don't lose the lesson!" Make the appropriate adjustment! We constantly have to make adjustments in when to talk and when to be silent; when to be assertive and when to be receptive. If we drive too fast in our car, we can get a ticket. Going faster is not better, and going slower is not better. Living in the Tao is better. When surfing a wave, if you get ahead of the wave, you will get dumped. If you go too slow, you will miss the wave. It is only when you remain in the Tao that you will catch the wave. Life is very much the same way. Life, in truth, is made up of an infinite number of adjustments in order to remain in the Tao. Learn to listen to this Tao and remain within its sublime rhythm. This is one of the keys to developing the Midas Touch! "Vast, indeed, is the ultimate Tao, spontaneously itself, apparently without acting, end of all ages and beginning of all ages, existing before Earth and existing before Heaven, silently embracing the whole of time." (Tao Te Ching)

*   *   *

The Universal Law of Life Being a Spiritual War

Earth life is a very tough Spiritual school, one of the toughest in the universe. The theme for our entire universe, in terms of the cosmic day we live in, is courage. To be successful in life and to own one's Spiritual power, you have to be very tough as well as loving. It is the integration of the "Spiritual Warrior" Archetype in its positive, uplifting aspect that will make you unstoppable! This becomes easier as time goes on. It becomes an ingrained habit once you have attained mastery over, and integration of, the subconscious mind, inner child, the Physical, Mental, Emotional Bodies and the ego. Djwhal Khul has called this the subjugation of the Dweller on the Threshold. Once this has been accomplished, life becomes a lot easier. Lessons will always arise, but once you are the captain of your ship, setbacks are temporary. Paramahansa Yogananda said in his writings that life is a battlefield. Krishna, in the Bhagavad-Gita, told Arjuna to give up his unmanliness and get up and fight, and that his self-pity and self-indulgence were unbecoming of the great Soul that he was. Krishna also said in the Bhagavad-Gita, "When you fight with love in your heart, no karma is incurred!" The Spiritual war in which all of us are involved is the battle between the lower self and the Higher Self; the battle between truth and illusion; the battle between negative ego thinking and Christ thinking. Paul Solomon said that the Spiritual Path was like climbing a mountain. It was up five steps, then knocked down two. Up seven steps, knocked down five. Since the theme for this cosmic day of our universe is courage, the Spiritual warrior Archetype is inherent in the way this universe was created! Don't be naïve! Every morning when you get up, prepare for battle by putting on your Spiritual armor, and declare war in the service of God! Your Spiritual armor is your personal power, your unconditional love, your protection, faith, trust, patience and forgiveness! The battle we are all in is to climb this mountain known as God Realization. It is not an easy mountain to climb, especially on this planet. It is not easy to master the mind, emotions, Physical Body, negative ego, inner child, Emotional Body and sexuality, to mention but a few. This Spiritual war is the fight to hold true to our Spiritual ideals under enormous obstacles. It is the fight to remain loving under all circumstances. It is the fight to transcend negative ego consciousness at all times. It is the fight not to go on automatic pilot, but instead remain vigilant for God and His kingdom at all times. It is the fight to bring one's Brothers and Sisters out of the seduction of glamour, maya, and illusion. It is the fight to remain in absolute mastery at all times in service of God and the Christ Consciousness. You may lose a few battles but you shall win the war!

*   *   *

The Universal Law of Loving One's Enemies

Did not Master Jesus say, "Love your enemies"? When you approach a person, neighbor, family member, stranger, or fellow worker on the job who is run by the negative ego, the first thing that GOD is teaching you is how NOT to be. You are also being taught to maintain and remain in your personal power. You are being taught by GOD to remain centered, and remain in your bubble of protection so other people's negativity slides off like "water off a duck's back." You are being taught forgiveness, and unconditional love, to respond instead of react. You are being taught to cause your own reality and to not let other people cause your emotions. You are being taught tolerance and patience. You are being taught to look at all things as teachings and lessons instead of bummers and problems.

You are being taught even-mindedness and to maintain inner peace in all situation. You are being taught to maintain your self-love and love from GOD within self, and not to seek it outside of self. You are being taught to remain right with self and right with GOD even though someone around you is not. You are being taught to remain whole in yourself and not seek wholeness outside of self. You are being taught to have preferences and not attachments. You are being taught to set a better example. You are being taught to let go of all attack thoughts and to be kind instead. In some cases, you are being taught humility and to turn the other cheek. In some cases, you are being taught to remain silent and unaffected. You are being taught to transcend duality: when truly centered in your God Self you remain the same when criticized or praised, in victory or defeat, in sickness or in health. In some cases you are being taught to speak up in a clam, rational, objective loving manner rather than a reactive, overly emotional, angry, attacking manner. In the ideal you are being taught to love your enemy and to see the diamond underneath the mud, or the light behind the lampshade. You are being taught to see the Christ within the other person, even though they do not see it in themselves and are not seeing it in you. As Christ said, "One can hate only the act or behavior to separate between the evil and the son of God who consciously or unconsciously chose to do this! A Spiritual leader must learn to love his enemies." What you see in others is a mirror of your own consciousness, since outer life is nothing more than a projection screen for your own thoughts. How you see your Brother and Sister is literally determining your oneness or lack of oneness with GOD. Your Brother and Sister are a Son and Daughter of GOD even if they are not acting like it. If you do not see this, it is you who have a lesson to learn in GOD's eyes. Be more concerned about learning your lessons than about whether your neighbor or friend learns theirs. Confucius once said, "When you encounter someone greater than yourself, turn your thoughts to becoming his equal. When you encounter someone lesser than you, look within and examine your own self." You are also being taught to remain in Christ Consciousness at all times even when under attack. You are taught to stay out of your negative ego at all times. In truth, you are being taught to be a Spiritual Master. From GOD's perspective you should bless your "negative" Brother and Sister for giving you the opportunity to learn such wonderful lessons! "If thine enemy be hungry, give him bread to eat; and if he be thirsty, give him water to drink." (Proverbs 25:22) "Let no one deceive another or despise anyone anywhere, or through anger or irritation wish for another to suffer." (Lord Buddha, Khuddakapatha 9) When life is looked at from the perspective of the Soul, everything is seen as a Spiritual lesson, challenge, and Spiritual test. Every interaction is seen as an opportunity to respond from the Christ Consciousness attitude rather than the negative ego attitude, from unconditional love rather than fear and attack. Every interaction is seen as an opportunity to choose oneness with GOD rather than separation from GOD, forgiveness instead of holding grudges. When you interpret your interactions with people from your Christ/Buddha Mind, each of our jobs Spiritually is to set a better example. In essence, your "enemy" or negative ego neighbor or friend is teaching you God Realization! The proper attitude to all situations in life is to say, "Not my will, but Thine, Oh Lord. Thank you for the lesson." As Sai Baba says, "Welcome adversity." Everything that happens in life happens for a reason. There are no accidents. Some interactions are actually set up by your Higher Self to test you to see if you are ready for higher levels of Initiation and Spiritual responsibility. Anyone can be Spiritual when things are going well. The true test is if you can remain in your Christ Consciousness when you are attacked. "So what that you gain the whole world but lose your own Soul," as the Bible says. "But love your enemies, do good to them, and lend to them without expecting to get anything back. Then your reward will be great, and you will be sons and daughters of the most high, because he is king to the ungrateful and wicked. Be merciful, just as your father is merciful." (Luke 6:35-36 NIV) "But I say unto you, love your enemies, bless them that curse you, do good to them that hate you, and pray for them which despitefully use you, and persecute you.

(Matthew 5:44) "Your worst enemy cannot harm you as much as your own thoughts, unguarded," as The Buddha said!

*   *   *

The Universal Law of Lower Psychism and Psychic Abilities

The psychic realm is not a Spiritual realm. It is a subconscious realm. The subconscious mind has certain abilities that can be tapped into, and psychic abilities are one of them. The glamour of psychic abilities sidetracks many on the Spiritual Path. Many psychics do not even believe in GOD! In this day and age, psychic abilities are often used for black magic, spells, omens, and negative forms of witchcraft or psychism. Psychic abilities are abilities that range far beyond the five Physical senses of taste, touch, hearing, seeing, and smell which allow for a wider range of perception that can transcend space, time, and dimension! Often those who have psychic gifts are very run by the subconscious mind because of their use of its gifts. This becomes a great blessing and great curse simultaneously. Very often to release themselves from this chronic victimization of the subconscious mind and Astral Body they actually have to let go of these abilities to learn to Spiritualize their whole program. Most Lightworkers don't realize that such Spiritual senses as Spiritual discernment, comprehension, healing, divine vision, intuition, idealism, beatitude, active service, realization, perfection, and all knowledge are much more advanced. Lower psychism is an Astral Level ability. To stay stuck there as a psychic rather than become a Spiritual teacher, is to stay stuck in the Astral Plane, which, in truth, doesn't even exist for a realized Ascended Master. Lightworkers should be much more concerned with developing the senses of the Higher Mind, the buddhic senses, atmic senses, monadic senses and logoic senses, than being enamored with the idea of being Astrally psychic. A person who is psychically developed and Psychologically and Spiritually unclear is going to have completely inaccurate and contaminated information anyway. Psychics often are under great psychic attack from Astral entities and from negative Extraterrestrials and they can't figure out why. They don't realize they are stuck in lower psychism, and don't understand what true mastery of the subconscious mind, Emotional Body, and Desire Body really is. Because the negative ego is in control, it clogs and contaminates the channel and attracts Astral and Mental Entities at best, to be one's inner guides. Often times these entities claim to be of the higher dimensions and ascended nature, when they are as confused or negatively manipulative as the people who are attracting them. People can only channel at the level of their clarity. In some cases there is an actual conscious pact made with the Dark Brotherhood. This is more common than people realize! Ponder on this!

*   *   *

The Universal Law of Magnetism and Attraction

The Universal Law of Magnetism and Attraction operates on a subconscious level. The subconscious mind continually attracts and repels things according to what has been programmed into it. A master is someone who uses this law to his own conscious benefit. Let's take the example of money and prosperity. If you have the subconscious belief that you will never have money, you won't. If, on the other hand, you think you will, the subconscious mind will attract those opportunities and possibilities to you. Whatever you want in life, you have to affirm or visualize this into the subconscious mind, and the subconscious mind will attract it to you. Carl Gustav Jung spoke of this when he talked about the collective unconscious. Your subconscious mind is interconnected to all other subconscious minds. You might say that all the sons and daughters of God have one great collective subconscious mind. You can learn to tap into the power of that collective. So, the subconscious is the real attracting and magnetizing aspect of your being. It is the real powerhouse of your energy. It is the seat of your feelings and emotions! It is the storehouse of your energies and all your programming. This is why it is essential to do affirmations and visualizations, and give your subconscious mind self-suggestions to program it to manifest what you want! It will attract to you that which you affirm and visualize into it. It will amaze you with its abilities. The negative ego sabotages you by having you forget to do your affirmations and visualizations. Remember that an idle mind is the devil's workshop. Keep your mind affirming and visualizing what you want. Use all five senses! Make it incredibly real! If you keep it up the subconscious mind will amaze you with its ability to manifest. You must just remember one thing, however. The subconscious mind has no reasoning, and is always manifesting every moment of your life. So if you are not affirming positive thoughts and images into it then negative ones are getting in. That is why some negative things are being attracted and magnetized into your life. Do not let the negative ego make you forget to continue practicing your affirmations, visualizations and continual positive self-suggestions! Heed this *Universal Law of Magnetism and Attraction*! It is the key to successful manifestation!

*   *   *

The Universal Law of Making Adjustments

The world we live in is not a very advanced Spiritual and Psychological world. It has the potential to become one but we are not quite there yet. A great many people are very stuck in their ways, run by their Emotional Body, run by their mind, not balanced in the masculine and feminine, opinionated, confused, unclear, not balanced in their Three-Fold Flame, not balanced and integrated in the Seven Rays, stuck in a great many subconscious patterns, operating out of victim consciousness, and run by the subconscious mind to a great extent. We even see these patterns in ourselves at times, so we have great compassion for others. Anyway, do not except others to live up to your ideals when, in truth, most people can't, even if they wanted to. If, for example, a person is run by their Emotional Body too much, all the attacking, criticizing or sharing in the world is not going to help for the most part. Instead of fighting with them, or instead of trying to teach them something they are not open to learning, or cannot learn, the true lesson is for *you* to make the adjustment, not them. If they are too run by their Emotional Body, make the adjustment to not let it bother you. If they have a habit of blowing off steam, you make the adjustment and let their negative energy slide off you like water off a duck's back, and just recognize that this is the only way they know how to be or can be! If the person you are dealing with is very ego sensitive, hypersensitive, and can't take criticism, then be sensitive and avoid giving them any. You make the adjustment, for they are incapable of doing it. You can take a horse to water but you can't make it drink. If someone around you is very run by the subconscious mind, scattered, forgetful, and prone to mistakes, accept this in your mind and allow them to be this way and don't let it bother you, for you recognize they are incapable of anything else. Instead of trying to change them, *you* make the change to not engage them and just look at it as a lesson in forgiveness and unconditional love. In this regard, you have the ability to make all relationships work, for you are willing to make the adjustment to achieve peace and harmony in the relationship even if they are not necessarily learning their lessons. This is the true attitude, perspective, and behavior of an "Integrated Spiritual Master." They know when to talk and when to be silent. They know when discussion is helpful and when it is not. They know when feedback to another person is appropriate and when the real lesson is making adjustments in self to keep harmony and peace. When one becomes an "Integrated Ascended Master," one has the ability to transcend any situation within their own consciousness by making attitudinal and emotional adjustments to maintain harmony and inner peace. Use whatever the other person is doing as a Spiritual test to teach you certain Spiritual/Christ/Buddha qualities you need to learn. Given how stuck in their ways most people are, with no judgement intended, this is an absolutely essential skill and psychospiritual ability to develop in your relationships if you want them to be successful and harmonious at all times!

*   *   *

The Universal Law of Making Spiritual Vows

Mahatma Karamchand Gandhi said, "A life without vows is like a ship without an anchor or like an edifice that is built on sand instead of a solid rock." Your salvation is not up to God. It is up to you. God has given you everything. What of yourself are you willing to give? Don't be wishy-washy or indecisive. Choose God 100%. By doing this you give God to yourself. Make up your mind to choose God in every moment for the rest of your life, holding to this conviction like a drowning man wants air, and you shall soon realize your heart's desire! Make a vow to never waste a single bit of time or energy. Make a vow to remain conscious at all times and not to think, say, or do anything you do not choose to do. Make a vow to be loving at all times and never to attack. If you make a mistake, instead of feeling bad about it, dwelling upon it and letting it get you down, immediately create a section in your journal for your Spiritual vows. Create a Spiritual vow that says something like, "I hereby 100% forgive myself and unconditionally love myself in regard to this mistake, I now learn my lesson and I will never allow this to happen ever again!" This simple little statement heals the whole process by creating self-forgiveness, and unconditional self-love, and affirms the lesson has been learned and that you will never allow this to happen ever again! This will put you back into your personal power and Spiritual Warrior battling spirit, which is absolutely essential to have every moment of your life. One's will to live is one's will to fight for GOD and everything you believe in. This short Spiritual vow will serve as alchemy to transform this negative experience into "Spiritual Gold." Because you have made this Spiritual vow it is almost good that this mistake occurred because you have now consciously learned this lesson, and your dedication to never allowing this to happen again is like steel which will serve you well in the future, and will save you untold suffering in the future because of the Spiritual vigilance you now hold and have because of this Spiritual vow. Hence that which could have impeded your progress has become a rocket launcher to take you to even higher and more refined levels of Spiritual growth and success. Master Jesus said, "Be ye faithful unto death and I will give thee a crown of life!" Be ye faithful to your Spiritual vows and ideals above all else, and you shall be given that crown of all crowns, The Crown of Life!

*　　　　　　　　　*　　　　　　　　　*

The Universal Laws of Manifestation

The first law of manifestation is that we must learn to manifest with all four of our minds—the conscious, subconscious, superconscious or Soul mind, and monadic mind. It is of utmost importance to use all four levels of our mind in perfect harmony, balance, and integration.

Be aware that you are the Soul and not the personality. If you manifest from the consciousness of the personality, you will see yourself as separated from your Brothers and Sisters—indeed, from Creation itself. That is an illusion. Your manifestation will be a thousand times more powerful if you recognize yourself as the Christ, the Buddha, the Atman, the Eternal Self, for in truth that is who you are. You are one with God and all of Creation; therefore what you are trying to manifest is nothing more than a part of yourself. This important point cannot be emphasized enough. The New Age laws of manifestation deal with this shift in the focus of your identity. Failing to use prayer and to not identify yourself as Soul rather than personality cuts you off to a very great degree from the source of energy for the manifestation of your desires. Ask for assistance from the Ascended Masters, angels, or your monad if you would like extra help.

Do not be attached to what you are praying for or are trying to manifest, or you will repel it from yourself. Make your choice for manifesting a preference, not an attachment. With this attitude you will remain happy until your preference is manifested.

Surrender your prayer request to God and leave it in God's hands. God is happy to help, but you must surrender your request. You can visualize your prayer request going up in a bubble of pink or golden light and melding with God's Light. Then it is your job to go about your business and do what you can on the conscious level of personal power and on the physical action level.

All that exists is perfection. God created you and you are perfect. Anytime anything but perfection manifests, immediately pray and/or visualize and affirm the truth instead of the illusion of the negative ego. Cancel and deny any thoughts that try to enter your mind other than this truth. If you are sick, affirm and visualize only perfection. If your bank account is low, visualize that it is full.

The thoughts and images that you hold in your mind create your reality. God's universe is abundant and limitless. We attract either poverty or abundance, depending on the attitude we hold. This brings us back to the Hermetic Law, "As within, so without; as above, so below." Your outer world and Physical Body are mirrors of the inner world of your conscious and subconscious thinking and imaging.

Have faith. You know God exists, and you know that God's Laws are perfect and work every time. So after you pray, know that your prayer has been heard and God's Law has been invoked. Nothing but perfect fulfillment of the prayer and law can happen as long as you have faith in God's Laws. If you give in to doubt and worry, you are blocking the energy manifestation that you just set in motion.

Be aligned and be committed. All four bodies must be in alignment for a quick manifestation of your prayer request. The mind must be attuned to God, Spirit, and the Soul so that its energy can flow through you. The Feeling Body must be attuned to the mind and then the Soul. The Physical Body must be attuned to the Emotional Body, which is attuned to the mind, which is attuned to the Soul, which is attuned to the monad, which is attuned to God in the same way that the lower minds are subservient to the ones above and to the Soul and God. After you pray, you don't want the subconscious mind acting against your interests by saying, "I don't believe this is going to work." If his starts to happen, push that out of your mind and say, "Get thee behind me, Satan." Then reaffirm God's perfection.

Everything in God's universe is energy, and all energy is God. Even physical matter is just energy vibrating more slowly. So all you are really doing in working the *Universal Laws of Manifestation* is changing or transferring energy from one form to another. This law deals with the fact that energy follows thought. What you ask for already exists on a higher level once the prayer, affirmation, and visualization have been done. Now you are just waiting for it to manifest into physical reality. Your attitude should be expectant. You are simply waiting for it to move down the dimensions and ground itself in physical reality. As long as you keep your Four Bodies and Four Minds in alignment, there is no reason for this not to happen.

The laws of manifestation operate whether you are consciously aware of them or not. They are perfectly happy to work with the negative as well as the positive, they do not discriminate. Whatever you give the subconscious, it will use. If you hold a negative thought and image for too long, it will manifest into your physical reality eventually. So if you are not working these laws of manifestation for the positive, they are going to work to your detriment.

Every moment of your life you are working the laws of manifestation, even when you are not praying, willing, visualizing, or affirming. Every thought you have in your mind as you go through your daily life and when you are sleeping is part of this process. If you never did any specific manifestation work but were vigilant about every thought that you let into your mind, allowing in only thoughts of perfection, God, love, and health, then you would have everything you needed. In this state the Four Minds are functioning as One Mind. Your Soul and Higher Self are doing your thinking, not the negative ego or personality.

Pray from your Soul and not the negative ego. Your Soul won't help if you pray for something that is not for the highest good of all concerned or that hurts someone else. If your prayer doesn't manifest exactly as you expected, there is a possibility it is not meant to be and not truly a part of your Divine Plan.

Perseverance pays off. On this Earthly Plane, time is slowed down so that we may practice these laws. In the higher dimensions of reality, things manifest instantly. We are on this plane of existence to prove our mastery of these laws so that we won't create havoc on the Higher Planes. We need to demonstrate endurance.

Manifestation knows no limits. If you are trying to manifest money, don't think or imagine it as only coming from working, for example. Maybe it will come from the lottery, or an inheritance, or you will find it, or someone will give you money. God works in mysterious ways, so don't try to outthink God. If you think your prayer can manifest in only one way, then you have limited God and your subconscious mind's ability to manifest for you.

We can receive as well as give. There are many Spiritual people who are great givers but do not know hot to receive. When they are offered a gift and say, "No, I can't accept this," they have just blocked their abundance. Receiving is an essential part of having prosperity consciousness.

Gratitude is good. Be humble and thankful for the abundance that God has bestowed upon you. Be thankful to God, the Soul, the Ascended Masters, the subconscious mind, the Angels, and the Nature Spirits for all the wonderful work they do for you. Make every day a thanksgiving.

Failure is not a possibility. How can you fail with God, the Soul, your personal power, the power of your subconscious mind, your Physical Body, and other people all helping you? Besides, you are the Christ, Buddha, the Atman, the Eternal Self. You are God. Can God lose against the forces of illusion and maya? The only thing that can stop your manifestation is the glamour, maya, and illusion of your own negative ego and lower self. The only thing that can stop you from manifesting anything you want is you. God has given you everything. You only have to claim it. That is the only thing that God can't do for you. We must claim God's abundance and then it is instantly ours.

To have all, give all to all. This is a law of manifestation made known *in A Course in Miracles*. We must learn to receive, but we also must learn to give in order to manifest effectively. We must keep our abundance in circulation. When we become selfish and stop giving, then the universe becomes selfish and stops giving to us. When we stop giving to the all, which is God, we are not able to receive as much. Keep giving and keep receiving; let the abundance flow freely in both directions. Also, what we are holding back from our Brother is what we are holding back from God and ourselves. To have all we must give all, for in reality we already are and already have everything. We have always been this and always will be this. It is only our belief in the ego as our guide and teacher that has made us believe otherwise.

Words have power. The power of your spoken words is even greater than the thoughts you allow to run through your mind. Every word you speak is a decree of manifestation. Consequently, you must be vigilant over your speech. Just because you are not focusing on your manifestation work doesn't mean that you are not doing manifestation work.

Positive affirmations produce positive results. For example, if you want to heal a broken leg, phrase your affirmation and prayer without saying, "I am now healing my broken leg." It would be better to say, "My leg is now powerful, healed and whole." The reference to the negative image can have a negative effect on the subconscious mind. The subconscious mind has no reasoning and will manifest anything that is put into it, so let only the positive in.

Vital force and energy are necessary ingredients. Before doing your manifestation work, build up your vital force and energy. Spirit and the Angels sometimes use the energy as well as the thoughts and imagery you send them in your prayer request. You can build up vital force by doing deep breathing or physical exercise for a few minutes before you begin praying.

Enthusiasm produces results. When you do your manifestation work, be enthusiastic. Your enthusiasm is part of the previous law of building vital force, and enthusiasm also incorporates your Emotional Body in the manifestation work, which will speed the process. The Emotional Body is connected to the subconscious mind, and nothing will manifest unless the subconscious mind is involved in the process. Remember, the subconscious mind is the powerhouse of attraction within your relationship to self. This is because it stores all the feelings and emotions. So to engage the subconscious mind you must manifest and do your Spiritual practices with Spiritual passion, enthusiasm, love, joy, happiness, and Spirit! If you are going to take the negative ego's view that this is drudgery and just go through the motions, it is not going to work. As *A Course In Miracles* says, "True pleasure is serving GOD"! Serving GOD is pleasure. Serving the negative ego is work! That is what is draining beyond belief! Serving GOD will give you infinite amounts of love, energy, joy and bliss! It will give you a peace that "passeth understanding"! So engage your feelings and emotions in this process, for by engaging the Emotional Body this engages the subconscious mind and Spiritually electrifies your whole being, which makes the manifestation infinitely stronger and faster!

There is just one universal subconscious mind. We each focus on one aspect of that mind while being simultaneously connected to the whole mind or, as Jung called it, the collective unconscious. This understanding and awareness in your manifestation work gets rid of the belief in separation that can slow down manifestation.

Only you can block your own manifestation. If you master your thinking and imaging and your Feeling Body, then nothing can stop the manifestation from occurring.

Grudges block the process. Be sure you have forgiven all people, situations, and yourself before beginning your manifestation work. Not forgiving someone builds guilt and other psychic blocks that make the subconscious mind unable to cooperate fully in the prayer process and affirmation work.

Love yourself. If you lack self-love, you feel undeserving. If you believe you are undeserving, you contradict what you ask for in prayer. If this is a lesson for you, seriously study Chapter 5 in the Revised Edition of *Soul Psychology*, which is on the Christ Consciousness.

Pray in proportion. Some people pray too much, which is a sign of lack of faith. In reality, once is enough. If, however, worry and doubt set in, there is nothing wrong with repeating a prayer as a reaffirmation of your faith. Each of us must achieve his or her own balance of prayer.

Put it in writing. Writing prayers and affirmations down on paper creates a stronger message for the subconscious mind than just thinking prayers or saying them out loud. Combining physical and mental actions exerts more force on the subconscious mind.

Meditate to manifest. Whenever you are in a state of meditation, or in an altered state of consciousness, you are also in a state of hypnosis, which allows suggestions to pass into the subconscious mind much more easily. A good time to do your manifestation work is just as you are falling asleep at night and when you are just waking up in the morning. This twilight state between sleep and waking is called the hypnogogic state.

Avoid talking about your manifestation work. Very often, talking with others about what you are trying to manifest can dissipate the energy. Another consequence of indiscriminate speech is the negative reaction that often comes from people when you share your vision. Guard against letting the negative energy of others penetrate your conscious and subconscious minds.

Positivity produces positive results. Until you achieve self-mastery, this is the single most important fact on one's Spiritual Path. In manifestation work you are trying to hold a certain thought form, energy, and vibration. You want to be around people who support this process. Being around negative people and negative environments tends to deplete one's energies Physically, Emotionally, Mentally, and Spiritually over time, and hence makes it more difficult to hold the vibration.

You possess all always. Since you are God, Christ, the Buddha, everything is yours, just as everything is God's. This has always been the case, but it is difficult for us to accept this because we are so used to believing the ego's interpretation of ourselves that tells us we are just a Physical Body, a personality, and are separate from creation. If we faithfully held the truth that we are the Eternal Self, then all our thoughts would stem from this basic understanding, and everything we need would manifest whenever we need it.

Ask only for what you need. If the ego becomes involved and starts asking for things you don't really need, then the prayer request is coming from glamour. This will sabotage your manifestation. However, as the Shinto saying goes, "A single sincere prayer moves Heaven."

Rely solely on God. God, your personal power, the power of your subconscious mind, and your Physical Body power are an unbeatable team. When you live this truth, your security is internal instead of external. No matter what happens to your external self, you know that you can manifest whatever you need with God's help, your will, and the power of your subconscious mind.

Four unified minds can move mountains. The Kahunas of Hawaii devised a special method of prayer utilizing all Four Minds. Their method required you to write your prayer down on a piece of paper very specifically, and with lots of colorful imagery. Make sure that you have built up your vital force and energy so that you approach this task with enthusiasm. When you have the prayer worded and imaged in a way that you feel good about, say it three times out loud, addressing the prayer to God, your Higher Self, monad, and one or more other entities. After saying the prayer three times, then command your subconscious mind, in a powerful but loving way, to take the prayer to your Higher Self and monad. Visualize this happening like the Old Faithful geyser, shooting up into the air through your crown Chakra. Then forget about the prayer and do whatever you need to do on the conscious and subconscious levels to manifest the prayer. in other words, make sure all Four Minds are working together in perfect harmony.

Use all five of your senses when visualizing what you want to manifest. See it, hear it, taste it, touch it, and smell it. Make your visualization so vivid that this meditation reality is just as real or more real than your physical life reality. Doing visualizations with all five senses engaged ensures your success.

Ask and you shall receive. Knock and the door shall be opened. If you don't ask for help, your Higher Self and the Ascended Masters and the Angels are not allowed to help you. If you don't ask, God doesn't help.

Tell your subconscious mind what to do. If you don't give it suggestions, affirmations, visualizations, and programming, then it will manifest whatever happens to be in it already, along with whatever you allow other people to put into it.

Be of service. Just because you are working with prayer and affirmation and visualization, this doesn't mean that you don't have to do physical work for a living. The Soul's perspective is that your work is your service to God and that true pleasure is serving God. Once you achieve some level of self-realization, there is no other reason to be here except to be of service to humanity, which is God.

Keep your mind steady in the light. By staying focused, you won't lose the idealized potential that you are in the process of manifesting. As you evolve you will not even have to be patient and wait, for what you choose to manifest will happen instantly.

Achieving emotional level manifestation helps you retain your childlike faith and devotion to God. The Bible says that true faith is like a mustard seed, which can when planted literally move mountains. Childlike faith in action is a wonder to see.

Stay attuned to the Soul Consciousness. Soul-Level manifestation requires you to identify yourself as the Soul, not as the personality. This allows the energies of the Soul to contribute to the manifestation of whatever you need. Working on the Mental, Emotional, and Physical Levels for manifestation and not utilizing one's Soul would cut us off from the source of all life.

Miracles are neutral. Miracles are the natural by-product of expressing and working through God's laws for the service of humankind.

Identify yourself with God. When you use the words "I Am" in beginning your affirmations, and when you are addressing God, you are affirming God's name, which is your own.

"Set your mind on God's Kingdom and His justice before everything else and all the rest will come to you as well (Matthew 6:33). What will a man gain by winning the whole world, at the cost of his true self?" (Matthew 16:26). True prosperity is being merged with the Soul and Spirit, which then leads to all your needs being taken care of in service of God.

It is okay to pray for material things. Some people in the Spiritual movement are confused by this point. It is perfectly okay and actually desirable for you to utilize the Soul's help in this capacity; however, don't be greedy. Ask for exactly what you need, no more and no less.

Focus upon service to humanity. An ancient metaphysical saying states, "When your heart is pure, you will have the strength of ten." When our work is for a noble cause and we are doing it with a pure heart and intent, we will have a much greater amount of energy to do what we need to do, for we are aligned with the universal force.

Be specific in your visualization and your affirmation. If you are too general, then by the laws of the universe you can manifest only a general solution, or one that is too vague to manifest in any recognizable way.

What we manifest is not really ours. You are simply a caretaker for all that is God's. There is no "yours" as separated form "God's."

Take good care of what you manifest. If you manifest a car and don't take care of it, then you are not deserving of the manifestation on the physical level. All levels need to be in alignment or manifestation can be blocked.

Be at one with the essence of all things. This law deals with what abundance really is. True abundance is not having everything, but rather being a source through which what is needed is made manifest.

Manifestation requires self-discipline. You must learn to discipline your mind, emotions, body, and consciousness to hold the proper vibration and attunement to the Soul. You must have self-discipline so that you won't let the lower self infiltrate the mind with its doubts and fears.

Having discipline gives us consistency. It allows us to stay continually in the light.

You are the authority and the Master. There is no force more powerful than your will, and to manifest effectively, you must own your full power and identity as the Christ. You must manifest with the full power of your self as Soul and as Spirit, and the universe will instantly comply with your command.

You have only one need. The negative ego would tell you that you have many needs. Your only real need is to own the truth of your identity with God. When this need is met, then all other apparent needs are instantly met as a by-product of this state of consciousness.

We lack nothing. Since everything you need is already part of you, the need for manifestation then becomes nothing more than an opportunity to demonstrate the presence of God. Manifestation is really just creativity at work.

To manifest as a group, all members need to share the same vision. If a group has differing visions, then the manifestation can be canceled.

Follow your inner promptings and intuitions after praying for help. Let's say you have prayed for a specific dollar figure for your rent check next month. The universe is manifesting this through a person you are supposed to meet at a party. If you get the guidance to go to this party but your lower self tells you that you are too tired to go, then you may miss the manifestation that was provided for you. This is where self-discipline dovetails with being obedient to your intuition and Soul and Spiritual guidance.

Honor *The Universal Law of Tithing*. This law states that if you give one-tenth of your income to a charitable or beneficial cause, you will receive a tenfold return on your generosity. As the Bible says, "Every man according as he purposeth in his heart, so let him give; not grudgingly, or of necessity; for God loveth a cheerful giver." This law is working with *The Universal Law of Karma*, which states that you sow what you reap; what you put out comes back to you. The giving of a tithe and/or seed money keeps the energy of money in circulation. If you are stingy with the universe, which is God, then the universe and God will be stingy with you. If you are generous with the universe, then the universe, by God's law, will be generous with you.

One of the keys to manifestation is to own the fact that you are God and you are serving God, and that you are one with that which you are trying to manifest. Being an incarnation of GOD, in truth you are and have everything already! You are God. All Creation is, in truth, contained within you. One of the blocks to manifestation is when the negative ego and personality try to manifest and they do so from the consciousness of being separate from Creation instead of a part of Creation! You are one with that which you are manifesting. Your manifestation will be infinitely more powerful if you remember that you are God, your Brothers and Sisters are God, you are one wit all Creation! So God is manifesting an aspect of self, to serve God, and GOD!

After prayer comes acceptance. This last law of manifestation is absolutely essential to follow. After praying, accept your prayer as answered. You have followed all the laws and principles of manifestation. You have fulfilled the law. Don't just believe that it is answered; rather, *know* it with every cell, molecule, and atom of your being that it has been answered. It is done. If is finished. So be it, for you have decreed it to be so. Your work is God made manifest. You are God, and you are one with God. You have fulfilled the law, so how can your prayer not be made manifest? Heed these words! They are literally the key to manifesting your heart's desire!

           *   *   *

The Universal Law of Mastering Addictions and Bad Habits

To understand addictions it is first essential to understand that the subconscious mind can also be referred to as the habitual mind. The subconscious mind is where habits are stored, both good and bad ones. One can have the habit of smoking, drinking, and thinking with one's negative ego mind, or the habit of eating right, exercising, meditating, and thinking with one's Spiritual Mind. So one of the main Spiritual practices of the Spiritual Path is to fill one's subconscious mind with good Spiritual habits! The problem is that in past lives we have had bad habits, and we bring these negative programs and bad habits with us when we incarnate into a baby's body. Second, when we incarnate into children's bodies we pick up both good and bad habits from our parents, family, school, television, peer, and mass consciousness. An addiction is an "attachment" or "bad habit" on a thought, feeling, or physical level. Most of the time we think of addictions as being focused on a physical or outer thing, like being addicted to cigarettes, alcohol, sex, food, to name just a few. The truth is, even though all these things are physical in nature, it is the "feeling" that is often addicted to. For example, the alcoholic tries to escape the pain they feel, and food may be used as a replacement for love, or to stuff feelings. So, we see that addictions are often to escape a negative feeling or to try and create a new one. A person can actually be addicted to a feeling: love, power, activity (and being unable to sit quiet). So we see people can be addicted to a ray in its lower aspect. Addictions can also be connected with energy, like people being addicted to doing dangerous things like bungie jumping, sky diving, or hang gliding. So we see that addictions can occur on a Mental, Emotional, Energetic, and Physical Level, and most often, all these aspects of self are interconnected to addictions.

Let's take the example of smoking. The addiction takes on a mental aspect because of the Mental habit of doing it. It takes on an emotional addiction because of the feeling it gives the person when they are feeling nervous, uptight or anxious. And smoking is addictive on a physical level because of the nicotine. The more you do it, the more it becomes engrained like a tape recording in the subconscious mind, and the more the nicotine gets into the cells. The same is true of heroin, alcohol, sugar, drugs, and so on. So what happens over time is the constant doing of these activities forms deeper and deeper grooves in the subconscious mind and a habit is formed and over time it becomes a very ingrained habit on a Mental, Emotional, Energetic, and Physical Level. The mind, emotions, and body actually crave toxicity because of the improper Mental, Emotional, Energetic, and Physical Programming. So, what is the cause of addictions? The original cause is always the same thing. It always begins with a negative ego/fear-based/separative thought which leads to a negative/fear-based-separative feeling! The person does not know how to escape this negative thought, feeling, and suffering, and begins to try and use an "outside source" to solve the problem instead of Spiritual mastery. So addictions can be caused by a way to escape pain and suffering or they can be caused by not having a healthy psychology, philosophy, and mindset! Most people are not in control of their minds. Their mind or subconscious mind runs them. Another case is that most people are run by their Emotional Body. They are not masters and causes of their feelings and emotions. Third, most people are run by their Desire Body. When you are run too much by your Emotional Body, you are also going to be run by your Desire Body, for the Desire Body is connected to the Emotional Body, and the Desire Body is always connected with addiction. When a person allows them-selves to be run too much by their Mental and Emotional Body, they end up being run by their desires. When the mind and Emotional Body run you too much, the negative ego mind becomes the director and program-mer by Psychological Law. If people allow themselves to be a victim rather than a master, then the negative ego will program their emotional life.

This causes negative feelings and emotions such as fear, worry, anger, depression, loneliness, frustration, and so on. These feelings can lead to addiction. Then what happens is because the Emotional Body is too much in control, the Desire Body automatically becomes too much in control which leads to overindulgence and getting involved with lower-self types of habits such as cigarettes, too much alcohol, drugs, overindulgence in sex, sugar, junk food, and so on. Lord Buddha said, "All suffering comes from attachments"! Attachments and addictions are very interrelated. People become attached to alcohol, sugar, or whatever, instead of it being an occasional preference. The negative ego mind causes the person to latch on and become attached or addicted to certain types of behavior which then forms a habit in the subconscious mind on a Mental, Emotional, Energetic, and Physical Level. It is all these factors combined together that form the root cause of all addictions. Addictions are really deeply ingrained mental and emotional negative habits of faulty thinking and emotional patterns, which have moved from the Mental and Emotional Plane also into the Physical Body and Material Plane. So an addiction in essence is a Mental, Emotional, Energetic, and Physical bad habit! Well, what can you do to master your bad habits and addictions? 100% fully claim your personal power and self-mastery over your every thought, feeling, word, deed, subconscious mind, Desire Body, Physical Body, inner child, and every aspect of self and Earthly Life. Make a Spiritual vow that as of this moment you are going to officially stop your bad habits. Monitor and remain Spiritually vigilant over your every thought and feeling, deny any thought/feeling not of GOD entrance into your consciousness, and replace it with the opposite Spiritual/Christ/Buddha thought or feeling. Do affirmations for personal power, self-love, Bubble of Protection, and Spiritual attunement twice a day! (See *Soul Psychology*) Call forth twice a day for 21 days the Core Fear Matrix Removal Program and ask Spirit and the Masters to remove the bad habit and addiction from your energy field and subconscious mind. They will do so! Ask and you shall receive! Pray to the Holy Spirit and ask the Holy Spirit to "undo" the original cause of the bad habit/addiction 100%. If you are ever tempted, immediately pray to God, Christ, the Holy Spirit, your Mighty I Am Presence and Higher Self to remove this temptation from your consciousness. Pray to Archangel Michael and ask him to cut all energetic cords within your being to this bad habit and addiction. Communicate with your inner child every day for 21 days and tell it that you need to be very firm in regard to stopping this bad habit and addiction, and ask for its cooperation! Call forth a "Golden Net" three times a day form your Mighty I Am Presence to cleanse your energy fields. Keep your mind steady in the light, keep a positive mental attitude at all times, and remain Spiritually vigilant for GOD and His Kingdom. Follow this simple program for 21 days (it takes 21 days to cement a new habit into the subconscious mind) and no bad habit or addition in this infinite universe will be able to withstand your power, and the Love, Wisdom, and Power of GOD and the Godforce! As the saying goes, "Know the difference between instinct and habit. Trust your instincts—question your habits."

*   *   *

The Universal Law of Mastering, Loving, and Taking Responsibility for the Earth and Earth Life

There are Four Faces of GOD: Spiritual, Mental, Emotional, and Material! One will not realize GOD fully without mastering, integrating, and fully loving Earth life! GOD exists as much in the Material Universe as He does in the Mental, Emotional, or Spiritual Dimensions! If you don't learn to master, integrate, and fully love the Earth, Earth

Energies, and Life, you will literally be missing one quarter of God Realization. Part of mastering, integrating and loving Earth and Earth life is loving the Earth Mother, the Animal, Plant, and Mineral Kingdom, Pan, the Nature Spirits, the Plant Devas, and the Elemental Spirits! Spiritually mastering the Earth and Earth Energies is just like Spiritual mastery, Mental mastery, Emotional mastery, Energy mastery, however, this is mastery in regards to the Mastery of the Physical Body, Earthly Energies, and Earthly Life! In terms of the Physical Vehicle, it means learning to Physically eat right, take care of Physical fitness, learning to develop good sleep habits, mastering the understanding of your body rhythms and learning to work with them! Mastery of Earth Energies deals with mastering money and developing prosperity consciousness, staying organized in your Earthly life and having proper time management, and prioritizing your goals and projects, and so on. To fully realize GOD, it must be done so on three distinct levels: on a Spiritual, Psychological, and Physical/Earthly Level! Each level is a doorway to God Realization! And each level is equally important! GOD is as much in the Material World as He is in the Astral, Mental, and Spiritual Realms! As we all know, ascension is descension. The purpose of life is not to leave the Earth, but to ground one's Mighty I Am Presence, Higher Self, and Soul fully into one's Physical Body and fully into the Earth and Earth life! We must love and care for Earth life! Many Spiritual people are not political, or don't care about social issues or changing our society, for they believe it is not important. They believe, only the Heavenly world is important, not what is going on in the Earthly world! This is faulty thinking! It is our purpose to love this world and turn it into a fifth dimensional society, a utopian society! "Hands that help are holier than lips that pray," as Sai Baba said. Politics is important. Mahatma Gandhi is quoted as saying, "Those who say that religion has nothing to do with politics do not know what religion means." Being politically active in some way is very important! Saving the whales, saving the rain forests, cleaning up the pollution, repairing the ozone layer, picking up trash off the ground, planting trees, Spiritually

educating our world, and manifesting Spirituality on Earth is just as
important as any Spiritual pursuit! That is why we have come! Not to
ascend, turn the body into light, and leave! That's illusion! You came to
descend and build a new Spiritual Civilization on Earth! Why have a
Physical Body if you are not going to Spiritually ground your mission?
You could have done Spiritual and Psychological work without a Physical
Body! Almost every institution on the planet is run from the personality
and negative ego, and not from the Soul and Spirit's perspective! We are
here to fix all this! Massive numbers of Lightworkers are focused on their
own Spiritual growth and are not focused on what they need to be focused
upon, and have their head in the clouds and are too ungrounded! So, the
first step is that we master the Earth and Earth energies within our own
being. Then we must always love the Earth, Earth energies, and Earthly
life! Then we must take responsibility and fulfill our Spiritual mission,
purpose, and puzzle piece on Earth! Part of mastering the Earth and Earth
Energies means anchoring your Spiritual mission on Earth and not just
talking about it, not just thinking about it, not just visualizing it, not just
getting excited about it, and not just meditating and praying about it! It is
now time for Lightworkers to get their acts together! Lightworkers are the
caretakers for Mother Earth and Earthly Civilization! Our civilization is
still backwards in a great many ways! If Lightworkers do not fix it, who is
going to fix it? It is our responsibility! We each have a Spiritual responsibility of making changes in this world and making changes in this society!
For some it will be through Politics, others through Spiritual Education,
others through Active Service in this world, others through the Arts,
through the Sciences, through Religion, or through Business, Economics,
and Changing the Institutions of our Civilization! One of the reasons that
a great many Lightworkers are not mastering Earth energies and are not
taking responsibility for the Earth is they are not balanced in the Seven
Rays! The Third Ray is about grounding Spiritual Energy Physically into
the world in the form of Active Physical Service. In a Lightworker who is
primarily Second Ray, the Spiritual Energy floats above the Earthly Plane

but never gets grounded! Another reason so many Lightworkers have difficulty grounding their Spiritual missions is that they are not only weak in the Third Ray of Active Intelligence, they are weak in their First Ray as well! They have not been trained how to fully own their 100% Personal Power at all times! This inability to own your Personal Power will of course make you completely unable to master Earth Energies or any type of energies for that matter. Life will push the person around instead the person mastering life! It is as important to take care of a person's physical needs as it is to take care of their Spiritual needs, Mental needs, and Emotional needs! In truth, it's even more important! If a person is physically ill, starving and malnourished, homeless, or living on survival mode, it is hard to focus on Spiritual Concerns! How is this world ever going to change if we each don't master Earth Energies, totally and completely love every aspect of the Earth, and take physical action to heal it! GOD and the Masters are not going to do it. They can't, they don't have Physical Bodies! Don't you see, that is why we are here! We are the instruments and channels of GOD and the Masters to make changes in this Earthly world! Ponder on this! It's time to get your hands a little dirty!

*   *   *

The Universal Law of Multidimensional Realities and Communication

In truth, we are multidimensional beings. This is true because we are Sons and Daughters of GOD, and we are made in His image and likeness. GOD is multidimensional and we are multidimensional! The

microcosm is like the macrocosm. We are constantly receiving hundreds
of different forms of communication on a subconscious and Spiritual
level. We are receiving thoughts, feelings, emotions, impulses, desires, sensations, energy, appetites, instincts, imagery from our subconscious and
Higher Self and/or Mighty I Am Presence. Each of these is a different
level, form, and mode of multidimensional communication! Our basic
forms of multidimensional communication with people begin with verbal
communication. Then we communicate reciprocally in a nonverbal manner by our gestures, expressions, and body language! We also communicate mentally or telepathically with others all the time, over short and long
distances. We communicate through our feelings and emotions, through
physical touch, just basic energy, and imagery. We also communicate with
our world through the five physical senses and their corresponding subconscious inner counterpart senses which allow us to inwardly see, hear,
taste, touch, and smell! This is why when we dream at night everything
seems so real! Our outer senses are asleep and instead we are using our
inner senses to see, hear, and so forth. This also explains why people can
still see, hear, taste, touch, and smell while Astral traveling, Soul traveling,
and when they physically die and translate to another dimension. These
are all subconscious inner senses that can be developed and it is what we
call being psychic! It also explains the process of channeling in a clairaudient or telepathic regard. Now, at any given moment we are also receiving
communication from our inner child, various subpersonalities, good and
bad habits, our negative ego and its illusionary thought system, as well as
the Christ/Buddha thought system. We also receive communication from
past life subpersonalities and/or aspects, and from the outside world or life
itself in the form of synchronicity and signs. We also receive dreams every
night as another means of communication and feedback on a subconscious and Spiritual level. Another form of multidimensional communication would be lucid dreaming where one can consciously awake in their
dreams and with the use of their will change the outcome of dreams. On a
Spiritual level, we not only communicate with our Higher Self and

Mighty I Am Presence, but we also communicate with the Inner Plane Ascended Masters, the Archangels and Angels, the Elohim Masters, and Christed Extraterrestrial races. If our psychology and Spiritual attunement and frequency is not of a totally Christ/Buddha nature we can also communicate with entities on the Mental and/or Astral Plane which is not recommended! This also explains why some people have to deal with abduction and negative implants! Then we also receive direct communication from GOD, Christ, and the Holy Spirit if we are open to hearing and receiving it! Our true identity is the Eternal Self, and given this fact, there are aspects of ourselves that exist in higher dimensions of GOD that are already functioning there which we may or may not be in communication with! Then, we communicate with our Soul and monadic family, with past life selves and future selves, and aspects of our parallel lives! We communicate with our Spiritual Teachers and/or Gurus, with past life friends and family, as well as future life friends and family. Then, we each multi-dimensionally communicate with Nature, Mother Earth, the Nature Spirits, the Devas, Tree Spirits, the Four Elements, and the Elementals—the Gnomes, Sylphs, Salamanders, and Undines. Crystals, gemstones, animals. On an Earthly level, we also have the ability to multidimensinally communicate with the subatomic particles of matter and our bodies. We can communicate with our electrons, protons, neutrons, molecules, DNA, and even subatomic particles known as quarks, and subatomic particles coming from outer space in the form of light particles known as photons. This explains how we each have the abilities to materialize and dematerialize and/or create substance or physical things right out of the ethers, as Sai Baba is demonstrating it. Then, we have hundreds of subtle Spiritual Bodies all of which have special abilities and functions in a multidimensional sense, that can and do communicate with us and we with them on a conscious or unconscious level. On a Spiritual level, we have multidimensional communication with GOD and the Cosmic Inner Plane Masters through the "Language of Light" which often manifests through the anchoring of Fire Letters, Key Codes, and Sacred Geometries!

Isn't life exciting? Our true multidimensional nature and communication seen from the Full Spectrum Prism Perspective makes *Alice in Wonderland* truly look boring! Enjoy!

*   *   *

The Universal Law of Nonviolence

This law includes nonviolence not only on a Physical Level, but also on the Mental and Emotional Levels in terms of transmuting all violent thoughts and emotions. When they do come up, don't listen to them, for they are a product of negative ego thinking. It is the negative ego that creates all negative emotions. When you think with your Christ Mind, your emotions remain loving, joyful, and peaceful. Never forget this! God lives in all things, even insects. If insects invade your home, you have the right to protect your space. Outdoors, however, you must respect their space! Practice nonviolence on all levels—Physical, Psychological, and Spiritual. Such is the behavior of a true Spiritual Master. Lord Buddha said, "The true master lives in truth, in goodness and restraint, nonviolence, moderation, and purity." And the master of nonviolence himself, Mahatma Gandhi, is quoted as saying, "Non-violence is not a weapon of the weak. It is a weapon of the strongest and the bravest." Ponder on this!

*   *   *

The Universal Law of Oneness

We are one with all life and all life needs to be honored as a part of God. You live in all things and all things live in you! Sai Baba is quoted as saying, "Nations are many, but Earth is one; beings are many, but breath is one; stars are many, but sky is one; oceans are many, but water is one; religions are many, but God is one; jewels are many, but gold is one; appearances are many, but reality is one." The Golden Rule states, "Do unto others as you would have others do unto you." If your true identity is the Eternal Self and all of Creation is part of that Eternal Self, then anything we do to any other part of Creation we literally are doing to ourselves. By the same token, to give something to another is literally to give love to oneself. If humanity would deeply understand and practice this one law, the entire world would change in an instant! Every person, every animal, every plant, every rock, is God. There is only one identity in the universe for all of life throughout Creation—and that is God. We all share that one identity. "The same current activates all." (Sai Baba) We must let go of glamour, illusion, maya and appearances so that we can see the true reality of life. Our true identity as the Eternal Self lives within all Creation. All Creation is a part of you. Strive to be harmless and defenseless in all things. Your Brothers and Sisters share your identity as the Christ with you. God had only One Son and One Daughter and we are all part of that Sonship or Daughtership. We each are apprentice Gods who are in the process of realizing this on deeper and deeper levels. This is the Initiation process. So, we are one with God, have always been and will always be! *A Course in Miracles* states that there is only one problem in life—separation from God. But the truth is that we will never be separate and never have been. This is illusion. The law of the mind, however, is that whatever we think is the reality we live in. The world is living in a mass negative hypnosis of separation that does not exist in reality. It only exists in our minds! In this moment, wake up from the bad dream and nightmare you have lived in for many lifetimes and realize the truth that passeth all understanding! We are all One! There is only One! You are the One! "Live a life worthy of the calling you have received. Be completely humble and gentle; be patient, bearing with one another in love. Make every effort to keep the unity of the Spirit through the bond of peace. There is one Body and one Spirit-one Lord, one faith, one baptism; one God and Father of all, who is over all and through all and in all." (Ephesians 4:1-6 NIV) "May the God who gives endurance and encouragement give you a spirit of unity among yourselves as you follow Christ Jesus, so that with one heart and mouth you may glorify the God and Father of our Lord Jesus Christ." (Romans 15:5-6 NIV)

*   *   *

The Universal Law of Opening the Third Eye

Many think the Third Eye is connected to clairvoyance. This is only an extremely small sliver of what the true full opening of the Third Eye is about! Never forget that you don't just see with your Physical eyes, you see with your mind. Part of opening the Third Eye is the Spiritual wisdom of esoteric knowledge and understanding. Part of this is wisdom on a Psychological Level. And part of this is wisdom on a Physical/Earthly Level. Psychological wisdom greatly opens the Third Eye. The thinking with your negative ego mind is what closes the Third Eye and causes blocks and imbalances in it. It is what creates blind spots, and limited lens seeing. Jesus is quoted as saying, "The light of the body is the eye: therefore when thine eye is single, thy whole body also is full of light; but when thine eye is evil, thy body also is full of darkness." (Luke

11:34) Every person either has negative ego vision or Spiritual vision. We don't just see with our Physical eyes, we see through our mind and belief systems. A person can have mystic clairvoyance, and can be a Spiritual, Psychological, and Physical/Earthly mess, and often is. See *The Universal Law of the Three Levels of Spiritual Vision.* This lack of clear Third Eye vision on these other levels also greatly contaminates and distorts their mystic vision. It is impossible to separate a person's consciousness from their mystic vision or channeling abilities. This is why there are many clairvoyants who are extremely unclear Spiritually and Psychologically, even though they can see into the Inner Plane. There are even psychics and clairvoyants who do not believe in GOD. Clairvoyance is actually a subconscious ability and/or inner sense. This is why many Lightworkers get trapped in the fascination of the psychic world, not realizing that this is a subconscious and/or Astral/Mental World and is not the true Spiritual World. This not only has very little to do with true Third Eye opening, but it is also often a psychic realm that has no connection to the Spiritual at all! The opening of the Third Eye also deals with the development and integration of the 22 Supersenses of GOD, such as intuition, knowing-ness, comprehension, knowledge, wisdom, Spiritual idealism, all knowl-edge, beautitude, active service, divine vision, revelation, healing, Spiritual telepathy, response to group vibration, Spiritual discernment, discrimina-tion, Emotional idealism, and imagination, to name but a few. A person could have their mystic clairvoyance opened and not be very developed in the rest of these inner senses that open the Third Eye. This is not even counting all the Spiritual and esoteric knowledge and wisdom, Psychological vision, and Physical/Earthly psychospiritual vision, and for that matter just plain Physical/Earthly vision, which is a type of Spiritual vision in truth. The ideal is to have good Spiritual vision in all these levels, and it is all of them that open the Third Eye and sixth Chakra. The Third Eye will never ever be fully open until all these factors are taken into con-sideration! Now, it is possible to open the Third Eye too much or too lit-tle. There is also a need for protection in life, which a lot of Lightworkers say is unimportant. This of course it not true. The Third Eye is like the Physical eye in some ways. The pupil of the eye opens and closes in terms of how much light is coming into the room. There are times to close the Third Eye a little. If you go to the movies and there are some violent scenes you might want to close it a little. Too many stimuli can be coming in at times. This needs to be monitored. There is also the aspect of overusing the Third Eye. Lightworkers may spend too much time working with this Chakra to the neglect of the others. This may cause headaches, eyestrain, or depletion of the pituitary gland. This is very important to not let happen, for this is the master gland of our body and affects all the other glands and organs. It is interesting that the Third Eye or Sixth Chakra is connected to the master gland, is it not? We see the incredible importance of having a clear Spiritual, Psychological, and Physical/Earthly vision in our lives. We see the enormous effect our Spiritual, Psychological and Physical/Earthly vision has on our lives. It is our thoughts and images in our mind that create our reality. Would it not make sense, given that the Third Eye and Sixth Chakra are connected with the vision for our whole life, that it would be connected to the master gland of the body, the pituitary? Is not GOD ingenious! So the key is not to underuse or overuse the Third Eye and Sixth Chakra, but to fully open it and keep it in balance with all the rest of the Chakras. We don't want to overactivate or underactivate the pituitary gland! Balance is as always the key!

*   *   *

The Universal Law of Optimism

You can take a person with a good attitude and put him in the worst situation and he may be disheartened for a little while, but he is going to be happy again. On the other side of the coin, you can take someone with a bad attitude and put him in the best outer situation possible, he will be happy for a while, but he will soon feel despair again. "All the days of the afflicted are evil; but he that is of a merry heart hath a continual feast." (Proverbs 15:15) The Spiritual attitude toward life is to remain optimistic at all times! Be happy and spread joy wherever you go! Sickness can be contagious if people are victims and have low resistance. Since so many people live in victim consciousness, why not "victimize" them into joy and happiness? The purpose of life is to spread joy and happiness and blessings and love everywhere you go so that when you leave the Earth, it will be a better place for your having been there! Become a walking "joy machine" blessing the face of the Earth. Remember the wisdom of Sir Winston Churchill, "A pessimist sees the difficulty in every opportunity; an optimist sees the opportunity in every difficulty."

*   *   *

The Universal Law of Owning One's Personal Power

Of all the attitudes and qualities we need to develop in our healthy personality, none is more important than personal power or the development of will. Personal power or will is the guiding force of the healthy personality. Personal power is first an attitude. We can choose to hold an attitude of weakness or of strength as we begin each day. Our power is the energy that we use to enforce our decisions. If you plan to do something at a certain time, you will need your power to make yourself do what you have committed yourself to do. You also need your power to control your subconscious mind. Your subconscious mind will push you around unless you own your own power, so personal power is the enforcing agent of the conscious mind. It is the energy that the mind musters to command and direct that personality. Personal power is expressed externally as assertiveness. Personal power is also very much tied in with decisiveness. If you are not decisive, then the subconscious mind or other people will make your decisions for you. But remember, the subconscious mind has no reasoning power, and other people's decisions are not always in your best interest. Consequently, if you are not decisive and assertive, you let others overpower you. If you don't own your power, then you end up giving it to the subconscious or to other people. We know that God has power. "The power we call God defies description." (Mahatma Gandhi) The fact is that you are a Co-Creator, so you have power, too. Gandhi is also quoted as saying, "God is not a power residing in the clouds. God is an unseen power residing within us and nearer to us than fingernails to the flesh." God helps those who help themselves and you can't help yourself if you don't own your power! Personal power is nothing more than channeling the energy in your Physical Body and subconscious mind to control your life. Owning your power is being a Spiritual warrior in your life. Never giving up and having the will to live is really possessing the will to fight. When you use your power over a long period of time, you develop what is called discipline. You will never progress on the Spiritual Path without personal power and self-discipline. When you don't own your power, you get depressed. Anyone who is depressed is not owning his power. There are two opposing forces in life: good and evil, light and darkness, positive and negative, illusion and truth, egotistical thinking and Spiritual thinking. Your power is your weapon with which to fight the negative and align yourself with the positive. As Edgar Cayce, the "sleeping prophet," said, "There is no force in the universe more powerful than your will or power." Edgar Cayce made another very important statement involving power. He talked about the importance of developing *positive anger*. Positive anger is controlled anger that is not directed at other people or yourself but rather at the dark force that is trying to push you down. It is used to catapult you toward the light and positivity. Anger has enormous power. The key is to channel this power constructively and creatively.

When one of Jesus' disciples started to complain, Jesus turned to him and said, "Get thee behind me, Satan." Rather than attack the man, he chose to do battle with the force behind the man. Earth is a difficult school, and we must be very tough in life or we can easily get overwhelmed. Always remember the words of Jesus, "Behold, I send you froth as sheep in midst of wolves; be therefore wise as serpents and harmless as doves!" Be wise as serpents and harmless as doves! Be a Spiritual warrior! The Bhagavad Gita, Krishna (Lord Maitreya) and Arjuna (Lord Buddha), Krishn'a disciple, are on the battlefield about to fight the evil enemy's army, when Arjuna comes apart Psychologically and falls victim to his negative ego. Arjuna is the head of the army of righteous men, and they are all depending on him. Krishna, Arjuna's charioteer and Spiritual Master, begins to lecture Arjuna on the folly of his ways in giving in to his negative ego and losing his power and control over his energies. Krishna is guiding Arjuna into the Spiritual mysteries, when Krishna says to Arjuna, "Get up now, and give up your unmanliness. Get up and fight. This self-pity and self-indulgence are unbecoming of the great Soul that you are." Arjuna was awakened by Krishna's Spiritual discourse and this statement, and he reclaimed his personal power and led his men victoriously into battle. Krisna's statements applies to each and everyone of us in our daily lives. So, every morning, the second you get up, claim your power by choosing to affirm the attitude in your mind that you possess it. Every morning when you get up, claim your power and commit yourself to becoming the Master of your life! A Spiritual Master and God-realized being remains in a state of personal power all the time. If you don't own your power, you give it to other people or to your subconscious mind. If we don't own our power, we can be run by almost anything in the universe. This includes disincarnate spirits, other people, the Dark Brotherhood, ego, thoughts, desires, impulses, Physical Body, past life karma, and mass consciousness. It is clearly dangerous not to own one's personal power. So, don't give your power away to anything! Don't give away your power to astrology, your dreams, the rays, to any Spiritual science or path or to the Ascended Masters. Do not give your power even to God. God doesn't want it. God wants you to use it and your love and your wisdom to become a Master. Pray with power, not like a weakling. Your prayers will be much more effective if you do so. Astrology is wonderful, but the bottom line is that you are God and God has created astrology! Dreams are wonderful, but don't give them your power and let an unsettling dream wreck your day! Also, do not give your power to any external channel even if they are saying, they are channeling the Ascended Masters. With all channeling, no matter who is doing it, the information is filtered through the personality, consciousness and information banks of that person—even if we are talking about Edgar Cayce, Alice Bailey or other great channelers. (Also, information may be valid at the time it was given, but not necessarily at a later time.) Again, you will never be able to manifest anything in your life inwardly or outwardly if you do not own your full personal power. Your personal power puts the force behind everything you do! Awareness without personal power is total victim consciousness. This is why some people lacking in personal power say, "Ignorance is bliss." No one who has personal power would ever say this! Your personal power is what allows you to be assertive in life but not aggressive! Personal power is what allows you to maintain self-mastery over your thoughts, feelings, emotions, subconscious mind, negative ego, inner child, Desire Body, Physical Body and Earth life! All manifestation begins with the need to own your personal power! Now the lesson in terms of power is to learn how to own it without abusing it. The ideal is to own it at all the time in a considerate, unwavering manner. It is through our power that we will attain self-mastery over our energies! "For God hath not given us the Spirit of fear; but of power, and of love, and of a sound mind." (2 Timothy 1:7)

*   *   *

The Universal Law of Past, Future and the Eternal Now

Think about the past. What is it? It is a memory. What is a memory? A memory is an image in our minds. What is an image? An image is a thought. So what this means is that the past is totally under our control, for it is nothing more than images or thoughts in our minds. You can be the Master of your past by learning to have self-mastery over the thoughts and images in your mind. Actually, thoughts and images are really the same thing. They are in a sense two sides of the same coin. Sometimes our thoughts come in thought forms and sometimes our thoughts come in thought images. The same applies to the future. The future is nothing more than thoughts and images in our minds. They are of a positive or negative nature, which determines whether we are worried or excited about it. This means that our future is totally under our control. The future does not really exist except as thoughts and images in our mind. The future is like a checkerboard grid. The grid is in place but most of the squares are not filled in. They are filled in by your free choice. "Stand up, be bold, be strong. Take the whole responsibility on your own shoulders, and know that you are the creator of your own destiny. All the strength and succor you want is within yourself. Therefore, make your own future." (Swami Vivekananda) "Each man carries his destiny in his own hands," as Sai Baba said. Excitement is looking forward to the future. Worry is dreading the future. All that really exists, in truth, is the Eternal Now. So we no longer have to be victimized by our past or by a worrisome future because it is all within our own mind. The proper attitude toward the past is to gain the golden nuggets of wisdom from the mistakes and from what we have done well, bring forth the positive memories we choose to keep, and release the rest. In Disney's *The Lion King*, Rafikki said to Simba, "The past, eh? The way I see it, you can either run from it, or learn from it." In terms of the future, the proper perspective is to create a plan for the future that serves us, and then leave the rest to God. The future is totally under your control. Remember the words of Mahatma Gandhi, "People become what they expect themselves to become." And Sai Baba said, "The attitude today is the root on which the future grows." Why worry when you can pray, own your personal power, and do affirmations and visualizations to attract everything you need? As an old adage says, "Master your past in the present, or your past will master your future." Or as Lord Buddha said, "The past should not be followed after and the future not desired; what is past is dead and gone and the future is yet to come." (Majjhima Nikaya III, 131) Heal the past. Live the present. Dream the future!

*   *   *

The Universal Law of Paying Attention to Details

GOD is in the details. GOD is not impressed with glamour. He is as much impressed with the little things as He is with the big things. GOD is just as impressed with a small act of kindness or attention to the small things, as with what we perceive as big things. To GOD the Earth is just one planet of billions of planets in this universe, and GOD has infinite numbers of universes within His Cosmic Omniversal Body. So GOD looks to the essence and motivation of things more than numbers. In truth, it is not about size, or numbers, it is about living each moment properly in service of GOD, be it communication with a flower, a rock, an ant, a cat, a dog, the wind, a nature spirit, one person, or one thousand people. GOD does not care about fame, or money, or so-called power, or social status, or perceived vanity. All GOD cares about is that you live each moment in a Godly manner, wherever you happen to be, with uncondi-tional love and true Spiritual sacredness. Did you remember to water your plants and feed all the animals? Did you remember to compliment an employee on how nice they look this day? Did you kiss and hug your loved one before they left in the morning and before bed at night and tell them how much you love and appreciate them? One of the real tests of the Spiritual Path is, will the Spiritual leader, teacher, and channel, if they move into a position of power and public recognition, all of a sudden stop doing these things? Will their personality change? If it does, it means neg-ative ego corruption has taken place. GOD would have you know that the "details", every moment of your life, "is your Spiritual Path"! Pursue excel-lence in everything you do! Part of paying attention to details is owning your personal power 100% of the time, and controlling your mind so you are not scattered, spacey, too right-brain, too ungrounded, too celestial, too caught in the subconscious, too run by the inner child, too caught up in your Emotional Body, or too caught up in your Desire Body. Part of "paying attention to details" is owning your 100% personal power at all times. Being in self-mastery 100% of the time. Being conscious 100% of the time and never allowing yourself to go on automatic pilot. Lightworkers should be reminded not to forget to fully own their Power Flame and Wisdom Flame along with their Love Flame. Then you will be able to pay attention to details in a balanced manner that is truly reflective of GOD. In conclusion, never forget that GOD is in the details. If you live each moment perfectly as GOD would have you live it in total focus, concentration, dedicated only to GOD and service of GOD, self and your Brothers and Sisters, then the rest of your life will unfold as it is meant to be! As Mother Teresa said, "Simple acts of love and prayer keep the light of Christ burning."

          *   *   *

The Universal Law of Perfection and Making Mistakes

Mother Teresa is quoted as saying, "Do not allow yourself to be disheartened by any failure as long as you have done your best." The Spiritual Path up the mountain consists of five steps forward, then four backwards. Seven forward, then six backwards. "Fall seven times, stand up eight," as the Japanese proverb goes. Don't buy into the ego's game of creating this impossible perfectionistic standard where mistakes are unacceptable. Spirit believes in striving for perfection but looks at mistakes as positive and unavoidable. So there is "Negative Perfectionism" of the negative ego and "Spiritual Perfectionism" of Spirit. Taking this understanding one step further, "true perfection does not mean never making mistakes, it mean never making *conscious* mistakes!" In other words, we all at times make unconscious mistakes. This cannot be helped, for we all become unconscious at times. The Spiritual ideal, however, is to not make conscious mistakes. In other words, each of us has a Spiritual ideal, moral code, ethics, and values that we live by. Ideally we want our every thought, word an deed to be in integrity with this Spiritual ideal. Unconscious mistakes can be cut down if you really try to live your life with full personal power, joyous vigilance, and total consciousness at all times. However, even if you do this to the best of your ability, mistakes will always continue to happen at all times. This is not a defect on anyone's part; it is just the nature of existence as GOD created it. As long as you are conscious, you choose to do the right thing. This takes enormous dedication and specified commitment to your Spiritual Path at the highest level. The negative ego, the lower-self, the Desire Body, and the indolence of the Physical Body will constantly give you reasons to not hold to your Spiritual ideal. So why do mistakes occur? First, people are not in control of their subconscious mind. They are constantly making mistakes, forgetting things, and spacing out because the subconscious mind is too much in control.

Secondly, most of the world still believes in victim consciousness—that outside things cause the way they think and feel—and does not understand that they cause their reality and that their thoughts create their feelings, emotions and behavior. Thirdly, people don't understand the difference between Spiritual thinking versus negative ego thinking. Fourthly, people lack the balanced development of the Three-Fold Flame of Love, Wisdom, and Power. See *The Universal Law of Balancing and Integrating the Three-Fold Flame.* Power without wisdom and love will lead to corruption! Love without wisdom and power will become corrupt and is not really love. Any combination you come with that is not totally balanced will lead to glamour, maya and illusion and the negative ego running the person whether they are aware of it or not. So to cut down on mistakes, you must get in control of your subconscious mind. Work on achieving absolute mastery over your every thought, feeling, emotion, word, and deed! Fully train yourself in the difference between Spiritual/Christ/Buddha thinking versus negative ego thinking. Work on perfectly balancing your Three-Fold Flame. Just using these points here as touchstones and Spiritual and Psychological ideals to focus on will help you to greatly cut down on the number of mistakes that you make in life. When mistakes occur, just accept this, learn from them, forgive self, unconditionally love self, do not judge self, and if your mistake has affected another, then consider if it is appropriate to admit that mistake and apologize for it. However, don't be neurotic about this admitting and apologizing business. It is not necessary to advertise your mistakes. On the other side of the coin, it is not necessary to hide form them. Remain in balance and Spiritual appropriateness on this issue. Now, there are Lightworkers who cannot admit a mistake if their life depended on it. Their egos are so defended that they live in complete denial. Their negative ego will go to any lengths to squirm out of taking responsibility. This shows a lack of GOD purity. People who can't apologize can't do it because they are run by the negative ego attitude system and live in a reality of thinking they are better than or worse than everyone else. So to admit a mistake makes them less than others, which of course is not true, but in their belief system it does. So they live in a reality of denial and ego-defendedness. Always remember, Earth is a school and our mistakes are not held against us. There are no sins, only mistakes. And there is no such thing as an original sin that some religions like to attribute to us. Every mistake is a blessing in disguise because there is always a golden nugget of wisdom to be learned from it. We are in this school to know ourselves and hence know God. God's universe is governed by knowable laws— Physical, Psychological and Spiritual Laws. We learn by making mistakes and then making adjustments. So whenever you make a mistake, forgive yourself and move on! As *A Course in Miracles* states, "Forgiveness is the key to happiness." Always forgive self for making mistakes, and forgive others as well. Do not fall into this glamour. Set the example to admit mistakes to others and they will follow in kind. "Anyone who has never made a mistake has never tried anything new." (Albert Einstein)

*   *   *

The Universal Law of Perseverance

The I Ching says, "Perseverance furthers success." Perseverance pays off! Given that the Spiritual Path is most often experienced as climbing a mountain or fighting a great Spiritual war, the qualities of perseverance and tenacity are some that everybody needs to develop. The Spiritual Path is like running a marathon; you do not want to burn out in the beginning. Many seekers are enthusiastic in the beginning, but they are not able to maintain the divine enthusiasm and perseverance over the long haul. This is because they are too anchored in the Emotional Body and not enough in the Mental and Spiritual Body. True Masters are unceasing in their efforts. They know when to rest, but nothing can stop their efforts. They are literally unstoppable no matter what the obstacle. They do not coddle themselves, and whatever the obstacle is, they find a way to make the appropriate adjustment, prayer, affirmation, visualization, and also take the action that is needed. Their faith, trust, and patience in God are unwavering. "That ye be not slothful, but followers of them who through faith and patience inherit the promises." (Hebrews 6:12) "For ye have need of patience, that, after ye have done the will of God, ye might receive the promise." (Hebrews 10:36) They are levelheaded and practical within their divine enthusiasm. Their efforts are like the ocean waves, which just keep coming until victory is achieved. The real Master will not take no for an answer, yet knows when to change course and direction when this is the divine guidance. The real Master remembers the words of Prophet Isaiah (Isaiah 30:21) "And thine ears shall hear a word behind thee, saying, this is the way, walk ye in it, when ye turn to the right hand, and when ye turn to the left." The real Master will always keep in mind what was put to paper a long time ago, "To those who by persistence in doing good seek glory, honor, and immortality, He will give eternal life. (Romans 2:7) May the Lord direct your hearts into God's love and Christ's perseverance. (2 Thessalonians 3:5) Consider it pure joy…whenever you face trials of many kinds, because you know that the testing of your faith develop s perseverance." (James 1:2-3)

*   *   *

The Universal Law of Polarity and Duality

The Biblical story of the Tree of Knowledge of Good and Evil is a most wonderful symbology and metaphor for understanding the

negative ego! In this story, Adam and Eve are told to not eat the apple of
Good and Evil, but they are doing so anyway as Eva is being tempted by
the snake. The eating from the Tree of Good and Evil as described in the
Bible is a metaphor for mankind using their free choice to think out of harmony with God's Will. The original Divine Plan was that we would make
choices within the realm of goodness only, without evil ever entering the
picture! But since we were given the free choice to think with our negative
ego   mind   instead   of   remaining   in   the   Spiritual
Buddha/Christ/Melchizedek Consciousness, fear, separation, and the
entire gamut of negative feelings and emotions began to be created. This
was as the Biblical story tells, the "Banishment from Eden!", Eden being
both, an allusion to Psychological principles, early Lemuria, and the First
Golden Age on this Planet. It was only because of this choice of misusing
free choice, eating the apple, and choosing negative ego thinking instead
of God thinking, that feminine and masculine energies got imbalanced,
all negative emotions began, the Patriarchy took over the Divine Mother
Energies and the Matriarchy was rejected. It is because of this that all selfishness began. It was why roses grew thorns! None of this would have ever
occurred if this choice had not occurred. Now do understand, that even if
Adam and Eve had never eaten the apple off the Tree of Good and Evil,
there would still be polarity, and there would still be an evolutionary
process, and there would still be the 352 Levels of Initiation. There would
still be Feminine and Masculine, God/Goddess, Priest/Priestess,
Yin/Yang. For this was all part of God's Divine Plan, however, all choices
would be made in the realm of polarity, however only in the context of
"Goodness". Darkness, or negative ego duality, was never meant to be part
of God's Divine Plan. Glamour, illusion, and maya was all a product of
this choice! The snake was on a Psychological Level the negative ego or
fear-based mind. Well, the good news is that after 18.5 million years of
living in the illusion of separation, we are now returning to another
Golden Age on this Planet, the Seventh Golden Age. It is in returning to
the "Garden of Eden Consciousness" that we can transcend all evil, all

darkness, all separation, all fear, negative ego, and all negative selfishness, negative feelings and emotions. It is then that we can transcend negative ego duality and live in the "Garden of Eden Consciousness" of old times!

＊   ＊   ＊

The Universal Law of Processing Life Properly on a Spiritual and Psychological Level

Processing is a certain type of thinking. There are different types of thinking that people do. There is a type of thinking that comes from the subconscious mind, types that come from the conscious mind, and types that come from the superconscious mind. Processing is a specific type of thinking that stems from the conscious mind that is for the purpose of Spiritually and Psychologically work on oneself to achieve clarity on any given subject. It is very important to learn to process life effectively, otherwise the mind and emotions will be constantly running and on a roller coaster. What is the natural state of one's consciousness in the ideal? The most basic state is your consciousness as a center of pure awareness: the mind is quiet, the emotions and feelings are calm; it is a state of no thought, or having a quiet mind with nothing going on. Now, many people only on occasion experience this. Instead of having a center of pure awareness and no thought as their baseline and core self, their mind is running a mile a minute and always active, always thinking on a subconscious and conscious level, and their feelings and emotions are always churning and/or on a roller coaster going up and down. The first goal of learning to process effectively is to use a certain type of thinking to requiet the mind, to get it back to this state of being a center of pure awareness and no thought. The second goal is to make sure the Spiritual/Christ/Buddha Mind is interpreting everything that is going in within self, life and all your relationships, so you can remain in a state of Personal Power, Unconditional Love, Happiness, and Joy. So the goal of processing is to requiet the mind and get the feelings and emotions back into a calm place, for if the feelings and emotions are agitated or in a negative place, usually the mind will be working overtime to try and get back to a state of pure awareness, with no thought first, and secondarily a state of inner peace and calm. Life is filled with choices, unexpected lessons, challenges, and life decisions. It's important to have Spiritual and Psychological tools to get yourself clear as quickly as possible. So when you are feeling a little out of sorts, what do you do? First, try to get centered in your consciousness through the process of self-introspection and self-inquiry. Examine what's going on and try to make the appropriate attitudinal adjustments to get yourself re-centered. Sometimes this is enough, and sometimes it is not. This is when processing comes into play. Processing is a more serious type of thinking and work to straighten out your consciousness, to get it back to is normally centered space. What do you do? Do Huna Prayers, ask for the "Core Fear Matrix Removal Program", call forth the Platinum Net from Melchizedek, the Mahatma, and Archangel Metatron. If feeling low self-esteem, make a list of all the reasons why you should feel good, if feeling sad, make a list of what you have to be grateful for. If something has gone wrong, make a Spiritual vow to forgive yourself, unconditionally love yourself and never allow this particular situation to ever happen again. Chant or repeat the names of GOD. Get organized inwardly and outwardly. Set up a Spiritual Battleplan which is a Spiritual list of every idea you can think of to correct this challenge or problem. Write a letter to your Higher Self. Practice attitudinal healing (go through what's on your mind and try and attitudinally adjust any attitudes or feelings that are bringing you down)! The goal of processing, in truth, is just "perspective". There is no situation in life for which GOD and your own creative mind cannot come up with a perspective to make you happy an joyous. One of the total keys to effective processing is learning how to NOT think, and put a certain lesson "on the shelf", so to speak. Other keys are to always remain in a state of 100% Personal Power and 100% Self-Love and unconditional love towards others. To only have preferences, not attachments. To pray, have faith, trust, and patience. The key to effective processing is to learn to do the smallest amount of processing necessary to get the quickest and greatest results!

*   *   *

The Universal Law of Prosperity

The Bible says, "And in every work that he began in the service of the house of God, and in the law, and in the commandments, to seek his God, he did it with all his heart, and prospered." (2 Chronicles 31:21) The negative ego's interpretation of life is that we never have enough. Spirit sees the universe as abundant, with plenty for everybody and no need for negative competition. The negative ego teaches both that money is the root of all evil and at the same time the answer to all problems. What a contradictory premise! Money, in and of itself, is divine. It is how you use it that determines whether it is good or bad. Spirit guides people to love money and make as much as possible, so that it can be used to make Physical changes in the world for a Spiritual purpose. The more you have, the more you can give. Prosperity Consciousness also encompasses the understanding or knowing that you can get a job or manifest a business and opportunities whenever and wherever needed. Who is more prosperous, a woman who lives in the ghetto with seven children and has total faith in God to provide her with everything she truly needs, or a stingy millionaire who worries about money constantly and makes a habit of stabbing clients and competitors in the back? You can be a multimillion-aire and live in total poverty consciousness! The first key to developing Prosperity Consciousness is to become right with self and right with GOD. By doing this you will develop the "Midas Touch." Secondly, let go of the belief that money and material success is bad. Money is Divine. Thirdly, let go of the belief that to realize GOD you have to give up all your possessions and be in poverty. This is a misinterpretation of the Bible and, in truth, just the opposite is true. Fourthly, deny any thoughts of poverty consciousness to enter your mind! Only allow those of a Prosperity Consciousness nature in! Fifthly, be creative and don't wait for GOD or the Inner Plane Ascended Masters to conk you over the head and tell you what to do. GOD helps those who help themselves. Pray for help but also be creative yourself. Sixthly, put GOD and your Spiritual Path first and have no false Gods and ideals; this includes money. Mother Teresa said, "I try to give to the poor people for love what the rich could get for money. No, I wouldn't touch a leper for a thousand pounds; yet I willingly cure him for the love of God." The only way to make lots of money is not to be attached to money. "Seek ye first the Kingdom of GOD and all thins shall be added unto thee", as the Biblical verse reveals. Seventhly, have a flawless character and integrity, always putting the cus-tomer first. Eighthly, dedicate your life to service 100%, which will ulti-mately cause you to have a pure heart and which will cause the universe to reward you. Ninthly, seed money to those in need, and it is totally your right to expect a ten-fold return! Tenthly, monitor your thinking and feel-ing to make sure that once you have prayed and done your affirmations and visualizations, that your daily thinking and feeling and speaking to others is not sabotaging the immaculate and perfected thoughtform you are trying to consciously hold. Eleventh, always remember that you are, in truth, one with all Creation. You are one with that which you strive to manifest. Twelfth, keep your money in circulation and don't overly hold onto it. Thirteenth, do not be afraid to take risks and make mistakes. Sometimes you may have to try five or ten ideas. Give up the word "failure" from your vocabulary. There is no such thing. Failure comes from a belief in judgement, which also does not exist. All that exists are mistakes, and mistakes are part of the Spiritual Path and are unavoidable and appropriate. True Prosperity Consciousness is rooted in the understanding that God, your personal power, and the power of your subconscious mind are your true source of financial security. The only security in life is a belief, knowingness, and understanding of GOD and GOD's Laws! GOD is your stocks and bonds and financial security. It is in the integrated understanding of these four levels that total faith and confidence in the ability to manifest money and wealth, no matter what happens in life, truly lies. God (prayer and meditation), your Personal Power (physical action), the power of your subconscious mind (affirmations and visualizations to program your subconscious mind to attract and magnetize monetary and material opportunities) are an unbeatable team! Practice these simple keys to prosperity and they will bring you not only untold prosperity and material wealth but they will also bring you, more importantly, inner wealth and success because you are dealing with money and material things from a GOD and Buddha/Christ perspective! "Wealth aquired unjustly will diminish; but he who gathers justly shall increase his wealth!" (Psalms 13:11)

*   *   *

The Universal Law of Protection

It is of utmost importance to protect oneself because there is a lot of negative energy in the world and a lot of people who are run by the negative ego! It is not only important to be Spiritually vigilant against allowing your own negative ego to try to enter your consciousness and mind; it is also essential to put your Golden Bubble of Protection up every day almost like a piece of clothing you put on every morning to keep out other people's negative energy. Because most people have no training in Spiritual psychology, even Lightworkers are extremely run by the negative ego. They are very advanced in their Spiritual Bodies or "Light Bodies", but they have a lot of rough edges around their Psychological Selves and Bodies from lack of proper Spiritual training. Because of this there are constant attacks, criticisms, judgements, put downs, self-righteousness, competitiveness, anger, intolerance, impatience, irritableness, and frustration, which of course are all negative ego qualities. If you don't keep your Golden Bubble of Protection up, these outside negative ego thought forms and energy can act as negative programming to try and counteract the Spiritual work you are doing. The key is to put this Golden Bubble on every morning from your "Etheric or energetic wardrobe," and place it around yourself so that when other people are manifesting this type of negative energy it just slides off your bubble like "water off a duck's back!" So, it is essential to develop an inner bubble to protect us from our own subconscious minds as well as to develop an outer bubble or shield to protect ourselves form other people's negative energy. The ideal is for us to be the programmer of the subconscious mind. Always remember that if we don't take responsibility for our own programming and protection, then the subconscious mind or other people will run our lives. The ideal is to be the cause, creator, and master of our own lives. If these Psychological laws aren't clearly understood, then other people will be our programmers. Let's say someone is judging or criticizing you. The ideal is to have an imaginary bubble or shield around you so that when criticism comes toward you, it hits the bubble or shield and bounces off, like water off a duck's back. It must be understood that this bubble is semi-permeable. In other words, it allows in positive energy but keeps out negative energy. You make a conscious choice as to whether to let others' energy into your subconscious mind or not. If you don't have this bubble of protection available to you at all times, then you can be victimized by another person's comments, statements, or energy. When your inner and outer bubbles are not functioning properly, you are letting yourself be hypnotized. Victims are in a sort of hypnotic state, letting another person program their emotions in a waking state. There is a time to be open and a time to be closed. It is necessary to close down and protect yourself if other people are being negative. If someone threw a spear to you, you would physically try to get out of the way if you could. The same thing is true when other people are directing negative energy toward you like a Psychological spear. You will be wounded if you let it in. You wouldn't let a person shove Physical poison down your Physical mouth. So don't let people shove Mental poison into your mind. You don't want your subconscious mind to run your life, and you don't want other people to run your life, either. Now, to make sure we cover every angel and lens of *The Universal Law of Protection*, let's go one step further and let's talk about invasion, for we all need to learn to protect our space from invasion of others and to always monitor our consciousness, thoughts, words, and deeds so we are not invading the space of others on any level! Invasion can occur Physically, Etherically, Emotionally, Mentally, Psychically, and Spiritually. On a Physical Level, be aware to of your Physical space and others' Physical space and be sensitive to both. On a Psychic Level, don't give psychic readings if you are not asked for one. On an Astral Level, don't send your Astral Body, consciously or unconsciously, into a person's home or bedroom and into their space. This is inappropriate and an invasion. Sometimes this happens unconsciously because the person is not in control of their Astral Vehicle. This can also occur in an inappropriate sexual fantasy about another. On an Etheric/Energetic Level, if one is sexually attracted to another, they may project their Etheric or Energetic Body, which is the same, onto that person without touching them Physically. On a Mental Level: sending negative thoughts to someone consciously or unconsciously. When you think a thought it does not remain in your Physical Body. All minds are joined. So, if you send someone a thought, that thought will instantly go to that person and either uplift them or do the reverse. This is why it is so important to be vigilant over the thoughts you allow yourself to think and even daydream about. Your thoughts affect people. If a person has a weak aura you may fill their liver and solar plexus with darts that can actually be seen clairvoyantly. On an Emotional Level, invasion occurs anytime one allows negative ego aggressive emotions, such as anger, impatience, manipulation, revenge, jealousy, and frustration, to manifest. These emotions can be felt immediately trying to penetrate another person's field. On a Spiritual Level one must be careful not to invade one's space either. One can travel in their Soul Body and visit others consciously or unconsciously. Make sure you are welcome! Once one becomes a full-fledged Ascended Masters, there are many gifts. You can read a person's mind or you could look into their Akashic records, to name just two. Just because one has these abilities doesn't mean that the negative ego can't misuse them for selfish purposes. We must be aware of the subtleties of invasion, for it isn't always as obvious as someone stealing from you or punching you in the nose. Negative ETs invade space by planting implants that suck energy, and Astral entities hang onto your aura like a parasite. Ponder on this, and make sure you protect yourself on all levels!

*　　　　　*　　　　　*

The Universal Law of Psychological Health

Psychological health can be likened to Physical health. If a person we know catches a cold or the flu, we certainly don't want to get it. We take extra vitamin C, eat well and try to get enough sleep. In other words, we build our resistance. If we keep our resistance, we don't get sick. There is no such thing as a contagious disease. There are only people with low resistance. This analogy is exactly the same on the Psychological Level.

There is no such thing as a contagious Psychological disease. There are only people with low resistance. How can we keep up our Psychological resistance so that we don't catch the infectious diseases of anger, depression, jealousy, hatred, and so on? We keep our Psychological resistance up by maintaining a positive mental attitude, by developing and maintaining the protective bubble, maintaining our personal power, unconditional self-love and self-worth, as well as faith and trust in God. "Activity must be dedicated to God, the Highest Good. Then, it will provide health to body and mind." (Sai Baba)

*   *   *

The Universal Law of Purity

Lord Buddha is quoted as saying, "As a silversmith sifts dust from silver, remove your own impurities little by little." Purity is one of the rarest qualities on Earth. Earth life can be a very tough school and the lessons of Earth life and the meanness and cruelty of others makes it hard for one to maintain their innocence and purity of character. What does it mean to remain one's purity? To remain pure means that one loves GOD to such an extent and to such an attunement that no matter how mean or cruel people are and no matter how tough the lessons of Earth life are, one holds to their unconditional love and faith, trust and patience in GOD. One holds to their Christ/Buddha Consciousness at all times, no matter how high the degree of momentary defeat of how high is one's Spiritual and Earthly success. Purity means that one's love for GOD and one's attunement to GOD is so great that the temptations, glamour, and false gods of the negative ego hold no interest. The development of purity means choosing the path of selflessness at all times, never giving in to an attack thought, admitting mistakes, never giving up, holding to one's

Spiritual ideals at all times, always being the one to apologize, being the first to forgive others and self, being constantly vigilant for GOD and His Kingdom and denying any thought not of GOD to enter one's mind. Maintaining humbleness and humility. Having compassion for other people's suffering and being willing to do something about it. Not gossiping or engaging in ego battles. Not competing with others. Always being the peacemaker and establishing harmony, oneness, and love in all situations. Purity means sticking to your ideals in thought, word, and deed, even when alone and even when Physically tired and/or exhausted. Purity means that you remain the same person no matter if you become the most famous person in the world in a Spiritual and Earthly sense, or if you live in seclusion and have a very small sphere of influence. Purity means examining one's motives in a thorough and honest manner! As we all know, the negative ego is very tricky. In the deepest recesses of our subconscious mind, what is it that truly motivates us to do what we are doing? It takes great courage to fully examine this. "Sincerity of conviction and purity of motive will surely gain the day, and even a small minority armed with these is surely destined to prevail against all odds." (Swami Vivekananda) To truly realize God and move into the highest levels of leadership, the conscious and subconscious minds must be cleansed of the impurities of the ego: selfishness, narcissism, lower-self desire, hedonism and materialism. To do so, one needs to be devastatingly honest with self! In conclusion, remain purity on all levels—purity in the Mental Body from impure thoughts; purity in the Emotional Body from impure, negative emotions and lower-self desires; and purity on the Physical Level in terms of diet, proper use of sexuality and proper action at all times. "Let all bitterness, and wrath, and anger, and glamour, and evil speaking, be put away from you, with all malice." (Ephesians 4:32) "Let us purify ourselves from everything that contaminates Body and spirit!" (2 Corinthians 7:1 NIV) "Purity of life is the highest and truest art!" (Mahatma Gandhi) Heed these words! They are worth its weight in platinum!

*   *   *

The Universal Law of Pursuing Excellence and Immaculateness in Everything One Does

The word *kaizen* is a Japanese word that means "constant improvement." The idea here is to appreciate the achievements of yourself, but on another level never be satisfied. This is the true pursuit of excellence. Cultivate this attitude of *kaizen* or "constant improvement", which means to do your best and then try to do better than your best. The foundation of all Spiritual work is the "God immaculateness and pursuit of excellence" that you maintain every moment of your life on every level of your being. What will manifest in your outer life is the clarity, pursuit of excellence, and immaculateness, or lack thereof in your consciousness. Many on the Spiritual Path do not hold themselves to the high standard and high calling of really trying to be God, be the Christ, be the Buddha, and be a Son or Daughter of GOD on Earth. This means monitoring every thought to make sure that it is a God thought and not a negative ego thought, monitoring every feeling and emotion to make sure it is stemming from your Spiritual Consciousness and not your negative ego consciousness, and monitoring and being vigilant over every word you speak, recognizing the power of the spoken word. Monitoring and being vigilant over your every action and behavior to make sure your every movement is representative of the Most High GOD! Keeping your word as GOD keeps His Word! Maintaining the highest level of integrity and honesty in everything you do, with yourself and others. Striving to be absolutely egoless and selfless at all times. And when it is right to be Spiritually selfish, it means to make sure that you are really being Spiritually selfish and not egotistically selfish. Pursuing excellence in everything you do means being devastatingly honest with self, and examining your every motivation for everything you are doing, constantly checking yourself to make your motivations are pure in GOD. Being able to admit mistakes to yourself and to others when necessary. Being willing to apologize for your mistakes. Putting GOD first and not having false gods before him in a Psychological sense (like power, fame, greed, and lower-self desire). Being consistent on a superconscious, conscious and subconscious level and Physical Body level, so that all Three Minds and the Physical Body are consistent with each other. It means every moment of your life trying to practice the Presence of GOD and to practice living like an Integrated Ascended Master on Earth. Sticking to your Spiritual and Psychological ideals on every level no matter what the circumstance, even when you are Physically exhausted, stressed out or overwhelmed. Not giving into temptation. Striving to live a life of perfection. Manifesting a flawless character to your highest ability every moment of your life. Recognizing that mistakes and adjustments are okay. Not being lazy or procrastinating. Making choices and standing behind them. Maintaining absolute mastery over your thoughts, emotions, feelings, subconscious mind, negative ego, inner child, lower-self desire, energies and Physical Body at all times in service of GOD, unconditional love and balance. Maintaining GOD Purity in every aspect of your life, every moment of your life. Treating others who are not at your level of Spiritual, Psychological and Physical/Earthly development with the utmost kindness, generosity, and compassion. Never judging another who does not hold the "Immaculate Standards and Demonstration" that you keep. Not giving in to the line of least resistance and the indolence of the subconscious mind. Getting back on the saddle when you fall off, and not indulging in self-pity or self-indulgence when you get knocked off or fall off the wagon, as you invariably will at times. It is to look at every moment of your life as a Spiritual test and to try and pass every test to the best of your ability. Pursue excellence in everything you do! Stay on top of things! The pursuit of excellence must be maintained on all three levels: Spiritual, Psychological, and Physical/Earthly at all times at a 100% level to the best of your ability. Do not settle for anything less in everything you do! Pursue excellence in your every thought, word, deed, and feeling, and you shall dance with God's Angels in Heaven sooner than you might have dreamed possible!

*   *   *

The Universal Law of Quieting One's Mind

The mind is a wonderful apparatus and as we all know, it is our thoughts that create our reality. So the key question is, how do we use this tool so it only works for us and not against us? There are two things we need to learn in this regard. First, we need to learn to think properly with our Buddha/Christ/Melchizedek Mind, and secondly, we need to learn how to quiet our mind and not think at all. This law shall explain in greater detail the latter. The first key to learn to quiet the mind is you must own your own personal power at all times and be conscious and aware of your content of consciousness (your thoughts, feelings, desires...). The owning of your personal power helps you to be the observer and have the needed detachment from the content of consciousness that is needed to have self-mastery over your content of consciousness. Learning this, more than half of this lesson of learning to quiet the mind will have been learned if proper joyous vigilance is consistently maintained. Always remember, the real you is the observer self, who controls, directs, chooses, and causes. The key to being the director is understanding the need to differentiate yourself from the content of your consciousness. You are not your thoughts, emotions, body, actions, personality, mistakes, successes, abilities, or beliefs. You are the essence and not the form. You are the consciousness, not the creation. You can direct and control only what you do not identify yourself with. Whatever you, as the consciousness or "I", are identified with will be your master. Identify yourself with only the Eternal Self for that is your True Self! The next insight that is important is that it is impossible to stop the mind completely from thinking and one should not desire to do so, for it is not GOD's Will that it be completely stopped. We are creative by nature and we create with our mind. The mind is always creating. The key insight, however, is that it can be quieted down and it can and must be mastered so we are not driven by it. Most people in the Western world are driven by the mind; the mind runs them instead of them running the mind. In the Eastern world it's the opposite. In truth, both are important and need to be balanced and integrated properly. So there is a time to think and a time not to think. Now here is the key insight. The subconscious mind is always thinking and creating in a negative or positive way because it has no reasoning. The key insight here is that the conscious mind does not have to engage the continuing string of thoughts, feelings, and impulses of the subconscious mind. So, it is as important in life to learn to think properly as it is to learn to not think at all. The mind is always striving for inner peace and understanding. The problem is, it is not possible every moment of one's life to have this understanding in every situation of life in any given instant. It is essential at times to put the mind on the shelf so to speak and to just be in the quietness and silence. If the mind is always chattering and the conscious mind is engaging the chattering, then how does the Holy Spirit, Mighty I Am Presence, and/or Higher Self enter the picture? They are the "still, small voice within." They do not fight for attention as the mind, emotions, and negative ego do. There is a time to identify and a time to disidentify with the content of consciousness. This brings us to the truth that the mind creates bondage or liberation depending on how it's used. Now, that we have this foundational understanding and perspective, here are some tools to achieving this quieter mind we all seek at times. First, write lists. The mind will be quiet as long as it feels honored to a certain degree. Keep a little notebook with you at all times and just write those things down that the mind presents you while watching TV or doing whatever, and your mind will be happy to be quiet as long as it is on the "tomorrow list." Secondly, have a journal section in your notebook, where if you are processing something and you do not want to think about it, you can write a little affirmation like, "I will not think about this until Monday morning." Even if something is really bothering you, as long as the mind knows that its agenda is being addressed, it will be willing to quiet and honor your affirmation not to think. The mind and emotions are amazing tools. In any given moment everything they create seems so important and real. The act of delaying thinking about different issues not always, but sometimes, resolves them without having to spend time thinking, processing, or doing anything. Issues that seemed so important in the moment, a week later you can't even remember. Time heals. Of course, there will be issues that do need to be addressed at a later time no matter how long one puts them off. One of the reasons that no thinking often resolves certain situations is that often an emotional charge seems extremely important, but a week later that emotional charge is gone and hence the thought or issue or thing to do may not need to be done. Well, here goes the third key to quieting the mind: sometimes you may be running errands or doing whatever and may not have a pen and paper. Make a number list in your mind from one upward. Each number will be one item on the agenda of the mind to think about or do. Fourthly, make Spiritual lists. There are an infinite number or kinds of Spiritual lists. When you are feeling unhappy, write a list of all the reasons you can think of that you have to be happy about. At Thanksgiving or any time you want some upliftment, create a Spiritual list of all the reasons why you have to be grateful. What does this have to do with quieting the mind? The mind is quiet when the Emotional Body and Mental Body feel at peace. When you are feeling negative about self or you are having negative interactions with other people or your world, the mind will be much more agitated and overactive. An overactive mind and too much thinking will exhaust your adrenal glands. So to learn to quiet the mind, it is essential to learn to think properly as well. The fifth tool to quiet to mind is making Spiritual vows. If you make a mistake, instead of feeling bad about it, dwelling upon it and letting it get you down, create a Spiritual vow not to let this happen again. See *The Universal Law of Making Spiritual Vows*. If you are depressed or agitated because of a setback or mistake, your mind is going to be overactive trying to get you back to equilibrium. Spiritual vows and Spiritual lists are a quick method to bring you back to this state of inner peace. In conclusion, too much thinking takes a toll on the Physical organs. When you consciously think and are constantly planning this runs energy through your liver and pancreas. The liver is known metaphysically as the organ of planning. Many people have digestive problems from overthinking because this is also running too much Third Chakra and Sixth Chakra energy. Too much thinking can create Emotional turmoil. Why? Again, since our thoughts create our feelings and emotions, the mind is always creating scenarios. Let's say you had a little spat with a friend. It is good to process this with your mind and come to a peaceful resolution. If there are any unresolved feelings, however, the mind will create scenarios of taking out its anger or telling people off. It's very important to shut these scenarios off for they are being created by the negative ego and not by your Soul! The key is to choose when you want to think and how you want to think and to be able to not think when you don't want to. Make the mind work for you rather than you working for the mind! As Lord Buddha said, " Wonderful it is to train the mind so swiftly moving, seizing whatever it wants. Good is it to have a well-trained mind, for a well-trained mind brings happiness." (Dhammapada 35) Ponder on this! This is one of the Golden Keys to enter the Kingdom of the Heavens!

*   *   *

The Universal Law of Reincarnation

To understand reincarnation, let's go back to the ancient times of Lemuria and Atlantis! The reason that the veil of reincarnation was placed upon the Earth and the people of the Earth began over 18.5 million years ago in Earth's history at the time of Lemuria, which predated Atlantis! This was the First Golden Age on this planet, and is referred to in the Bible as the Edenic State! This was the time on Earth when the Earth and the people of the Earth were more Etheric in nature! The world was not as Physically dense as it is now. Earth and Earth life was a Garden of Eden! There was no separation between Spiritual worlds and the world on Earth! There was no stepping into the world of negative ego duality, only making choices within the Mind of GOD! Then came the eating of the fruit from the Tree of Good and Evil, and the choice to think with one's negative ego mind! This was the choice to overidentify with the Physical Body, and people forgot that they were God living in a Physical Body! As this negative ego thinking and feeling spread, the world began to densify and Physical Bodies began to densify. This was not part of the Original Plan. Pretty soon most of the world had fallen asleep! And so 18.5 million years ago, Sanat Kumara and his fellow Kumaras from Venus came to rectify and heal this problem! Part of the Plan that was set up by GOD and the Godforce to remedy this descent into forgetfulness and Spiritual sleep was reincarnation. The plan was that all those Souls who had fallen asleep would reincarnate over and over again until the seven Levels of Initiation were completed in an integrated and balanced manner so liberation from the wheel of rebirth and/or graduation would be achieved! The idea was that having time on the Inner Plane between lives would give Souls time to remember who they were, and give them time to introspect and reflect before incarnating again! Any Soul who does not master the Psychological Level (mind and emotions) will be forced to reincarnate again on the Mental or Emotional Plane even if they have completed their seven Levels of Initiation! This will only occur if there is somewhat of a serious issue of nonintegration, victim consciousness, negative ego contamination, and corruption or fragmentation. "There are two paths, Arjuna, which the soul may follow at the time of death. One leads to rebirth and the other to liberation!" (Krishna to Arjuna in the Bhagavad-Gita) Achieving your seven Levels of Initiation in an integrated and balanced manner will bring you liberation from the wheel of rebirth. The purpose of life is to achieve liberation from the cycle of rebirth, to realize God and to be of service to humankind. "I am easily attained by the person who always remembers me and is attached to nothing else. Such a person is a true yogi, Arjuna. Great souls make their lives perfect and discover me; they are freed from mortality and the suffering of this separate existence. Every creature in the universe is subject to rebirth, Arjuna, except the one who is united with me!" (Krishna to Arjuna) One does not have to be perfect to achieve full liberation, you just must be in the "ball park", so to speak, of "Integrated Ascension". Isn't this an interesting view on that whole issue? Complete your seven Levels of Initiation in an integrated and balanced manner, and liberation from the wheel of rebirth shall be yours!

*   *   *

The Universal Law of Relationships

The two most important relationships in our lives are our relationship to self and our relationship to God. Actually, our relationship to self is even more important than our relationship to God. If we are wrong with ourselves and allow ourselves to be run by the ego, then we will project this wrong relationship to self onto everything in our lives, including our relationship to God and the Inner Plane Ascended Masters. This lack of a right relationship with self is the cause of the angry Old Testament

God. It is also the cause of concepts such as original sin, the idea that we are lowly, sinful worms, and the judgmental and self-righteous qualities of some fundamentalist religions. So, get right in these two relationships first and all other relationships will come into divine order. Before we are ready to serve others, we need to self-actualize. There are many people who are trying to serve from a place of not being right with self and right with God. It is noble that they want to be of service, but they would be better off getting right with themselves first. This law of becoming right with self and God as the two most important relationships in your life is a golden key to God Realization! "Live every second in the consciousness of your relationship with the infinite universe." (Paramahansa Yogananda)

*   *   *

The Universal Law of Releasing Anger

Sai Baba says, "Anger is the worst exhibition of the ego." To release anger from our lives, it is just a matter of understanding what attitudes, thoughts, and beliefs create anger. The definition of anger is "a loss of control and an attempt to regain it"! If you always remain in your 100% personal power then you never have to lose control. Many people on Earth use anger as a replacement for true personal power and this is not good. Anger is not personal power and self-mastery, it is a demonstration of being out of control. It is a false sense of power that stems from the negative ego. To truly become a Spiritual master you must replace anger with true personal power! If you always own your personal power then you will never have to be angry! If you ever do start to get angry, channel that energy immediately into a creative usage of personal power! Just redirect it with the power of your mind, so it becomes true personal power and Spiritual warrior energy instead of anger. Mahatma Gandhi said, "I have learned through bitter experience the one supreme lesson—to conserve my anger; and as heat conserved is transmuted into energy, even so out anger controlled can be transmuted into a power which can move the world." This is called "positive anger." The Buddha said, "Anger is like a chariot careering wildly. He who curbs his anger is the true charioteer. Others merely hold the reins!" So firstly, own your Personal Power 100%. Secondly, keep up your Golden Bubble of Protection 100% at all times! Without this protection, other people's attacks, criticism and negative energy can lodge in your subconscious mind and solar plexus and cause a defense and anger reaction. The ideal is to respond in life and not react. Thirdly, let go of attachments. As Lord Buddha in His Four Noble Truths said, "All suffering comes from attachments". Whenever you are angry, you are attached, and this is a fact. The Spiritual ideal is to change all attachment attitudes to preferences. See *The Universal Law of Having Preferences Rather Than Attachments*. Fourthly, look at everything that happens in life as a Spiritual test and lesson, not as some kind of bummer and problem. Every time you get angry you are forgetting to look at life as a Spiritual test and lesson! Everything that happens in life is happening for a reason! Everything that happens is GOD and/or life teaching you something! The real purpose of Earth life is nothing more than to see if you can respond to everything that happens in life in a centered, unconditionally loving, and forgiving manner. In every situation of life you either respond from your negative ego/fear-based/separative mind or the Spiritual/Christ/Buddha Mind. You either realize GOD in that moment or lose GOD in terms of your realization by how you respond! Fifthly, always remember that you cause your own reality, your feelings and emotions by how you think. No one can make you feel angry but yourself! They may have attacked you or criticized you unfairly, but that did not cause you to feel anything! That is what is called the "catalyst"! Sixthly, always seek to maintain love within self and from GOD first before seeking it from others. In other words, unconditionally love yourself and your inner child. Also fully allow yourself to receive GOD's and the Masters' love for you. This way, before you enter the world you are totally complete and whole within yourself. This way you go into life feeling filled with love! If you don't do this you are not feeling loved, and hence will seek love from others instead of finding it first within your relationship to self and GOD. Perfect love casts out fear! Seventhly, always remember that anger is a form of attack. Anytime a person attacks, they are feeling fear! There are only two emotions: love and fear. An attack is a call for love! Anger is the negative ego thought system's misguided and faulty thinking way of trying to get love! Anger will not get you what you want. It will create the opposite. The key is to transcend both fear an anger, which are the two sides of the negative ego philosophy and thought system, and to instead think with your Spiritual/Christ/Buddha Mind, which only thinks from the heart and unconditional love. As Master Yoda of Star Wars said, "Do not give into your anger and fear and become seduced by the dark side of the force!" Do not look back in anger, or forward in fear, but around in awareness!

*   *   *

The Universal Law of Releasing Fear and Worry

Worry is negative affirmation and meditation. "Worry is wasting today's time to clutter up tomorrow's opportunities with yesterday's troubles," as the saying goes. The first key to releasing fear and worry is to always own your personal power and Self-Mastery. The second you lose your Personal Power and Self-Mastery, fear based thinking and feeling will begin to creep back into your consciousness. You must be in control of your thoughts, feelings, emotions, energy, and Physical Body to not have

fear! The second key is to place around yourself, every morning to start
your day, a semi-permeable Golden Bubble of Protection that keeps out
negativity from self and others and allows in only Spiritual and positive
thoughts, feelings, and energies. This will give you the appropriate sense
of invulnerability. Thirdly, it is impossible to release fear unless you adopt
an attitude of unconditional love at all times. This is because the opposite
of love is attack and fear! If you don't approach self, people, and life with
unconditional love then you will approach it with attack and judgement.
By the law of karma within your own mind you will live in fear. Fourthly,
pray! Why worry when you can pray? Fifthly, do affirmations. Every time
a fear-based thought or feeling arises, push it out of your mind, and
replace it with a love-based thought or feeling and/or affirmation. Doing
this, all fear will be released over time. Sixth, have faith! Constantly affirm
your faith in yourself and your own abilities to master, cause, and create
your life and your faith in GOD, the Ascended Masters, and the Angels.
Your thoughts create your reality. If you affirm this it will be so! Whenever
thoughts of doubt arise, remember the Biblical verse, "And I will bring the
blind by a way that they knew not; I will lead them in paths that they have
not known; I will make darkness light before them, and crooked things
straight. These things will I do unto them, and not forsake them." (Isaiah
42:16) Have faith! Seventh, maintain Spiritual attunement with GOD,
your Mighty I Am Presence, the Inner Plane Ascended Masters, and the
Archangels and Angels. What manifests in life is where you put your attention and consciousness. If you keep your mind steady in the light, what is
to fear? As the old adage goes, "Focus on the positive in your life, for what
you focus on increases." As Jesus said on the Mount of Beatitudes which is
traditionally thought to be the place where he gave his Sermon on the
Mount, "Do not worry about what you wear or what you eat and drink.
The birds in the air do not sow wheat or store it in barns, and yet the heavenly Lord feeds them; the lilies of the field do not spin or weave, and yet
not even Solomon in all his glory was as magnificent as one of these."

*   *   *

The Universal Law of Renunciation or Involved Detachment

A renunciate is one who renounces the material world and gives first priority to the Spiritual world. Now, this does not mean that one does not remain involved with the material world. The idea is to be involved but not attached. You might call this involved detachment. The key is to let go of all material attachments, for that is what leads to suffering, as Lord Buddha described so beautifully in one of his Four Noble Truths, "All suffering comes from attachment. And all suffering comes from wrong points of view." To realize God it is necessary that at some point you let go of all attachments, and put material life, and this includes all relationships, on the Spiritual altar and surrender them to God. Put your Spiritual life first, and release all false gods and idols. By doing this you will save yourself much suffering. So make material things just preferences and happiness and inner peace shall be yours forevermore!

*　　　　　*　　　　　*

The Universal Law of Resolving Conflicts

One of the most important understandings and skills in one's Spiritual Path is the ability to resolve conflicts in yourself and your relationships. It is of the highest importance to resolve conflicts within self as quickly as possible. This is necessary to remain in a state of personal power, self-mastery, and decisiveness. Too many conflicts in your conscious and/or subconscious mind begin to drain your energies over time.

Agree to disagree. Frame the discussion in a win/win manner. Spirit's philosophy is a win/win philosophy, whereas the ego prefers a win/lose philosophy. We will see what we look for. When we see fault and judgment, we are in reality faulting and judging ourselves, for what we see in another is just a mirror of our own state of mind. When we see only God, love, and blessings, that is what we give to ourselves. Whether we see it or not, that is what is there, for that is what God created. Faulty perception doesn't create truth; it just creates the reality we live in! Respond instead of react. Be the first to apologize and admit your mistakes. Be the first to forgive no matter how much you have been wronged. Choose your battles carefully, for there are certain battles that are just not worth fighting. Always remember, there is a time to talk and a time to be silent, and sometimes the best form of communication is silence. Honesty does not mean you have to say everything. True mature honesty means you say what is appropriate, as GOD would have you say it, to gain maximum results in a Spiritual and Earthly manner. If the other person starts getting angry, attacking or coming from their negative ego, don't catch their Psychological disease. Set a better example. It takes two to have a war! Always remember that the person you are in conflict with is an incarnation of GOD, the Christ, the Buddha, the Atma. Treat them as such even if they are not demonstrating it. Turn the other cheek when appropriate and necessary. Be more concerned about learning your lessons than teaching other people theirs. Leave that to GOD. Always remember the words of Mother Teresa:

People are often unreasonable, illogical, and self-centered;
Forgive them anyway.
If you are kind, people may accuse you of selfish, ulterior motives;
Be kind anyway.
If you are successful, you will win some false friends and some true enemies;
Succeed anyway.
If you are honest and frank, people may cheat you;

Be honest and frank anyway.
What you spend years building, someone could destroy overnight;
Build anyway.
If you find serenity and happiness, there may be jealousy;
Be happy anyway.
The good you do today, people will often forget tomorrow;
Do good anyway.
Give the world the best you have, and it may never be enough;
Give the world the best you've got anyway.
You see, in the final analysis, it is between you and God;
It was never between you and them anyway.

Use every conflict as a Spiritual challenge, test, and Spiritual opportunity to practice the Presence of GOD and Godliness. By doing this you will not only help yourself Spiritually, you will also be giving yourself unconditional love, inner peace and oneness. You will also be setting a wonderful example to your Brothers and Sisters, and by doing so, you will have brought unconditional love, oneness, and peace into the world. How can we have peace between nations, if we do not know hot to create unconditional love and peace between ourselves and our Brothers and Sisters when conflict arises? Each of these conflicts are just mini Spiritual tests, Spiritual challenges, and Spiritual opportunities to practice this. In all conflicts and situations in life, it comes down to, do I want GOD or do I want my ego in this situation? Do I want unconditional love or fear and attack? Do I want oneness or do I want separation? The choice is yours! The paradoxical nature of life, however, is perfectly stated in the Biblical verse, "Seek ye the Kingdom of GOD and all things shall be added onto thee." Those that choose GOD and the Path of egolessness may at times look like they are losing from the limited third dimensional perspective. But that is illusion, of course. The truth is, you have gained and realized GOD in that moment and series of moments. In the long run you will not only realize GOD, which is the greatest gift of all, but your egoless, selfless example will bring to you material gain as well. For the Bible verse ends with the words, "All things shall be added onto thee"! In the bigger picture choosing the path of ego and selfishness will only cause you ultimately to lose material wealth, and not gain it. Choosing GOD and unconditional love in this manner will allow you to "Gain the Whole World and not lose your own Soul." For does not the Bible also say, "What does it profit a man that he gains the whole world but loses his own soul." The consistent choice to choose your Soul and Spirit every moment of your life, and especially when conflicts arise, will bring you a Spiritual, Psychological, and Earthly wealth that "passeth understanding"! Finally, remember the words of the Buddha who said, "He who does not strike nor makes others strike, who robs not nor makes others rob, sharing love with all that live, finds enmity with none." (Lord Buddha, Itivuttaka 22)

*   *   *

The Universal Law of Respecting Each Person's Unique Point of Balance

Everyone has their unique point of balance in all aspects of life. It is very important in life that everyone speaks only for themselves, and never tries to impress their point of balance on another person. The Physical, Emotional, Mental and Spiritual Bodies must all be respected, balanced, and integrated properly. If what you are doing in your life is hurting your Physical Body, then stop. The Physical Body is a face of God. Listen to the wisdom of your Physical and Emotional Bodies and do not try to override them. Always remember, GOD didn't create everybody the same. Every person has a different Monadic Ray and Soul Ray.

Some people were born to be mystics and some, occultists. Some people were born to do Physical work, and some people Spiritual work. Some people were created by GOD to be artists, and others, scientists. There are many people in this world who are run by the negative ego and are very self-righteous, and go around telling people how everyone should follow their point of balance. This is illusion, and nothing more than a massive ego trip. Be vigilant against the negative ego if it ever tries to do this. People's points of balance are greatly affected by their Physical health or lack thereof. A person's point of balance is also enormously affected by their Spiritual development. The more advanced you become Spiritually, often the more unconventional some of your habits may become. Also, what must be factored in here is that people's points of balance are constantly changing. Follow the beat of your own drum. Do not compare yourself with others, but rather trust your own point of balance. Most of all do not let your negative ego tell you that the point of balance you have found for yourself is the point of balance everyone else should follow. Every person is at a different state of evolution, which also greatly affects one's point of balance. This is why it is often dangerous to make fast and hard rules. One man's meat is another man's poison. Never forget this!

*   *   *

The Universal Law of Romantic Relationships

In *A Course In Miracles* it says that "relationships are the temple of the Holy Spirit." As already explained, the two most important relationships in your life are those with yourself and with God. A relationship partner is third on the list. If this is not clear, you are headed for some suffering. The danger here is trying to find your wholeness in another person, rather than finding your wholeness within yourself and God. If you don't do this, your relationship turns into a type of addictive love. One of the most important prerequisites to a healthy love relationship with another person is self love. The ideal is for you to love your inner child and to allow yourself to feel and receive God's love. If these aren't established first, then you end up seeking love, worth, approval, and acceptance from another person instead, which again will turn into a type of addictive love. Virginia Satir, the well known family therapist, said, "Communication is to a relationship what breathing is to living." This statement brings us to the next important ingredient to a healthy romantic relationship. Communicate with your partner about your feelings, or the relationship wont' work! A romantic relationship is said to be the Master of all relationships! Your partners are master teachers in everything they do. Even when they are misbehaving, they are giving you the opportunity to practice Christ Consciousness and to demonstrate qualities your Soul would have you develop! You are constantly being taught to stay in your power, to be loving, to forgive, to practice humility, to turn the other cheek, to remain the cause of your own emotions! A romantic relationship provides you with lessons in patience, emotional protection, honesty, communication skills, nonattachment, egolessness, unconditional love and staying centered, to just name a few! It's easy to remain in Christ Consciousness living in a cave, but it's a whole other story to practice the Presence of God while in a relationship! Now, this brings us to the next issue which is divorce. *The Universal Law of Romantic Relationships* stresses the importance to never leave a relationship until you have learned the lessons of the experience. Otherwise, you are likely to have to repeat the lessons in a new relationship. It will be a different Physical Body, Soul extension, and personality, but the same psychodynamics will occur. So, in all relationships there are times when your ego or lower self is triggered. How do you respond? The Soul's perspective on this is not to talk! When you are caught in your ego, all that happens is that you hurt each other emotionally. You say things you don't really mean in a vain attempt to get back at the other person. The negative ego's game is not love, but who is "right". You must ask yourself whether you want to be right or to have love. You can't have both! When both partners are caught, sometimes the best thing to do is take time alone to calm down, get re-centered, and attune to self and God. One other key lesson in romantic relationships is to focus on your own lessons and not the lessons you think your partner needs to learn! As Master Jesus said, "Do not condemn: as you judge others, so will you yourself be judged. Before you criticize the speck of sawdust in another's eye, first remove the plank of wood in your own." You are not responsible for your partner's lessons, only for your own lessons! So what do you do if your partner has a Psychological disease such as judgementalnesss, anger, depression, worry, lack of self-worth, lack of faith, self-doubt? The ideal is that you not catch the disease, but maintain a strong Psychological resistance. When your partner is Physically sick, you also do everything to build up your resistance! You take extra Vitamin C, get enough sleep, exercise, and sunshine, and keep a positive mental attitude, and don't catch it! Now, how do you build your Psychological resistance? You do so by staying in a place of personal power and self-love, using a protective bubble, a positive attitude, meditation, prayer, Spiritual reading and journal writing, to name but a few. If you maintain this Psychological resistance, negative energy does not hook into your subconscious programming. You are setting an example and hence helping the other to come out of his or her off-centeredness! Otherwise you can catch the Psychological disease. The world is like a hospital that is run by the patients: the purpose of life is to be a healer and a teacher of God so you can set a good example! Now, what do you do when you and your partner disagree about the perception of a given situation? It's easy! Agree to disagree, and stay in love and in oneness. This is possible as long as you don't let the ego in. No two people see things the same way all the time. Remember that you see with your mind, not just with your eyes. You see through your belief systems, since it is your thoughts that create your reality! Aren't relationships the best testing ground for helping you to get out of your ego? In the beginning of this paragraph we mentioned the importance of yourself and God being the two most important relationships in your life. What happens if you don't do your inner work and achieve these two right relationships is, that you form father-daughter, mother-son relationships! The ideal of course is to form mutually independent adult-adult relationships, not dependent relationships. If you don't find your wholeness within and oneness with God, then you will end up seeking it within a partner. And this will lead to two halves joining together, instead of two whole people uniting. If you are a daughter or son Psychologically, then by the laws of energy you will attract people who want to be mothers or fathers within the relationship. And if you are a father or mother Psychologically, the only type of people you can possibly attract are Psychological sons or daughters! So how would the ideal relationship now look like? The Dalai Lama said, "Remember that the best relationship is one in which your love for each other exceeds your need for each other." The ideal relationship is one in which both individuals are in right relationships with themselves and with God. Both people are whole and complete within themselves, and then they will attract a whole person who realizes his/her oneness with God! They are both causes of their own realities, not victims! Both individuals put their Spiritual Paths first! And the reason they are together is that they can grow faster and experience more love and joy by sharing the path together! The key to finding your true mate is to focus completely on your Spiritual Path and on service of humanity. Your total commitment to God and your Spiritual Path will attract the ideal Spiritual mate.

*   *   *

The Universal Law of Safety and Security

The negative ego creates insecurity because it teaches you to find your security outside of yourself in other people, possessions, houses, money, and so on. The only true security that cannot be taken away from you is security that is grounded in your personal power, in God, in the power of your subconscious mind, and in God's Laws! "True security is not the absence of danger, but the Presence of God, no matter what the danger!" The following quotes taken from the Bible speak for themselves and do not need any further explanation. "For we know that if our earthly house of this tabernacle were dissolved, we have a building of God, a house not made with hands, eternal in the heavens." (2 Corinthians 5:1) "As I walk through the shadow of death, I hear no evil, speak no evil for the Lord is with me." "When thou passest through the waters, I will be with thee; and through the rivers, they shall not overflow thee: when thou walkest through the fire, thou shalt not be burned; neither shall the flame kindle upon thee." (Isaiah 43:2) "He shall not be afraid of evil tidings: his heart is fixed, trusting in the LORD." (Psalms 112:7) "The LORD shall preserve thee from all evil: he shall preserve thy soul." (Psalms 121:7) "The name of the LORD is a strong tower: the righteous runneth into it, and is safe." (Proverbs 18:10) "The Lord will rescue me from every evil attack and will bring me safely to his heavenly kingdom." (2 Timothy 4:18) Always remember those words in times of need! They are worth its weight in gold!

*   *   *

The Universal Law of Salvation

One of the lessons of *A Course in Miracles* is, "My salvation is up to me." This is confusing to some, for most feel that GOD gives salvation. The truth is, GOD does not need to give salvation because GOD never took salvation away. As *A Course in Miracles* also says, "The fall never really happened, we just think it did." In other words, we have always been the Christ or the Buddha; always have been and always will be. No matter how much we indulge in negative ego thinking, which tells us we are separate from GOD and each other and are just Physical Bodies, this does not change the truth. As the introduction to *A Course in Miracles* says, "Nothing real can be threatened. Nothing unreal exists. Herein lies the peace of GOD." So, God has already given us everything. It is we who have separated ourselves from God by listening to the voice of the ego, by thinking that we were just a Physical Body. The truth is that we have never been separated from God, however, in our consciousness, or perception of reality, we are. We can easily remedy this situation by changing our thoughts. The Bible instructs us, "Be ye transformed by the renewal of your mind." Change your thoughts and you change your reality. The negative ego tells us that God doesn't exist because we can't see Him with our physical eyes and hence the ego is the ultimate authority. The ego tells us that each of us is just a Physical Body, not the Christ living in a Physical Body. We have been letting the ego be the ultimate authority. It's time for us to recognize and own our authority over ourselves and to gain mastery over our mind, our emotions, our physical body, and our ego. It is not God's job to get rid of the ego, it is our job. We created it, so we can get rid of it. God could do it, but this would be like giving birth to a child and doing everything for the child. If we did that, the child would grow up to be completely incapable and there would be no reason to incarnate into this school called Earth Life. God doesn't need to learn these lessons—we do! So recognize and own your personal power and gain mastery over your mind, emotions, physical body and ego, and "salvage yourself". Your salvation is up to you! God has given you already everything! "The LORD is my rock, and my fortress, and my deliverer; my God, my strength, in whom I will trust; my buckler, and the horn of my salvation, and my high tower. (Psalms 18:2) And being made perfect, he became the author of eternal salvation unto all them that obey him." (Hebrews 5:9)

*   *   *

The Universal Law of Self-Actualization

There are three distinct levels of our Spiritual constitution—monad, Soul, and personality—and hence there are three distinct levels of self-actualization. Our true identity is the monad—an individual Spiritual spark of the Creator representing our first core intelligence and our first individualized identity. There are 60 billion monads in our planetary system, and each of these monads created 12 Oversoul projections, each of which in turn creates 12 Soul extensions or incarnated personalities. We on Earth are personalities, or Soul extensions of our Soul, just as our Soul is an extension of a greater Consciousness which is our monad. Our monad is an extension of an even greater Consciousness which is GOD. A self-actualized person at the personality level would be someone who is Psychologically self-actualized, but not necessarily Spiritually self-actualized—for example, a famous movie star or psychologist. The second level of self-actualization would be self-actualization at a Soul level. A self-actualized person at this level has become one with the Soul and Higher Self and is living this reality in daily life. A self-actualized person at the third level of self-actualization, the monadic level, has become one with the monad and Mighty I Am Presence and is living this reality in daily life.

*   *   *

The Universal Law of Self-Inquiry

This law states the importance of developing an unflinching commitment to self-inquiry! Self-inquiry is the commitment to monitoring one's thoughts and being Spiritually vigilant at all times. This means never going on automatic pilot. This also means not allowing any fear thought or any other thought that is not of God to enter one's mind. This Spiritual practice is of such importance that Sai Baba actually says it is 75 percent of the Spiritual Path. It is the practice of recognizing that there are no neutral thoughts. All thoughts are either from the Higher Self or from the ego. It is the ego that fears, for the Higher Self knows that it is eternal. It is up to each one of us to choose who we will serve.

*   *   *

The Universal Law of Service

Mahatma Gandhi is quoted as saying that the best way to find yourself is to lose yourself in the service of others. There is an ancient proverb that states, "One who is pure of heart has the strength of ten." Your powers of manifestation are increased a thousandfold if your life is focused on God and serving your Brothers and Sisters in Christ. "True pleasure is serving God", as Jesus says in *A Course In Miracles*. Is there anything more exciting than serving the One who created and embodies all of

Creation? Isn't serving God the most glorious thing in the universe? And he sat down, and called the twelve, and saith unto them, "If any man desire to be first, the same shall be the last of all, and servant of all!" Don't go to work! Go to service! It does not matter what you do. You could clean toilets, or collect garbage. This is a most holy and sanctified service of GOD. All cleanliness and purification on every level is a Spiritual practice. It does not matter what type of work you do, it is the attitude and perspective you take towards it! Mother Teresa said, "Love cannot remain by itself—it has no meaning. Love has to be put into action and that action is service. Whatever form we are, able or disabled, rich or poor, it is not how much we do, but how much love we put in the doing; a lifelong sharing of love with others." Sai Baba said, "Love must express itself as service." See each customer as God, which is who and what they are, and treat them as such. See yourself as God! See the process as Son and Daughter of GOD serving Son and Daughter of GOD in service of GOD! Gandhi said, "I am endeavoring to see God through service of humanity, for I know that God is neither in heaven nor down below, but in every one." Now, being of service is a noble thing. Nevertheless, there is one little thing that you should consider. There are many people who are trying to serve from a place of not being right with self and right with God. If you are operating out of a cracked mold, so to speak, how can you possibly be really of service, and stay centered and whole and complete within self? It is a noble thing wanting to be of service, but they would be better off getting right with self first! "Secure Spiritual bliss first and then try to convey it to those who thirst. When the tank is dry how can the taps give water," as Sai Baba put it. Once we become Spiritual Masters, however, the main reason for being here is to serve! Taking this attitude makes work not work, but makes work a Spiritual practice which is the joy of serving GOD and the joy of serving your Brothers and Sisters in GOD! Krishna said, "Work becomes consecrated and purifying when it is done as service unto God." Always make sure that when you serve, you do so from a pure heart, with pure motivations! In the Bhagavad-Gita, Krishna instructs Arjuna "to serve and to not focus upon the fruits of the service." And the Bible teaches us, "Therefore, my beloved brethren, be ye steadfast, unmoveable, always abounding in the work of the Lord, forasmuch as ye know that your labor is not in vain in the Lord." (Corinthians 15:58) We do not serve for power, fame, self-love, self-worth, approval, or praise; we serve because "true pleasure is serving GOD." So, get right with self and GOD, and be about your Father's and Mother's Business! "As for me an my house, I serve the Lord!"

*   *   *

The Universal Law of Sevenfold Protection Against Psychic Attack on All Levels

The first level of psychic attack is when we are being attacked by our own negative ego. This is very common and a great many people in the world are suffering from this in the form of the critical parent, lack of self-love, negative ego thinking, and sabotage, to name a few. The second level of psychic attack comes from people in the world who attack you either in your verbal conversations with them, or are doing this on the psychic plane without your awareness. They may do this either consciously or unconsciously. Always remember, that since most people on Earth have not been properly trained in how to master their mind and emotions and transcend negative ego thinking and replace it with Christ/Buddha/Spiritual thinking, they live in fear. Fearful people attack. So everyone on Earth will have to deal with being attacked and criticized at times! It is important to be able to receive constructive criticism in life, and it is even important to learn from people's feedback even if they express it from their negative ego. Do not, however, let disturbed negative, egotistical people who are manufacturing things to attack you about, have any effect on you. Stand solid in our truth and let their negativity slide off your Golden Bubble of Light like "water off a duck's back." The third level of psychic attack comes from some lower Astral entity, or a group of entities, on the Inner Plane. The fourth kind of attack is from negative Extraterrestrials. Why are so many people suffering from this problem? The key understanding here to become invulnerable to psychic attack on any level is that you must create a protection on seven levels. These seven levels are the Spiritual, Mental, Emotional, Psychic, Etheric, Physical, and Earthly Levels. The reason a great many Lightworkers are suffering from psychic attack is they are requesting projection, but are not doing it on all seven levels! The most important level to prevent psychics from occurring on any level is to learn to master your own thoughts, emotions, desires, subconscious mind, inner child, physical body, energy, and most of all, negative ego mind and thinking. If you do not learn how to do this, all other forms of protection will be extremely limited in effectiveness. Most people in this world are under psychic attack or psychological attack from their own thoughts, emotions, inner child, and negative ego mind. When the negative ego is programming your thoughts and emotions instead of the Melchizedek/Christ/Buddha Mind, this will not only make you miserable, it will also leave an opening for you to be attacked by other people, Astral entities, or negative Extraterrestrials. If this first level could be mastered, almost all psychic attack would stop without doing anything else. Mastering this level takes a little time however, and does not happen in one day. It takes great focus, commitment, and Spiritual vigilance. So, on the Mental Level you are going to deny all negative ego thoughts from entering your mind and you are going to reply them with Spiritual Melchizedek/Christ/Buddha thoughts. On an Emotional Level, you are going to only create Melchizedek/Christ/Buddha Emotions for you are only going to think with your Melchizedek/Christ/Buddha Mind. You realize that your thoughts create your feelings and emotions. You take responsibility that if you feel negatively or positively, you are creating it by how you are interpreting the situation. Once you have focused your energies to try and completely master the Psychological level, then it is time to call in the Spiritual forces for protection. Do a meditation called "The Cosmic and Spiritual Hierarchy Protection Meditation" (see *Ascension Activation Meditations of the Spiritual Hierarchy: A Compilation*) which will create a force field of protection that is so profound that nothing will be able to get through unless you choose to allow it! It enormously invokes the help of the Cosmic and Planetary Hierarchy and Archangels Michael and Faith, whose job—since they are First Ray Archangels—it is to protect. On a Physical/Earthly Level you are going to strengthen your Physical immune system through proper Physical diet, Physical exercise, sleep habits, rest, sunshine, fresh air, positive affirmation, positive visualization, and calling on the Inner Plane Ascended Masters and Angels to keep your Physical Body and Etheric Body (energy Body) in perfect radiant health. This is important because the Physical Body can be attacked as well by bacteria, viruses, parasites, fungus, and so on, and keeping a strong Physical immune system will fight any potential diseases off! Keeping the Physical Body strong also allows you to not be Physically tired and it makes it easier to remain in your personal power, self-mastery, and joyous vigilance at all times! On an Earthly Level, lock your car, lock your house door. You pray to Allah but you also make sure to tie up your camel! On an Energetic Level, the calling in of GOD, the Masters, and the Angelic energies, as well as your own ability to shift and change the energy in your auric field and body, will keep your Etheric Body clear, strong, and full of energy and vitality! On a Psychic Level, do the Meditation, practice the other levels spoken of in this paragraph, do a prayer of protection and put on your Mental Armor, so to speak, every day and every night. What does it mean to put on your Mental Armor? It is not enough to just ask GOD and the Masters to protect you. You must consciously do your part as well on the Psychic Plane. GOD helps those who help themselves! A great many Lightworkers pray their hearts out and can't understand why Spirit and the Masters won't help them. This, of course, is a projection, for Spirit and the Masters are helping them. However, the problem is not a Spiritual one, it is a Psychological one. That is what is allowing the Psychic attacks to continue! Even Spirit and the Masters cannot fully stop the Psychic attacks if one's psychology is not mastered. So, when you first get up every morning, visualize in your mind's eye claiming your sword of power, your golden bubble of protection that you create yourself with the power of your own mind and heart. Put on your self-love, maybe by putting a red rose in your heart. Visualize your attunement to GOD and the Masters by seeing your Antakarana or tube of light from your Heart Chakra back to GOD. Put on your Melchizedek/Christ/Buddha thinking and see yourself getting rid of all negative ego thinking. Visualize the Three-Fold Flame of Love/Wisdom and Power burning bright in your heart! This will keep you protected on the Psychic Plane! In conclusion, the first type of Psychic attack is that of your own negative ego thoughts, emotions, and inner child. You deal with it by releasing all negative ego thoughts and only thinking with your Christed Mind. When attacked verbally by other people, you are prepared for that, as long as you put on your Mental Armor every morning, do your prayer of protection and do your homework on a Psychological, Spiritual, and Physical/Earthly Level. Why? Because if you fully own your personal power and have a bubble of protection around you, and you have self-love and self-worth within you and your attunement to GOD and the Masters, then other people's negative verbal attacks will slide off your bubble like water off a duck's back. You will not have allowed them to cause your emotions or hurt you in any way! You have not reacted as a victim, you have responded like a Spiritual Master! Look how the Master Jesus responded when attacked and crucified. "Love your enemies," as Jesus put it. See *The Universal Law of Focusing on Your Own Lessons Rather than Being Concerned about Teaching Other People Theirs.* See through the negative ego veil they are manifesting, and give them unconditional love they are truly asking for. People attack because they live in fear. An attack is a call for love! Now, what do you do when attacked by a negative Astral entity? The only way an Astral entity can remain connected with you is if you allow yourself to be run by your negative ego, negative thoughts, negative emotions, and you do not parent your inner child with firmness and love. If you do these things, it is impossible for an Astral entity to remain in your aura. What attracts the Astral entity to you is your own negative thoughts, negative emotions, and negative ego. In terms of attack coming from negative Extraterrestrials in the form of negative implants and abductions, listen very closely! No one in life is a victim! No Extraterrestrial can abduct you or place implants within you unless you let them. GOD did not place you on this Earth to be a victim or to be victimized. GOD placed you on this Earth to be a Spiritual Master and the complete cause of your reality on every level. This is your birthright as a Melchizedek/Christ/Buddha, which is who you are. GOD is not victimized by negative ETs and neither are you, if you claim your birthright! If you claim your 100% Personal Power, 100% Unconditional Love, and 100% Spiritual and Psychological Wisdom, and never let go of it, then you cannot be touched! You are invulnerable! Ponder on this!

*   *   *

The Universal Law of Sexuality

Are we the masters of our sexuality, or is it the master of us? Does the flow of our sexuality serve the lower self or the Higher Self? Which comes first, God or sexuality? Are we moderate in our sexual practices? Does our sexuality serve love and intimacy or just materialistic animal pleasure? A selfish purpose or a selfless purpose? Is our sexuality used also for the raising of our Kundalini and brain illumination, or just for a Second-Chakra release? Sexuality is a wonderful thing. God created it for us to enjoy as a communication device in the service of love. Sexuality is not bad, becomes negative, however, when it is used by the lower self, or carnal self, or negative ego. Lord Buddha said, "If one, longing for sensual pleasure, achieves it, yes, he's enraptured at heart. The mortal gets what he wants. But if for that person—longing, desiring—the pleasures diminish, he's shattered, as if shot with an arrow." (Sutta Nipata IV, 1) Use it in service of the Higher Self and love, and it becomes a most sacred consecration! One of the great tests of the Spiritual Path in regard to sexuality also comes when we achieve power, money, and fame. How do we deal with our sexuality then? A great many Spiritual teachers have fallen when confronted with this situation, and used their power to have sex with their students and/or devotees. "Learn from the mistakes of others. You can't live long enough to make them all yourself," as the saying goes. Learn through grace instead of karma. Grace erases karma. Ponder on this!

*   *   *

The Universal Law of Silence

ai Baba instructs us to "practice silence: for the voice of God can be heard in the region of your heart only when the tongue is stilled and the storm is stilled, and the waves are calm." There are two ways to look at the subject of silence. These would be the horizontal view and the vertical view. The vertical view deals with one's relationship with GOD. The horizontal view deals with the issue of silence in a more interpersonal and social sense. On a horizontal level, there is a time to talk and a time to be silent. Most people on Earth talk way too much, because they are lacking in self-mastery and self-control, and are run too much by their Emotional and Mental Bodies which causes them to talk much more than is appropriate. The Emotional Body and the mind always want to engage and respond so they can feel good about themselves. In every situation of life there is an appropriate response and there is an inappropriate response. Silence can be the strongest and most powerful statement you can make. However, be sure to step forward and communicate when need be. Edgar Cayce called this "sins of omission and commission." Remember, the inner voice is often called "the still small voice within." The negative ego yells and screams but the "still small voice within" just waits in silence and does not compete for attention! On a deeper level, *The Universal Law of Silence* does not only deal with the importance of learning when it is appropriate to communicate and when it is appropriate to remain silent, it also deals with silencing the mind and the emotions. If your emotions are always agitated you will never appreciate the silence; most people's minds are going a mile in a minute. See *The Universal Law of Quieting the Mind.* Now, on a vertical level, inner peace comes in two ways. One is learning to think properly and have things in proper perspective. The second way is to have no thought and just be in the silence, which is where GOD, the Holy Spirit, your own Mighty I Am Presence, your Higher Self, and the Ascended Masters can be found. "Silence is the altar of God." (Paramahansa Yogananda) "God's Presence is felt in Silence." (Sai Baba) The mind will always be active to a certain extent. That is its nature. The mastery comes in learning not to engage it at its every impulse. The conscious mind has a choice as to whether to engage with the constant flow of input from the subconscious mind. There is always a balance of when to identify and when to disidentify. Silence is learned by learning to disidentify. Do not be afraid to enjoy the silence! It is a place of peace and rest! "The Divine Radio is always singing if we could only make ourselves ready to listen to it, but it is impossible to listen without silence." (Mahatma Gandhi)

*   *   *

The Universal Law of Soul Retrieval and Soul Fragments

In life as we connect with other people we create cords and threads, and leave aspects of our energy with them. This is a good thing and a gift from one God to another God, in a sense. Sometimes, however, there are certain energy pieces that it may be Spiritually appropriate to draw back to one's Soul. They are called Soul Fragments. This is not something you have to figure out consciously yourself, you can just ask God, the Mahatma, Melchizedek, Metatron and Archangel Michael to do it for you. The basic request should be to return to you all Soul Fragments that are Spiritually appropriate to return, and to leave the ones as Spiritual gifts that are pieces of energy that are meant to stay with all the people you have loved and touched in some way. In a similar vein, also call in Archangels Michael and Faith, and request that all energy cords and lines of energy from this life, all past lives, and all inner plane connections between lives since your creation be cut that are not Spiritually appropriate. Again, this is not something you have to consciously figure out, it can just be requested, and by the Grace of Archangels Michael and Faith, can be done in an instant! Simple but profound!

*   *   *

The Universal Law of Spiritual Alchemy

One of the absolute Spiritual keys to effective Self-Mastery and Self-Realization is the ability to turn lemons into lemonade! This is called the process of Spiritual Alchemy! It must be understood that life will never always go according to our preferences. This is why the concept of having preferences rather than attachments is so important. If one is attached to having things go the way they want, this person is going to have an enormous amount of suffering in their life. When we only have preferences we are happy, no matter what happens. We still want our preferences met, but our happiness is not based on achieving them. Besides the concept of preference, which is essential, we must also understand that from GOD's perspective everything that happens is positive and should be looked at as a gift. The proper attitude to everything in life is "Not my will but Thine, thank you for the lesson!" No matter what happens in life, no matter how horrific the example, this is the proper attitude. As His Holiness, the Lord Sai Baba has said, "Welcome adversity." From GOD's perspective, there are no accidents in the universe and everything happens for a reason! The reason is always to Spiritually teach a lesson that needs to be learned! Now sometimes the "negative" things that happen are caused from personal karma, sometimes planetary karma, and sometimes they are caused by past life karma! The truth is, it doesn't matter why it happened or where it came from, for if it happened, you can be assured that you needed that lesson for some reason and the proper attitude is to welcome it, accept it, and look at it as a gift. From GOD's perspective, everything that happens in life is a Spiritual test. In every situation in life, we can respond from GOD Consciousness or negative ego Consciousness. So, Earth is a school to practice demonstrating GOD, a Melchizedek, the Christ, and/or the Buddha. Now the truth is that life is constantly throwing us lemons. The key principle here is, will you turn it into lemonade, or will you keep tasting the bitter taste of the lemon? Now the question is, how does one turn something negative that has happened into a positive? The first thing that turns every situation of life that is not your preference into something positive is looking at it as a Spiritual lesson and Spiritual test. The second thing that causes this Spiritual Alchemical process is forgiveness and unconditional love towards self and others. The third thing that turns any negative into a positive is the "Golden Nugget of Wisdom" learned from your mistake or the mistake of others and/or the Spiritual tests you get to practice! Fourthly, recognizing that everything works for the good in GOD's infinite universe and that GOD always makes good out of everything. We have all heard the expression, this was a "blessing in disguise." No matter what happens in life, the key is to focus on what you can do instead of what you can't do! Focus on what you have gained, not what you have lost! If you lose your voice and can't speak any-more, then become a writer. If you have an illness and can no longer go outside, then dedicate your life to developing your inner life! If you lose a large sum of money and someone rips you off, you are being given the wonderful opportunity not only to practice forgiveness, but also to not be attached to money. No matter how much is taken away and no matter how many things you cannot do, there is always something you can do. Focus yourself and your consciousness on that which you can do! A person with a negative, pessimistic attitude will find a way to feel unhappy even if outwardly things are going well. A person who has an optimistic positive attitude will ultimately remain so, no matter what happens in their life. A person practicing a Buddha/Christ/Melchizedek philosophy could go to jail and would look at it as a Spiritual retreat. They would say, my meals are taken care of. I don't have to work. What a great opportunity to prac-tice forgiveness and unconditional love. They would say, I will spend my days Physically exercising, reading, studying the Bible or some other book, like *The Universal Laws of God*, and bilocating to the Ascension Seats of GOD. Calling in light showers and love showers from the Masters. Doing inner plane service work. Looking at everything that happens as a Spiritual test. Seeing how Christ-like they could be under the worst circumstances. Mahatma Gandhi, when they came in the middle of the night to arrest him, said, "I am at your service. I am ready now." He brushed his teeth, prayed briefly, and went off to jail. Gandhi could not be imprisoned, in reality, for he saw imprisonment as a state of mind, not a set of bars. The physical prison was called Yeravda, so Gandhi referred to it as Yeravda

Temple! The AIDS patient ends up totally changing their priorities. Living in the moment. Appreciating life a million times more. Christ was crucified and killed, and used it as an opportunity to practice forgiveness. "Forgive them Father for they know not what they do!" A person loses their leg and becomes a Special Olympics athlete! If you have chronic health problems, "join the club." So did Mother Teresa who had a failing heart. So did Saint Francis! All these so-called challenges, or crosses to bear are temporary. Life in truth goes by in a twinkling of an eye. GOD deals in expanses of time such as "100 billion years of Brahma." One lifetime is like a grain of sand in relationship to the infinite universe! What's the worst that could happen anyway? Isn't death the worst case scenario? If it is meant to be that we go (early) then so be it! This may not be our preference but there is no such thing as death and you will see all your family and friends soon on the inner plane anyway! Some would look at it as a blessing, for we are visiting here and this is not our true home. Our true home is in Heaven! You are fully capable of passing any test, for if you weren't, GOD would not have sent you! The world is nothing more than a projection screen for our attitudes and interpretations! GOD would have us be 100% positive and optimistic no matter what happens in life, no matter how morbid the example! Whatever happens in life is there to teach us certain Christ/Buddha qualities. Everything that has ever happened in this world, is happening, or ever will happen, is a blessing (sometimes in disguise). If it happened, it means our Soul needed that lesson. One cannot cry over spilled milk! It is spilled and nothing is going to change that! There is no such thing as good luck or bad luck in this world. This is total illusion! The concept of luck is an illusionary fabrication of the negative ego thought system. Everything in GOD's Universe operates out of Laws on a Spiritual, Mental, Emotional, Etheric, and Physical Level. If something happened then there is a cause. This is the immutable Law of Karma, or Cause and Effect. We cannot always control what comes into our life on an outer level, however, we can control 100% our attitude, interpretation, and perspective of what happens to us. "Never let life's hardships disturb you. After all, no one can avoid problems, not even saints or sages." (Nichiren) He continues, "Life isn't about what happens to us. It's about how we perceive what happens to us." So no matter how sour the lemons are that you are given, you can thank GOD and bless this experience, for it has given you the opportunity to transcend your negative ego and practice Melchizedek/Christ/Buddha Consciousness. Even if everything is taken away on every level, then all that is left is GOD, and you can say, "Naked I came from my mother's womb, and naked shall I leave. The Lord giveth, and the Lord taketh away. Blessed be the name of the Lord."

*   *   *

The Universal Law of Spiritual Assignments

In the process of the unfoldment of your Spiritual Path, Integrated Ascension, and God Realization unfoldment and evolvement, Spirit and the Masters will give you certain "Spiritual Assignments" for you to complete on the Earthly Plane! Spirit and the Masters watch very closely how you fulfill and accomplish these Spiritual Assignments, and it is by how you accomplish them that you are being "groomed" in a sense to take on bigger ones! The first step on the Spiritual Path is to become right with self, right with GOD, and the Masters, and right with other people! Then it is to complete your seven Levels of Initiation in an integrated and balanced way. As you are going through this process, Spiritual Assignments will be given to "Spiritually test" your Spiritual Leadership ability for Planetary World Service! It is by completing each Spiritual Assignment properly, with a pursuit of excellence, that Spirit and the Masters can see that you are ready for the next step! They only give you what you are ready to handle. However, they are willing to stretch you. Do understand that as you evolve, much has been given, and much will be expected! The more advanced you become, the more Spirit and the Masters will expect of you in terms of stepping forward in Spiritual Leadership and Planetary World Service! There are many Spiritual Leadership Posts that the Masters are looking to fill! It must be understood that the Inner Plane Spiritual Masters cannot move onto their next position on Solar and Galactic Levels until they find suitable replacements from the Earthly ranks of Masters, Initiates, and Disciples! So Spirit and the Masters watch and monitor your progress in terms of each Spiritual Assignment you are given! If you do it competently, your next Spiritual Assignment will be enlarged! So, completing your Seven Levels of Initiation and Ascension is not the end, it's just the beginning! Then comes "Spiritual Leadership and Planetary World Service"! It must also be understood that the Inner Plane Ascended Masters are going through the same process as well, in terms of the concept of Spiritual Assignments! Masters like Lord Buddha, Mother Mary, and Quan Yin, for example, all have their Spiritual Assignments, and they are being overlighted by Galactic or Universal Masters who are guiding them! For example in 1995, Lord Buddha took over the position of Planetary Logos which Sanat Kumara held for 18.5 billion years. Sanat Kumara now has moved to his next Cosmic Position and Spiritual Assignment. Even Melchizedek, the Universal Logos, has a Spiritual Assignment and Cosmic Position to run the entire Universe! And when he completes this Spiritual Assignments, He will also move on and be given an even more expanded Spiritual Assignment. Eventually, as we fulfill our current Spiritual Assignments and Positions properly, we will be given Spiritual responsibilities for Planets, then Solar Systems, Galaxies, the Universes, Multiuniverses, and then for the Cosmos Itself! That is our destiny! Well, but before we shall do so, let's master the Spiritual Assignment that is in front of us first, and then more will be given! Also, don't wait for the Masters to conk you over the head with a hammer and say, "This is your Spiritual Assignment! Voilà!" GOD has given you a Christed Mind that is incredibly creative just as GOD's and the Masters' are! One of the keys to catching the Masters' attention is to create your own Spiritual Assignments so the Masters take notice! This idea that we are just supposed to be channels and robots for Spirit and the Masters is illusion! They want each person to become a full-fledged Spiritual Master in their own right! So the key here is to create those Spiritual Assignments and to ask for Spirit and the Masters to give you your current Spiritual Assignment. Do them as perfectly as you can, for new Spiritual Assignments will be given as you complete the previous one. Make yourself useful to Spirit and the Masters! Isn't Life exciting? As for me and my house, "Yippee and Hurray!"

          *   *   *

The Universal Law of Spiritual Discernment and Judgement

The development of Spiritual discernment is one of the most important Christ/Buddha attributes a person needs to develop to become a full-fledged Ascended Master. Many Lightworkers have not developed enough Spiritual discernment to see through claims that certain people are making. Certain people claim to have realized GOD on the 352nd Level, when they have not. Some people claim they are married to the Inner Plane Ascended Masters, and others still complain to have completed their Cosmic Ascension. And many people think that if people claim such things, it must be true. Nothing could be further from the truth! The lengths that the negative ego will go to make itself feel important is mind-boggling. Lightworkers are also way too naïve when it comes to reading books. Half the channeled information out there is ridiculous and inaccurate, yet, the book says it's channeled, "so it must be true." Or the person has some fancy Spiritual name, so it must be true. The negative ego's need to feel important fills people with so much garbage, glamour, and illusion, it is unbelievable. Spiritual discernment is essential because the negative ego comes up with the most bizarre philosophies and belief systems for seeing life. Just think for a moment of the very naïve and Pollyannaish philosophy of some groups, who in the pursuit of their Spiritual Path do not want to allow themselves to see anything negative. It is absolutely essential to know how the negative ego works within self and to see it operating and demonstrating within others. If one doesn't, not only will karma and imbalance be created, but one will get involved in all kinds of interactions and relationships that will be detrimental to that person, because their faulty thinking and belief system is blocking their willingness to have Spiritual discernment in the vein of trying to be Spiritual. Without Spiritual discernment one cannot weed out all the delusion and illusion of the negative ego thought system in its infinite forms of corruption. To make it through an entire lifetime with all the lessons which life brings on this planet and all the lessons that Spiritual leadership brings, takes enormous Spiritual discernment and discrimination. Now there are corollary issues that are related to this, which the negative ego has distorted because of not understanding it. One is the issue of Spiritual discernment versus judgement. There are many that think that we should never even have discernments, that any time you observe negativity it is a judgement. So they try to blind themselves to seeing any negativity. There are others who judge, which means they are discerning with no unconditional love. "If you judge people, you have no time to love them." (Mother Teresa) Remember the words of Master Jesus on the Mount of Beatitudes, "Do not condemn: as you judge others, so will you yourself be judged. Before you criticize the speck of sawdust in another's eye, first remove the plank of wood in your own." "Judge not, that ye not be judged. For with what judgement you judge, you will be judged; and with what measure you mete, it shall be measured to you." Both of these are the negative ego. To blind yourself to the existence of evil is a prescription to be run by it. To blind yourself to not being allowed to have Spiritual discernments is also a prescription to be totally run by the negative ego. To judge others with "Innocent Perception" or unconditional love for everyone, no matter how evil, is a prescription to be totally run by the negative ego. The proper integration comes in allowing yourself to have Spiritual discernments and observations while simultaneously seeing each person as God and the Christ, and only making these observations through the heart and unconditional love. Never forget the masterful words of Jesus Christ, "Take heed lest any man deceive you for many will come in my name saying, 'I Am Christ'; and will deceive many. Be aware of false prophets, who come to you in sheep's clothing, but inwardly are ravening wolves. You shall know them by their fruits!" Let those words of Jesus Christ always reverberate throughout your being, and let them serve as a loving reminder to always be Spiritually discerning.

*   *   *

The Universal Law of Spiritual Honesty

There are two kinds of honesty. There is the honesty of a child and the honesty of a Spiritual Master or adult. The child's form of honesty is to say everything. A child has not developed their reasoning mind or finely tuned their intuition. Whatever is inside of them comes out. The honesty of a Spiritual Master and adult is based on the proper integration of one's attunement to GOD and intuition, reasoning mind and Spiritual discernment, and emotional and psychic feelings. From GOD's perspective, in every situation in life there is an appropriate response and an inappropriate response. You can respond from your negative ego or from your Soul and Mighty I Am Presence. True Spiritual honesty is sharing that which creates unconditional love, and not fear; that which creates oneness, and not separation; that which heals rather than hurts others. A child will blurt out something regardless of whether it hurts others, or whether it is appropriate to do so. If what you have on your mind to share is just going to hurt someone, create a war, and not get you what you want, then why say it? Then silence might be the appropriate action to take. A Spiritual Master understands that this is true honesty. In other situations, childlike honesty is inappropriate because the person is not trustworthy to receive your honesty. They will not keep it confidential, or in the future they will use it against you. As Master Jesus put it, "Don't cast your pearls to swine." Also, examine your motive for sharing and being "honest." Often when people are being "honest"", they are indulging their Emotional Bodies and negative egos by using "honesty" as an excuse at the expense of another person to let out anger, punish, or win an ego battle. Heed the holy words written down in the Bible, "Nothing in all Creation is hidden from God's sight. Everything is uncovered and laid bare before the eyes of Him to whom we must give account." (Hebrews 4:14 NIV) "O Lord, thou art my God, I will exalt thee, I will praise they name, for thou hast done wonderful things; thy counsels of old are faithfulness and truth." (Isaiah 25:1)

*   *   *

The Universal Law of Spiritualizing the Ego

Everyone has an ego or personality which the Soul and Spirit work through. What is the ego? The ego is that part of self that gives us a sense of identity and individuality. Having an ego goes along with having a Physical Body. The ego's true function is to be a retriever of information and to remind the Soul extension who is living in the body to take care of its Physical Body. The ego is the material-plane expert. If we didn't have an ego we might forget that we are even incarnated. The ego reminds us that we need food, water, and sleep. Now the problem arises because the ego was never meant to interpret the rest of our lives for us. The rest of our lives were meant to be defined and interpreted by the Soul and Spirit. We have let the ego interpret our reality, which interpretation is based on the faulty belief that we are bodies (because that is all it knows about), and we have let the ego override intuitive ways of processing information of Spirit. In interpreting our realities, the ego has misused the conscious, reasoning mind and created an illusionary belief system based on fear, separation, selfishness, and death. Hence we have the negative ego/fear-based/separative mind. The Fall that the Bible refers to occurred when we as monads, or individualized sparks of God, chose to come into matter. It wasn't the coming into matter that caused the "Fall" but the overidentification with matter. It was that moment when we thought we were a Physical Body rather than a God-being inhabiting or using this Physical Body. In thinking we were a Physical Body, we fell prey to the illusion of separation from God and separation from our Brothers and Sisters. Then came selfishness, fear, and real death. From these faulty premises a whole thought system developed that was based on illusion, maya, and glamour. The amazing thing *A Course in Miracles* teaches us is that the "Fall" never really happened. We just think it did. The basic law of the mind is that it is our thoughts that create our reality. Our feelings, emotions, behavior, and what we attract and magnetize into our lives all come from our thoughts. Our thoughts create our reality, but our thoughts do not create truth! The negative ego didn't come from God, it came from man's misuse of free choice! We have always been the Christ, the Buddha, the Atman, the Eternal Self, and have always been one with God. All of our negative egotistical thinking has not changed this one single bit! The "Fall" never really happened! So if you think that you are just a Physical Body rather than Spirit living in a Physical Body that will be the reality you will find yourself in—a reality based on fear, separation, and self-centeredness, which is illusion, in truth. For you have always been one with GOD and have always been the Christ, or Sons and Daughters of GOD. However, our thoughts create our reality. As Sai Baba said, "Your mind creates bondage, or your mind creates liberation." He also said, "God, if you think, God you are. Dust, if you think, dust you are. As you think, so you become. Think God. Be God." To interpret reality through the ego is to interpret reality through the physical eyes only. We have not allowed the ego to become spiritualized; it has become a negative ego. So our job now is to spiritualize the ego. How do we accomplish this? Since our thoughts create our reality, the key is to deny any thought not of GOD to enter your mind. The key is to be vigilant for GOD and His Kingdom at all times and never to go on automatic pilot. Whenever a negative thought tries to enter your mind just deny it entrance and push it out. Switch your mind like a channel changer to a positive thought. This is the concept of denial and affirmation. You are the executive director of your personality and it is your choice to think with your illusionary/negative ego/fear-based/separative mind or with your Spiritual/Christ/Buddha Mind, understanding that you are the Christ, the Buddha, the Atman, the Eternal Self. GOD and the Ascended Masters will not do this for you no matter how much you ask. This is your job! Every person on Planet Earth only has one real problem: you can call it negative ego, fear, or separation. It is all the same thing. Every problem in life will find its initial source and cause in this place. The negative ego is the cause of all negative emotions, all negative thoughts, all negative behavior, all Psychological diseases, all relationship problems, poverty consciousness, war, and terrorism. In essence, the negative ego is blocking you from God Realization. Sai Baba says, "God is hidden by the mountain range of ego!" It is the negative ego in all its infantile variations and manifestations that leaves us open to negative implants and elementals, parasites, negative imprints, Etheric damage, Etheric mucous, Astral entities, core fear, gray fields, and negative Archetypes. It all comes down to which voice you are listening to. Are you listening to the voice of separation or oneness, the voice of fear of love? As *A Course In Miracles* says, "Choose once again." Every moment of our lives we are choosing either GOD or ego. As Yogananda Paramahansa said, "If you want to realize GOD you must want Him like a drowning man wants air." You will not find GOD, being indecisive or sitting on the fence. Now, there are corollary lessons that are also required that emanate out from this initial lesson of denying the negative ego and choosing Buddha/Christ/Melchizedek Consciousness. The main corollary lessons are: learning to balance your Four-Body System, learning to integrate your Three Minds, learning to properly parent your inner child, developing Self-Love and Self-Worth, learning to own your Personal Power at all times, learning to reprogram the subconscious mind, proper control of sexual energy, psychic self defense, right human relationships, proper care of the Physical Vehicle, and mastery of the Desire Body. Just taking heed of and practicing *The Universal Laws of God* as outlined within these pages will spiritualize your ego in a Full Spectrum Prism Manner! Choosing GOD in every moment of your life will spiritualize your ego! Living a life in accordance with Sai Baba's definition of God will spiritualize your ego: "God equals man minus ego! Ego lives by getting and forgetting; love lives by giving and forgiving; love is expansion; self is contraction; self is lovelessness; love is selflessness."

*   *   *

The Universal Law of Subconscious Interference

If you take 12 people who see an accident, all 12 will tell a different story. How can this be? Is it the Physical eyes? Well, maybe a couple of people had poor Physical vision, but this could not be the case with all of them. No, it usually is one's Psychological Consciousness that is distorting a true efficient perception of realty. This is called subconscious interference, and this is, in truth, an entire new study in the field of psychology and vision. This is what dyslexia is. This is why when people read something out loud they add and subtract words. This is why often when we type something there is the adding and subtracting of words that were not even meant to be typed! Or, we are all aware of the process of "Freudian Slips," where words come out that a person doesn't mean to say, but slip out anyway to show one's true thinking and meaning. A person can park their car in the mall and on their return from shopping look for it, but they have a fixed idea in their mind where the car is and so they walk right by it even though it is right in front of their Physical eyes. We all know the game of telephone where a message is passed along to someone to give to someone else, and when it finally goes around the circle the message is nothing like the original message. This is subconscious interference. People are constantly projecting their thoughts and images on a conscious and subconscious level onto the world and something that is not there. They are also constantly allowing other people to plant thoughts and images into their minds and seeing things that are not there. A person goes to see a scary movie, and then all night after the movie they think they are seeing and hearing possible scary things. Are you fully getting the point here? People are constantly hallucinating and seeing, hearing, tasting, touching and smelling things that are not there, which is being caused by "subconscious interference." How come? The reason for this is that most people on Earth live in hypnosis 99% of the time, even though their eyes are wide open. Most of what the people on Earth are seeing, including Lightworkers, is a massive hallucination of their subconscious mind. In the field of hypnosis which we have all seen demonstrated in stage shows, by a mere suggestion to the subconscious mind, a person can be made to hallucinate any of the five senses and any thought or image that is planted in their mind. They actually see these things and they are not there. Most people being under hypnosis, they are constantly seeing, tasting, touching, smelling and hearing things that are not there because of subconscious interference. People are constantly hallucinating things from thoughts and images that are being programmed into their minds, from the past, by themselves, and from other people in the present, that are not really there. When a person is run by the subconscious mind they are also automatically run by the Emotional Body, Astral Body, and Desire Body. This means that you do not cause your emotions, they are victimizing you. This also means that the negative ego is running the person and their life, for if the Emotional Body is in control then that automatically means the negative ego will also be the programmer. This is an indisputable fact and law of the mind. If you allow your feelings and emotions to run you, the Desire Body will be too much in control. In most cases this will also mean that the inner child will be running the person's life. This will also mean the mind is running the person and the person will not have inner peace. This will lead to unbelievable numbers of mistakes. The subconscious will be creating havoc. And the person cannot figure out why. It is because they are not in control of the subconscious mind, the Emotional Body, and their conscious mind. Hence the negative ego is in control and is sabotaging the person right and left. The person is letting a non-reasoning mind run their life and does not even realize it. Ponder on this!

*   *   *

The Universal Law of Success

That which you hold in your consciousness will eventually manifest in your outer reality! GOD is 100% successful in everything GOD does. You are God so you have to be successful in everything you do! How can GOD, which is everything, not be successful? "My ally is the Force. And a powerful ally it is. Life creates it. Makes it grow." (Yoda, Star Wars Trilogy) So hold this Spiritual Ideal or Perfection and know that you will be successful in everything you do, and it is impossible for anything but this to happen. Yet be balanced and integrated in the process of how you do this! Work on all levels of GOD to achieve this. Yet hold the perfected ideal! What the bank account is saying, or what your outer life experience is saying in terms of success is meaningless! Don't let your outer circumstance determine what you are. Let your consciousness, which is attuned to GOD and your true identity as a Son or Daughter of GOD, determine who and what you are. It is impossible for GOD and God not to be wealthy and successful in every aspect of life! The key to success is to hold the Perfected Ideal, but also have common sense and practicality while doing it! For some hold the ideal of perfection, but are not integrated and get all fouled up. And others strive for integration and balance, yet do not always hold the Christed or Perfected ideal! So, honor the need to be integrated and balanced in everything you do, and recognize the need to utilize all levels of GOD to truly be successful and not just get stuck in one! The four keys to success lie in the following statement: "GOD, my Personal Power, the Power of my Subconscious Mind, and my Physical Body power are an unbeatable team!" There is much profundity in this affirmation and you should say it often! This is how the Integrated Ascended Master manifest. He or she works on all four levels. They use personal power and Spiritual/Christ/Buddha thinking and feeling on the conscious level, prayer on the Spiritual level, affirmations, visualizations and self-suggestion on the subconscious level, and right Physical action on the Physical level. Always remember, that each of us carries within us an aspect of God's Mind. So, the key to success is Co-Creation—calling on God and the Masters' mind power and utilizing our own mind power to cause the reality we wish. The negative ego will try to make you forget one of these levels. If you do, it will sabotage the process. All four levels must be maintained and continued in a structured, self-disciplined and continual manner and if you do this, success will be assured! "This book of the law shall not depart out of thy mouth; but thou shalt meditate therein day and night, that thou mayest observe to do according to all that is written therein: for then thou shalt make thy way prosperous, and then thou shalt have good success." (Joshua 1:8)

*   *   *

The Universal Law of Taking Physical Action

Great thoughts speak only to the thoughtful mind, but great actions speak to all mankind! The Buddha said, "One is not low because of birth nor does birth make one holy. Deeds alone make one low, deeds alone make one holy." (Sutta Nipata 136) One of the many ways the negative ego thought system sabotages your ability to manifest is by making you passive, indolent, and procrastinating. As Carl Gustav Jung, the famous Swiss psychologist, said, "Man's greatest sin is his indolence"! Don't putt off later what you can do now. He who hesitates is lost! Part of manifestation is owning your power and taking Physical action. This is called "Active Intelligence"! It is not enough to just own your personal power (first ray) and love yourself and others (second ray) . You also must take Physical action (third ray). Many get the opportunities they seek, however they don't take action when the opportunity arises! "There are risks and costs to a program of action, but they are far less than the long-range risks and costs of comfortable inaction!" (John F. Kennedy) In order to create Heaven individually within our own consciousness and collectively on Earth, we need to take Physical action! We are the hands and feet of GOD and the Masters on this Earthly plane. "We are all pencils in the hand of God," as Mother Teresa put it. "Mere brave speech without action is letting off useless steam." (Mahatma Gandhi) Remember the wisdom of Saint Germain as brought forth through Godfrey Ray King, "I am the presence of God in action this day!" May this be your new mantra!

*   *   *

The Universal Law of Temptation

What is temptation? Temptation is the negative ego trying to steer you away from the straight and narrow path. Temptation is the negative ego's inappropriate thinking and misinterpreting reality. Temptation is the negative ego trying to get you to indulge in negative emotions, trying to pull you into your lower-self, trying to a take the low road where GOD would always have you take the high road. Temptation is the negative ego trying to make you indulge in carnal sexuality where GOD would have you use sexuality only in service of unconditional love and in an appropriate and non-overindulging manner. It's the negative ego trying to make you follow the path of hedonism and overindulgence and pleasure seeking. GOD would guide you that there is a higher purpose to life than just pleasure seeking. Temptation is the negative ego guiding you to indulge in bad habits where GOD would guide you towards self-mastery, self-realization, and moderation in all things. Temptation is the negative ego guiding you to pollute your body, mind, feelings with things not of GOD, where GOD would guide you to maintain purity of consciousness on all levels. In Christianity they would refer to temptation as stemming from the devil or Satan which is nothing more than a symbol and metaphor for the negative ego. In Hinduism the negative ego would be called illusion or maya. In Western esoteric teachings it would be called glamour. When temptation occurs, the key is to pull your attention away from it. It can be done in your consciousness and/or by partaking in a different Physical action. It can be done through doing a positive affirmation or visualization, through prayer, through repeating the names of GOD, by just telling it to go away. It is always a process of denial and affirmation. An idle mind is the devil's workshop. The key to successful living is to keep your focus and attention always on GOD in thought, feeling, and action. There is no sin in temptation, it is acting on temptation that is the lesson. The key is, when you become conscious that you are indulging in the negative ego and/or temptation, just stop without judgement and with forgiveness. Perfection is not, not making mistakes. Perfection is not making conscious mistakes. GOD does not expect perfection even consciously. Even if we consciously give into the negative ego or temptation, it is not the end of the world. It is just a mistake and mistakes are okay. Righteousness in the eyes of GOD is trying. You must own your personal power. A lot of people have consciousness, but they do not have personal power. They are victims, they are conscious of it, and this makes it even worse. A true Spiritual Master has consciousness and 100% personal power, wisdom, and unconditional love to enforce his or her conscious discernments. Some people make the mistake of becoming aware they are giving in to temptation and then the negative ego says that you have already totally blown it, and now you might as well just continue. Do not compound a smaller mistake with a bigger one. All is forgiven by GOD. The key is forgiving yourself. As *A Course In Miracles* states, "My Salvation is up to me". GOD has already given us everything, the question is, will we give GOD to ourselves. We do this by choosing to not give into the negative ego and temptation, and if we do, to forgive ourselves, unconditionally love ourselves and learn from our mistakes. "No temptation has seized you except what is common to man. And God is faithful; he will not let you be tempted beyond what you can bear. But when you are tempted, he will also provide a way out so that you can stand up under it." (1 Corinthians 10:13 NIV)

*   *   *

The Universal Law of the Goddess

There was a time on Earth during the time of the ancient civilization of Lemuria which predated Atlantis when the God/Goddess energies were in perfect balance. However, when there was the first eating of the fruit from the "Tree of Good and Evil", what happened was that for the first time on Earth, man misused his free choice and thought out of harmony with GOD. This was the beginning of negative ego/fear-based thinking. It was this choice of fear, separation, selfishness, lower-self desire, conditional love, guilt, hurt, depression, and anger that also began the process of rejection and abuse of the Divine Mother and Goddess energies on Earth. It also began the process of mass consciousness on the Earth to identify with masculine energies over feminine energies. mind over heart! Thinking over intuition! Thinking over feeling! Thinking and science over Spirituality! Thinking, selfishness, and technology over anything in regard to Mother Earth and Nature! This caused an overidentification with the Patriarchy over the Matriarchy! Left brain became more important than right brain! Men began to control society and women were not seen as equals! Women were forced to become subservient and lesser class citizens. The cutting off of the feminine also cut off Spirituality to a great degree. It caused a total disconnection from Mother Earth, the Animal, Plant, and Mineral Kingdom. Even GOD was seen as being masculine. We were taught to call "Him" the Heavenly "Father". The Feminine aspect was seen as Mother Earth. In the New Age Movement there is a great focus on Spirituality but there is an overidentification with Heavenly energies and a lack of appreciation for the Material Face of GOD! There are millions of examples. The Divine Mother was completely rejected from Spirituality! The feminine path to GOD needs to be much more developed in people and Lightworkers around the globe to hence then find the proper God/Goddess balance that true Gods and Goddesses both want! The feminine path to GOD has been disowned. Lightworkers on Earth are extremely imbalanced. Their Spiritual Bodies are highly developed, but their bank accounts are not. Their Light Bodies are highly developed but their Love Bodies may not be equally as balanced! The Divine Mother and Goddess energy brings us not only a reconnection to our feeling nature but also the ability to ground our Spirituality. The Divine Mother and Goddess energies help us also to fully realize GOD through embodying God on the Earth. Well, women, of course, now have to be careful not to overidentify with the Goddess path and not become matriarchal in nature, feminist in the sense of anti-masculine, overemotional where we are victims of the Emotional Body, and negative ego mind. Women have to be careful to avoid being too right brain where they lose common sense or logic, and become too empathic. The true Goddess Path does not try to oppose the masculine path of GOD, but to just properly integrate it. The same is true of the masculine path of GOD. God Realization, the Divine Plan, and Integrated Ascension will not be achieved if the Divine Mother, the Goddess energies, the Lady Masters, and Mother Earth, Pan, the Nature Spirits, Plant Devas and Elementals are not brought back into their rightful Divine place within yourself and our society as a whole. No one on Earth will achieve true God Realization in the fullest sense of the term, which integrates all Four Faces of GOD (Spiritual, Mental, Emotional, and Material), if they don't fully embrace the masculine path of GOD and the feminine path of GOD! It is only then that you will know the "Wholness of GOD!"

        *   *   *

The Universal Law of the Holy Encounter

Every time we meet another person, it is a holy encounter. Each encounter with another person is, in reality, Christ meeting Christ, Buddha meeting Buddha, Atman meeting Atman, Eternal Self meeting Eternal Self, God meeting God. Every person we meet, whether we know him or not, is God visiting us in Physical form. This concept applies to the animal, plant and mineral kingdoms too. There is only one being in the universe, and that is God. So every encounter is indeed a holy encounter. See beyond the appearances of the Physical, Emotional and Mental Bodies and see the true core of every being. The world is a mirror of our own thinking. What we see in our Brothers and Sisters is, in truth, what we are seeing in ourselves. You cannot realize GOD unless you also see your brothers and sisters as God! We are all Gods whether we like it or not. We have no choice in this, because we didn't create ourselves. GOD did. This is a fact, and all negative ego thinking in the infinite universe will not change that truth! "Be not forgetful to entertain strangers: for thereby some have entertained angels unawares." (Hebrews 13:2)

        *   *   *

The Universal Law of the Holy Spirit

In some ways the Holy Spirit is the ultimate Spiritual Master, for it is the aspect that GOD created right out of Himself to, in essence, be the "answer" to all our challenges and lessons in life. GOD has divided Himself into three aspects. This is the Trinity of GOD, Christ, and the Holy Spirit, the Holy Spirit being the aspect of GOD that He has placed within us as the answer to all our problems. In truth, all problems are created by the negative ego or separative mind. All answers and solutions come from the Holy Spirit. "When you are brought before synagogues, rulers and authorities, do not worry about how you will defend yourselves or what you will say, for the Holy Spirit will teach you at that time what you should say." (Luke 12:11-12 NIV) The Holy Spirit speaks for the "Atonement" or the "At-One-Ment." To atone means to undo. Of the many gifts of the Holy Spirit and the infinite wisdom, knowledge, love and power it possesses, one of the most profound ones it has is its ability to undo past mistakes and negative interactions and situations. The Holy Spirit cannot only undo it in your subconscious and unconscious minds and auric field, it can also undo the effects that your mistakes may have caused to other people or other situations. There is no situation in life that it cannot undo or rebuild if you call upon it. There is no situation in life that it does not have the answer for. Call on GOD and the entire Godforce, however, don't forget to call on the Holy Spirit. The Holy Spirit is the ultimate Cosmic Master that GOD has placed inside of you to be the answer to all your challenges and lessons, and the ultimate power in the universe to undo obstacles in every aspect of life. This applies to the Physical Level, the Etheric Level, the Astral Level, the Mental Level, and the Spiritual Level. As long as your requests are sincere and pure, and are not negatively ego motivated, it will help you and it is literally the arm of GOD. Let's remember the words written down in the Holy Bible, "May the God of hope fill you with great joy and peace as you trust in Him, so that you may overflow with hope by the Power of the Holy Spirit." (Romans, 15:13) "And hope does not disappoint us because GOD has poured out his love into our hearts by the Holy Spirit whom he has given us." (Romans, 5:5)

*   *   *

The Universal Law of the Incredible Power of Ideas

Most people do not realize that they are literally an incarnation of God and have an aspect of God's Mind within them. This Mind is filled with the inspiration and creativity of God, if each person will use it. The power of one good idea can completely change and revolutionize the world! The power of one good idea can make you rich and successful. Most people do not realize and acknowledge what a rich resource they have within them. All of Creation began as a single thought in God's Consciousness. We have the same power to cause and create our reality as God does. We are in essence miniature Gods growing to be like God. Every single thing that has manifested on the Earth began as a thought. The Sistine Chapel of Michaelangelo began as a thought in his mind. Jesus raised the dead with the power of a thought. "When you are inspired by some great purpose, some extraordinary project, all your thoughts break their bonds; your mind transcends limitations, your consciousness expands in every direction, and you find yourself in a new, great and wonderful world. Dormant forces, faculties, talents become alive, and you discover yourself to be a greater person by far than you ever dreamed yourself to be!" (Patanjali) With the power of Your Mind, God's Mind, the

Masters' Minds, your Monadic Mind, your Higher Self Mind, and your Subconscious Mind (see *The Universal Law of Balancing and Integrating Your Four Minds*), do you realize how much creative thought, inspiration, and ideas can potentially flow through you every day? Write all your ideas down on paper, for the nature of the mind is very fleeting and if you don't write them down you will lose them as the mind floats off to another area of creativity and expression. God gives creative expression to the infinite universe through the power of His Mind. We give creative expression as incarnations of God to our lives through the power of our minds. Harness and utilize this power for it is a golden key to Realizing God, being happy, successful, and fulfilling your Spiritual mission on Earth!

*   *   *

The Universal Law of the Merkabah

The Merkabah is like a Body that surrounds the auric field of every person. Contrary to popular opinion, it is nothing that has to be consciously built by the person for it is automatically built in the process of evolution! The Merkabah is used for a number of things. One is greater protection of the energy fields. Another is as a means to travel in. It is a vehicle of light that operates automatically even if one is never trained consciously how to use it. When each person Soul travels at night, or even consciously Soul travels, they are in their Merkabah. It is not anything one has to consciously do for it happens automatically! The Merkabah changes its shape after each Initiation you take. Every person's Merkabah is different for its shape is created at Initiation according to the development of your consciousness. So, at each Initiation it changes to reflect the growth in your consciousness. There is no need to spin the Merkabah to clean your fields. Calling in the Platinum Net works much better. However, once in a while it is a good idea to ask for an alignment and clearing of the Merkabah. Part of the building of the Light Body is the anchoring of Higher Light Bodies one by one into the energy fields and the entire system, the Merkabah being the outermost body that surrounds all one's energy fields. The Merkabah is semi-permeable in nature and allows one's other Light Bodies to extend out as far as they are able while simultaneously still providing total protection. When one is sitting and not thinking, the Merkabah field extends like 10 to 50 feet outward. Depending on what you are thinking it extends out much farther. Potentially, as one expands in Spiritual evolution, the Merkabah field can extend infinitely. If one on Earth is an extremely highly advanced Master, an "Integrated Spiritual Master", and totally in integrity and transcending the negative ego to a very high degree, then it is possible for this Earthly Master to extend their Merkabah to a Universal Level! This is all governed by one's thinking process and the level and degree of one's Spiritual Leadership and Planetary World Service work! The Merkabah is indestructible and is created by God. Where the other Light Bodies can potentially get out of balance, the Merkabah does not. It also helps to channel the energies of the Light Bodies and is automatically programmed by God to function with all the codes, frequencies, functions, and wisdom of all the different Light Bodies at all 352 Levels of God! For those who are integrated and balanced as Spiritual Masters in total service of God and the Masters and pure of heart, the Merkabah can allow service work and lightwork to be done beyond one's level of Light Body integration at the discretion of God and the Masters; however, this can only take place if the person is truly operating as an "Integrated Spiritual Master"!

     *   *   *

The Universal Law of the Platinum Net

L iving on the Earth where there is so much negativity, it is essential to find tools to constantly clear your fields. The easiest way to do that is to call forth Melchizedek, the Mahatma, and Metatron, and ask for a Platinum Net. This Platinum Net will move through your Twelve-Body System and cleanse it of impurities. The color platinum is the highest color frequency available to the Earth. Upon request, the Platinum Net can be placed in all the doors, windows, and arch ways of your home and office. That way, every time you walk through a doorway or archway, you are immediately cleansed by the Platinum Net, and any and all negative energy is transformed by this net into the Higher Light Frequency of the Divine! It ensures the cleanliness of your auric fields, and also protects your home from any unwanted energies entering in! Simple but profound!

*   *   *

The Universal Law of the Potential Glamour of Spiritual Gifts

T his is indeed an interesting law we are about to discuss! There are an enormous number of people who have various kinds of Spiritual gifts that have been developed in this life or past lives which are wonderful! It is essential, however, to understand that just because someone has a Spiritual gift or Spiritual power in some area, it doesn't mean that they are a Spiritual Master or are integrated and skilled in other areas of their life. Lightworkers must be more Spiritually discerning and discriminating in regard to this! For example, someone can be a channel for the Ascended Masters and be completely run by the negative ego, a total emotional victim, and on a massive ego trip and path of self-aggrandizement, yet still at times bring forth beautiful channelings! Half the time these channels are not even channeling the Masters, they are channeling their own belief systems and calling it the Masters. This whole process is unconscious, of course. Or, another person may have written a very popular book that has made them famous, when the truth is, if you read the book with real Spiritual discernment and know the person, there is much negative ego contamination and the person is not even close to being any type of integrated Spiritual Master. Another example might be a person who has had past lives as one of the Disciples of Christ or some other great Saint or guru. Half the time people say it, it is total illusion and a massive ego trip and information they received from another contaminated external channel. Even if, however, this was true, the Masters care less for what you have done in the past as to what you are doing in this moment! Well, there are many, many examples, but I think you get the point! Well, in conclusion, in India they call these Spiritual gifts and/or Spiritual powers "Siddhas". There is nothing wrong with having Spiritual gifts or powers, however, don't make these gifts or power your goal or aim. If they come, so be it. If not, so be that. Let your goal be God Realization in an integrated and balanced manner. Also, do not put other people on pedestals and do not project powers, gifts, and levels of Spiritual mastery onto people just because they have a wonderful Spiritual gift in one or two areas of their life. Be Spiritually discerning and street smart on a Spiritual, Psychological, and Physical/Earthly Level! Let your Spiritual discernment not overestimate any given individual and not underestimate any given individual. Let your Spiritual discernment see on these four levels exactly as things are, in unconditional love as GOD would have you see!

*   *   *

The Universal Law of the Spiritual Purpose of Life

The negative ego's purpose in life is essentially hedonistic—it seeks pleasure, gratification of carnal desires, power in a top-dog sense, material wealth, and control over others rather than control over self. The Spirit's answer to this is the biblical statement, "For what profit is it to a man if he gains the whole world, and loses his own soul?" The Spiritual purpose of life is to achieve liberation from the cycle of rebirth, to realize God, to become an Integrated Full Spectrum Prism Ascended Master, and to be of service to humankind. The Spiritual purpose in life is also to be happy and to enjoy oneself, in balance with our Spiritual growth. Swami Sivananda uncovered the mystery of life. He is quoted as saying, "You have come to this Earth to attain spiritual perfection. You have come here to attain supreme and unalloyed bliss. The purpose of this human birth is the achievement of divine consciousness. The goal of life is self-realization!" His Holiness, Sai Baba, teaches, "The purpose of living is to achieve *the living in God.*"

*   *   *

The Universal Law of the Spoken Word

Those who are able to see with "inner vision" would see as do the Masters, that words are far more than they seem to be. Every single word has not only frequency of vibration but also, upon the Etheric realm, literally has weight, shape, form, color, and tone. Each and every word uttered is a power packed force of singular substance. When we string words together in sentences, particularly when formatted with Emotional and/or Mental Imagery, we, as human beings, harness and make manifest a great and dynamic powerhouse of force. "Thou shalt also decree a thing, and it shall be established unto thee: and the light shall shine upon thy ways." (Job 22:28) It is time for us all to be aware of the vital force and power of the spoken word, so this abundant energy is neither wasted in idleness, not worse, used unthinkingly and unintentionally to do harm. "Do not use poisonous words against anyone, for, words wound more fatally than even arrows." (Sai Baba) In point of fact, as a race in general, we speak far too much and think about what we are saying far too little. We all know from direct experience the impact hurtful words from others have had upon ourselves. We likewise have seen the effect our own negative and deleterious words have had upon our fellow human beings. As is written in the Holy Bible, "Not that which goes into the mouth defiles a man but that which comes out of his mouth, defiles him." Think before you speak! Preceding even this, meditate and attune with your Soul, monad, and Mighty I Am Presence before you even think. Mother Teresa said, "Before you speak, it is necessary for you to listen, for God speaks in the silence of the heart." This will align your motive and intent with that of GOD. The thoughts that then enter your being will be even of a higher order and the words that therefore follow these thoughts will be synchronistic with them. They will carry with them the shape, tone, color, and frequency of that which, for you, is the highest and best expression of GOD. Your words then will be an upliftment, not only to humanity, but also to every kingdom and evolution that exists upon the planet. "For verily I say unto you, That whosoever shall say unto this mountain, Be thou removed, and be thou cast into the sea; and shall not doubt in his heart, but shall believe that those things which he saith shall come to pass; he shall have whatsoever he saith." (Mark 11:23) "In the beginning was the word and the word was with GOD and the word was GOD." This is the force we wield with every single utterance we make! Ponder on this! Let us all choose our words wisely! "Thy word is a lamp unto my feet, and a light unto my path." (Psalms 119:105) "It is written that man shall not live by bread alone, but every word of God." (Jesus)

         *   *   *

The Universal Law of the Three Levels of Spiritual Vision

There are three levels of Spiritual vision. When most people think of Spiritual vision they think of someone being clairvoyant. Someone being able to see auras, Spiritual beings, and into the inner Spiritual worlds. Spiritual vision is not necessarily a sign for advanced Spiritual growth. Spiritual vision on this level is connected with the development of one's subconscious inner senses, not any superconscious level necessarily. There are people who are schizophrenic who are clairvoyant and see into the Astral world. It must be understood that there are thousand different degrees of Spiritual vision at this level. Everyone's clairvoyance is not the same. Some people can see into the Astral Plane, some into the Mental Plane, some into the Buddhic or Causal Plane, some into the Soul Plane, some into the Spiritual Plane. Some people can see one layer of the aura, another person two, another person three, and so on into infinitum. Some people can see into Chakras and other people can't. Some people can see Spirits and other people can't. Some people see lots of light and color, other people can see clearly the inner plane worlds. There is one thing that must be understood, and that is one cannot separate the development of consciousness from one's clairvoyance. How developed or undeveloped one is will totally affect one's clairvoyant abilities. This is because one's thoughts create one's reality, and this will act as a lens and filter for one's clairvoyance. It will attract and magnetize certain types of sight and repel other types. So, it is of the highest importance that every person develop their consciousness on a conscious, subconscious, and superconscious level, for that is what you are causing manifesting, creating, and filtering everything in your life through, every moment! Well, now the second type of vision is Physical vision. This is also a type of Spiritual vision for GOD is as much in the Physical Body and Material Universe as He is in the Heavenly Universe. Just as Spiritual clairvoyance can give important information about what is going on in and around one's reality, Physical vision gives equally important information. There are all kinds of things going on in one's Physical reality that gives all kinds of important Spiritual information. The appearance of any given person, their body language, the way they talk, the way they sound, the clothes they wear, their demeanor, their posture, their eyes, their stride, how they decorate their home, their desk, just to name a few. The third level of Spiritual vision is the most important level and profoundly affects the other two types of vision. As stated often before, we just don't see with our Physical eyes, we see with our minds. We also see with the images in our minds and through our feelings and emotions. We also see through not only our conscious minds, bur we see thought our subconscious minds. The last one is the kicker. For the subconscious mind is the storehouse of all our programming from all of this life and even past lives. So most people don't see in the Holy Instant, most people see through their past programming. This is a very profound statement. Take a moment and ponder on this! In this Holy Instant I am the Christ, you are the Christ, and we are all one with each other and one with God. In reality all else is illusion. This is why *A Course in Miracles* says, "Nothing real can be threatened. Nothing unreal exists. Herein lies the peace of God." You do not have to try and become God. You already are God *now*, in this Holy Instant. This third type of Spiritual vision profoundly affects the other two types of vision because a person's channeling and clairvoyance are filtered through the consciousness and/or subconscious programming of the person who has these abilities. This is why very

Psychologically disturbed individuals with these abilities are usually tuning into the Astral Plane and channeling Astral entities even though they have these gifts. Their consciousness attunes them to and attracts its level of understanding and development. The world, in truth, is actually a neutral screen and we each project our thoughts and programming onto this world, and we see, experience, and feel what we are projecting, but it all happens so fast we think it is coming from outside of ourselves. We give the meaning the world has for us. All the feelings and emotions we feel in relationship to the world and all people are coming from ourselves, not from anything outside of ourselves. Why? Because you either interpret life from your Spiritual Mind or your negative ego mind. This, not what is coming from outside of self, governs what you experience and how you feel in life. All meaning of the outside world comes from your interpretations, perception and belief system. It is not in the world, it is in your Psychological vision, perception, interpretation, programming and belief system. See *The Universal Law of Developing a Healthy Psychoepistemology*, *The Universal Law of Hypnosis*, and *The Universal Law of Subconscious Interference* to gain an understanding of the mechanics of Spiritual vision. For our purposes, however, other lenses are our religion, race, socioeconomic level, country and city we live in, schooling, parents, Spiritual psychology, philosophy, past life programming, subconscious programming, gender, profession, friends, political affiliation, education, astrological horoscope, numerological configuration, archetypal identification of the Twelve Major Archetypes, to name just a few. Adding all of these restricting factors of Spiritual vision, you can see now how much our Psychological vision affects our Physical vision, and that most people on Earth see life through one one-millionth of the lens that GOD is looking at life from. Does not the Bible speak of this when it says, "If people have the eyes to see and the ears to hear"? Everyone has eyes and ears, but most people cannot see or hear. This is because this Biblical verse is speaking of your Spiritual and Psychological eyes and ears, not just our Physical ones. The truth is, if Christ was to return to Earth he would not be known or recognized and would be completely rejected by the majority of the world. Most people in this world think they have excellent Spiritual vision and think they are seeing exactly what is going on. The truth is they do not have the slightest idea how their negative ego is controlling them, or how much their belief systems, philosophy, Psychoepistemology, subconscious programming, subpersonalities, Ray structure, Archetypes, Four-Body System identification, Horoscope, lens background, education, just to name a few, are restricting their vision. People cannot see their own blind spots and limitations so they do not think they are there. Heed this law! A Spiritual Psychologist sees a great many things that others do not see because of their training. An artist sees a great many things that others do not see in the realm of beauty. A clairvoyant sees many things that others do not see. What does this show us? Because of our training and focus in this life and past lives, we see through that which we have been trained in, and we have blind spots in areas we have not been trained in. It unlocks the key to understanding the unbelievably profound effect your psychology and consciousness has upon your vision and the effect it has on all channeling, clairvoyant and Spiritual work, as well as the extraordinary effect it even has upon your Physical vision of reality. If you truly want to realize GOD and have true Spiritual vision then you must do this at the highest possible level Psychologically and in your consciousness on the Spiritual level and on a Physical/Earthly level as well. The ideal is to develop an efficient perception of reality. One cannot do this without being balanced and integrated, Spiritually, Psychologically, and Physically. It is only then you can become a fully realized "Integrated Melchizedek/Christ/Buddha" on Earth.

*   *   *

The Universal Law of the Twelve Strands of DNA, the Biostratus, and the Super Genetic Super Helix

Normally we have two strands of DNA. The belief we once had twelve strands of DNA and Extraterrestrials in our ancient past came and took it away is an illusion. This never occurred and is a myth a great many Lightworkers have accepted as a fact! It never occurred! Yes, they have tampered and worked with the DNA, but they never reduced us from twelve strands to two! Secondly, a great many Lightworkers are trying to establish more than two strands of DNA. It is possible to establish twelve strands of DNA, however, this begins first on the Etheric Level! So, if you were medically tested it would not show up! It is only possible to physicalize up to seven strands. This is the limit that Earthly existence allows at this time. So, people going around saying they help physicalize all strands are, with no judgment, faulty in their understanding! Now Metatron in the *Keys of Enoch* refers to the anchoring and activation of the Super Genetic Super Helix as the anchoring and activation of "Biostratus"! To fully incorporate and physicalize the seven strands of Physicalized DNA and Biostratus, and anchor "new electrons" into one's energy field which you can request from Archangel Metatron, the person must become an "Integrated Spiritual Master." They will be given this if they ask for it—in a step by step graded process—if the High Level Initiate and Master on Earth is deemed worthy to receive it by the demonstration of Spiritual Mastery, Spiritual Leadership, and Grounding of their Spiritual Service Mission on Earth! This is the key!

*   *   *

The Universal Law of "Thou shall honor thy father and mother!"

This is the Fifth Commandment! This is a very wonderful and appropriate commandment in a literal sense ad bears heeding! In an esoteric sense, also all the fathers and mothers you have had in your past lives! Honor Mother Earth! Honor Father/Mother GOD! It is time to properly honor the Divine Mother and the Goddess energies! This commandment also means to honor not just the male Masters but also the female embodiment of the Mother, like Mother Mary, Quan Yin, and Isis, to name just a few! Honor Helios and Vesta, our Solar Divine Mother and Father! The same applies on a galactic, universal, multi-universal, and cosmic level! Honor GOD, Christ, and the Holy Spirit, the Holy Spirit being a more feminine aspect of creation! Honor the mother and father within self and/or yin and yang, feminine and masculine energies! It also means to learn to be a proper Spiritually balanced parent to your inner child! Honor thy father and mother!

*　　　　　　　　*　　　　　　　　*

The Universal Law of "Thou shall not be a false witness against thy neighbor!"

This is the Ninth Commandment. From an esoteric point of view, any time anyone is out of integrity or is dishonest with another person they are being a false witness! Any time you are out of integrity or dishonest with yourself you are being a false witness to self! Above all else, to thine own self be true!

*   *   *

The Universal Law of "Thou shall not commit adultery!"

This is the Seventh Commandment! The outer meaning is obvious! The esoteric meaning is to not commit adultery as well in your thoughts, feelings, and energy! Lust, pornography, carnal desire are all forms of adultery! When fantasizing sexually one must be very careful for all are GOD, and when you fantasize, your thoughts, feelings, and energy affect that person! Even if you don't commit adultery Physically, it is also possible to be doing it Mentally, Emotionally, and Energetically! Mental adultery is thinking or imaging about having sex with someone inappropriately, even if you don't do it Physically! Emotional adultery is not only doing it Mentally but doing so Emotionally as well. Energetic adultery is doing the same thing with your thoughts, images, feelings, and all your energy as well! Spiritual adultery might be someone who has not committed adultery Physically, but might be Soul traveling to the person and trying to have sexual contact out of body! Sounds strange but it can and does happen, and it is not Spiritually right! So, it is always important to keep your energies consistent on all levels! This means if you are not going to commit adultery on a Physical level, then don't do it as well on a Mental, Emotional, Energetic, Etheric, or Spiritual level either! It means always being decisive in life! Whatever you do on one level must be done on all levels consistently! You must be 100% decisive in all that you do on every level of your being! This is one of the keys to achieving God Realization!

*   *   *

The Universal Law of "Thou shall not covet thy neighbor's house, wife, man, servant and/or maid servant!"

This is the Tenth Commandment. The esoteric meaning of this is getting into the realm of Psychological coveting! Any time you are jealous, have envy, are competitive in an egotistical sense, you are also coveting! You want what they have, in a selfish way, and are not truly happy for them, as you would be for yourself! If everything is GOD and we each are incarnations of GOD, then when others achieve happiness and success, if you are in your Spiritual/Christ/Buddha Consciousness, then you should be totally happy for their success! Another example of coveting is anytime you are attached to something, be it a person or anything! You are coveting that thing for you want it too much! Turn your attachments into preferences!

*   *   *

The Universal Law of "Thou shall not have any other Gods before me!"

This is the first of the Ten Commandments given to Moses on Mt. Sinai by GOD. It has classically been interpreted in peoples' minds at the time as Physical Bodies. In this modern day and age this is much less prevalent. However, what is prevalent and much more "insidious" is another form of idol worship and false gods! It's the worship of "power, fame, money, greed, lust, attachment, lower-self desire, anger, selfishness, false pride, self-glory, materialism, vanity, egotism, overindulgence", to just name a few! These are much more dangerous false gods than physical idol worship ever was. Everything you make an attachment to instead of a strong preference is a false god and idol worship! There is nothing wrong with money, success, and material things. However, you must ask yourself what comes first, GOD or these things. What are your true motivations, not just consciously but also subconsciously? Are you really being honest with self? Do you seek GOD above all else? Do you have these things in proper perspective or do you want those things more than GOD! Whatever you put first in life is the God you worship! Some people make false gods out of people, out of their relationships, children, or friends! This was the whole story of the Abrahamic Initiation in the Bible. Who came first, GOD or is son Isaac? For a time, Abraham put his child before GOD! When finally forced to choose, he chose GOD first and then he did not have to kill his son! It is not that GOD will kill that which you put before Him, you will! Your own negative ego attachment and thinking will repel that which you want! Have you passed the "Abrahamic Initiation"? Does not the Bible say, "Seek ye the Kingdom of GOD and all things shall be added unto thee!" One of the keys to manifestation is to seek only GOD and GOD will be the only thing that manifests back! Make GOD your number one in life, and all things shall be added unto thee!

        *   *   *

The Universal Law of "Thou shall not make any graven images!"

This is the Second Commandment. The deeper esoteric meaning of this commandment is not just physical idol worship but the worship of materialism. Some people make graven images of the car, the physical appearance of others. It's the accumulation of material things above the importance of GOD and your Spiritual Path! The overemphasis on appearances! Judging people by their looks, and not seeing every person as the God/Christ/Buddha. In truth, any form of materialism and getting caught up in appearances and glamour, instead of seeing the truth and essence, is what this commandment and law speaks to.

*   *   *

The Universal Law of "Thou shall not murder!"

This is the Sixth Commandment! The overt meaning of this lesson is obvious! However, killing can also occur on much more subtle levels as well! This is what the esoteric meaning has to do with. For example, when we as the people of this planet abuse the Earth by dumping toxic wastes, polluting rivers, lakes, oceans, cutting down the rain forests, and creating holes in the ozone layer, we are killing the Earth by doing so! This commandment and law has application in not killing even insects or bugs if they are not invading your house! Also, on the Mental and Emotional Level, do not kill thoughts of GOD in your own heart! Jesus said, "You have heard it said, you shall not kill. But those who keep murderous thoughts in their minds are also to blame. You must be able to forgive whoever has made you angry." Do not kill your connection to Spirit by getting lost in glamour, illusion, maya, and negative ego thinking and feeling. Do not kill in relationships by being attacking and hurtful which can kill the trust, kill unconditional love, and friendships! Do not kill self through abusive habits such as smoking, alcohol abuse, or drug addiction! Do not kill by misusing your personal power in an abusive way! Do not kill your feelings and emotions through numbing things as a method to avoid pain. Learn to master your feelings and emotions, yes, but also learn to properly integrate them!

*   *   *

The Universal Law of "Thou shall not steal!"

This is the Eighth Commandment. The esoteric understanding of this law focuses not just upon the stealing of material things, but rather the stealing of thoughts, ideas, feelings, or energy from others! This happens all the time in the world! A person has an idea for an invention and another person steals it. People read books or go to workshops and then claim the information as their own and don't give credit! This is a very subtle and tricky issue! People steal energy from other people! People also Emotionally steal from each other. Using people Emotionally for an ulterior motive happens all the time! People can steal from each other Spiritually or Physically as well. People with Psychic or Spiritual gifts might read a person's mind without their permission. They may try to get certain information without their permission! This is stealing!

*   *   *

The Universal Law of "Thou shall not take the Lord's Name in vain!"

This is the Fourth Commandment. The overt meaning of course is to not misuse GOD's name in how you speak! There are all kinds of cussing and expressions that people use that are not the proper use of GOD's name! The esoteric meaning takes this to an even deeper level. Do not also use any incarnations of the names of GOD in vain either, like the name of Jesus or others like it. GOD's name is a mantra and it is holy, and all His incarnations are holy as well! This commandment and law also speaks to the "Power of the Spoken Word" and how important it is to carefully monitor and control every word that comes out of our mouth. For we are Gods in truth and our words have power! This commandment also applies to people's names in vain, for all people are incarnations of GOD as well! Do not, in truth, use any name of anything in GOD's Infinite Universe in vain, for GOD incarnates and lives within all beings! So in truth, any cursing, swearing, and attacking, using a person's name or at a person's name, is the breaking of this commandment as well from this esoteric understanding! For everything that is named is in truth an incarnation of GOD, for all substance is made of GOD and we live and move and have our being in GOD, and we in truth are incarnations of GOD who are in the process of fully realizing GOD!

$$*\qquad\qquad *\qquad\qquad *$$

The Universal Law of "Thou shall remember the Sabbath Day and keep it holy!"

Classically it has been thought to mean to take one day off and not work and have one Holy Day for GOD! The esoteric meaning of this lesson is that people in life get very busy and involved with third dimensional reality and life! This law is a reminder to not get so caught up in life that you lose remembrance of the purpose of why you are doing all that you do! Keeping the Sabbath is to remind us to remember that everything that happens is a Spiritual test and lesson! In getting involved with all that goes on in life, this can be forgotten in a heartbeat! So keep the Sabbath burning at all times in the "Altar of your own Heart", so you always remember the reason and purpose of what you are manifesting in your every thought, word, and deed!

*　　　　　　　*　　　　　　　*

The Universal Law of Transcending Armageddon within Self and Society

Few people have ever thought of Armageddon occurring within themselves, but Armageddon couldn't happen on a Planetary Level if it was not first happening within the consciousness of the people of the Earth. In truth, one of the main purposes of life is to transcend Armageddon Consciousness within self and within the Planet as a whole.

So what is Armageddon Consciousness within self? It is the battle within
every person between negative ego thinking and Christ/Buddha thinking,
between the lower self and Higher Self within each person's consciousness.
In Christian terminology, it is the battle between Satan, Lucifer and/or the
devil, and the Christ. In Buddhism, it is the battle between truth and
ignorance, and in Hinduism, it is the battle between Brahma, Vishnu, and
Shiva, and the forces of illusion. In laymen's terms, it is the battle between
good and evil, evil being nothing more than an extreme case of negative
thinking. The devil is just a metaphor for the negative ego or separative
mind. Now, in truth, the negative ego and its thought system do not even
exist. It's illusion. So, the Battle of Armageddon is the battle in your own
consciousness every moment of your life as to if you are going to listen to
the Christ/Buddha interpretation of every situation of life, or the negative
ego interpretation of life. Our thoughts create our reality. Think with your
negative ego mind and you will have negative emotions. Think with your
Christ Mind and you will create Christed feelings. So, understanding this,
we see that transcending Armageddon Consciousness is nothing more
than transcending the negative ego duality within self! Once you transcend Armageddon within self, you will find inner peace. It is not possible
to have peace in the world, if people don't have inner peace. The first step
is gaining a right relationship to self and a right relationship to GOD, and
gaining inner peace within self. The second step is then forming peaceful
unconditional loving and harmonious relationships with your spouse,
children, parents, friends, and so on. Doing this you will become a beacon
of light, love, and wisdom to the world. If everyone would practice this
within themselves, we would have peace on the planet. On a planetary
level, World War I was the first Armageddon. World War II was the second Armageddon.! We warned against prophets of doom. Some are
unconsciously holding on to an old thought form. Others are consciously
or unconsciously doing this to achieve power over others by creating fear.
There won't be another war of this kind! Fortunately, we don't have that
many wars going on on the planet. Unfortunately, there still is a great lack

of unconditional love and Christ/Buddha Consciousness between the nations of the Earth and the people of the Earth. So it is now time to transcend the Psychological level of Armageddon Consciousness, not just the Physical violence level. And this begins with each person doing this within self, and demonstrating this example! Well, it must be understood that the Battle of Armageddon occurs not only in GOD's Infinite Physical Universe—on Earth, the Orion wars and other galactic battles—but occurs on the Inner Plane or Inner Dimensions as well. Those who have Physically died from this planet or other planets and live on the Astral or Mental Plane are still in a battle between their lower self and Higher Self. Just because you Physically died does not mean the Battle of Armageddon is over. This is why suicide is not an escape from one's lessons, in truth. The same lessons you have not mastered on this side, will continue on the other side. Even in Spiritual dimensions of reality, the negative ego can still manifest. The reason this is the case is that GOD created all His Sons and Daughters throughout the Infinite Universe with free choice and free will. We are the only beings who can create a will separate from GOD's which is the will of the negative ego as opposed to GOD's Will. So GOD didn't create negative ego, people did with the misuse of their free choice. As *A Course in Miracles* says in its introduction, "Nothing real can be threatened. Nothing unreal exists. Herein lies the Peace of GOD." The ultimate goal of GOD's Creation is to end Armageddon Consciousness within every Son and Daughter, within every Planet, every Solar System, every Galaxy, within every Universe, every Multiuniverse, and within every Dimension in GOD's Infinite Body. And be assured, Victory is ours! For could GOD and GOD's Creation lose this battle with the forces of illusion that don't even really exist, in truth? Of course not! All we are fighting is the illusion of negative ego thinking, which is nothing more than a paper tiger! The outcome for all Souls in this journey is inevitably a return to the Godhead. So be of good cheer, for the battle is as good as won!

*　　　　*　　　　*

The Universal Law of Transcending Duality

As for those who seek the transcendental reality, without name, without form, contemplating the Unmanifested, beyond the reach of thought and of feeling, with their senses subdued and mind serene and striving for the good of all beings, they too will verily come unto me! (*Bhagavad-Gita*) Transcending duality is one of the key teachings of all Eastern religions. Duality could be another way to describe negative ego. One of the clearest ways of understanding how the negative ego works has to do with the understanding that the negative ego has an upper and lower side to it. They are like two sides of a coin. If you get caught on one side of the coin, you will also unavoidably get caught on the other side of the coin. The negative ego reality offers you only an either/or option. Love or fear, holding grudges or holding the thought of forgiveness, guilt or innocence and so forth. We can't allow ourselves to flip back and forth between the two. The negative ego *wants* us to be caught in duality. We need to transcend the whole system! This is the only way to achieve true Christ Consciousness and inner peace! To transcend negative ego thinking you transcend both sides of the negative ego, both upper and lower. As the Bible says, "After pride cometh the fall." You must learn to laugh both sides off the stage. This is called transcendence. This is a way of thinking that transcends this state of consciousness. So the key lies in the transcendence of duality. Krishna spoke of this in the *Bhagavad-Gita*. He would counsel us to maintain even-mindedness, equanimity, peace, joy and love at all times, regardless of profit or loss, pleasure of pain, sickness or health, victory or defeat, praise or criticism, good weather or bad weather. It is fine to have preferences, but if it isn't realized, we can still have joy and inner peace. This is the secret to God Realization. And this way of thinking allows us to remain in inner peace regardless of what is going on outside of self. It is a state of consciousness that is unaffected by the turmoil of the world or the negativity of others. Djwhal Khul has called this state of consciousness Divine Indifference. Others have named it Involved Detachment. In essence, it is a state that transcends duality! Lower forms of consciousness focus on duality and polarity. When we move into fully realized consciousness, we use our Christ Consciousness or Buddha Consciousness, and this can help us transcend dualistic thinking while we remain fully involved with life! The Christ Consciousness allows us to be unceasingly the same, always in our power, always loving, always happy, always even-minded, always with equanimity, and always forgiving, regardless of the fluctuation of the dualities of life. This is the Consciousness of the God Self. This allows us to remain the same whether people praise us or vilify us. This is possible because the negative ego does not become engaged. The storms of outer life do not affect the stability and even-mindedness of our thinking process. "Let the wave of memory, the storm of desire, the fire of emotion, pass through without affecting your equanimity." (Sai Baba) It is not what is going on outside life that should be our concern, but rather our inner attitude toward what is going on. Everything in life is perception, interpretation, and our belief system! Our salvation is not up to God, it's up to us. God has given us everything from the beginning. The question is whether we will give ourselves salvation by releasing our negative ego completely and fully embracing Christ Consciousness. The process is very simple! Every time a negative ego thought or emotion comes up in your consciousness push it out of your mind and replace it with the Christ Consciousness attitude and antidote. By not giving energy or water, so to speak, to that weed it will die within three weeks time. That is how long it takes to cement in a new habit into the subconscious mind. By not giving water to negative ego thinking and emotions and watering Christ Consciousness attitudes and feelings they expand and grow, and soon you have a habit of Christed thinking and feeling and a habit of being in inner peace and joyous all the time. The happiness you seek is an attitude and perspective that is attached to nothing outside of self, and has nothing to do with another person. Change your thoughts and you change your life, for it is your thoughts that create your reality, your emotions, your behavior, and what you attract and magnetize into your life! As the Bible says, "Be ye transformed by the renewal of the mind." "Let this mind be in you that was in Christ Jesus." Heed this Law! The decision you make this day to transcend the negative ego may be the single most important decision you will ever make in your entire life! "As long as we think we are the ego, we feel attached and fall into sorrow. But realize that you are the Self, the Lord of Life, and you will be freed from sorrow. When you realize that you are the Self, Supreme Source of Light, Supreme Source of Love, you transcend the duality of life and enter into the unitive state!" (The Upanishads)

*   *   *

The Universal Law of Truth

What is truth? There is a common believe in this world that truth is relative! Now from a certain lens this is true, however, from a more Full Spectrum Prism Consciousness Perspective and Higher Perspective this is totally not true! From a singular lens, there is such a thing as relative truth! We are all aware of the sayings, "Beauty is in the eye of the beholder!" or, "In matters of taste there is not dispute!" Many disagreements that people have are not because one is right and one is wrong, but is because they are seeing the situation through different lenses, because of maybe race, creed, color, or religion. Most people on Earth think everything they think or say is the truth! This is because our thoughts create our reality and even if we think with our negative ego mind or from a limited lens perspective it feels totally 100% true to us! Many people base truth on how they "feel" and in truth this is not a good barometer of truth for our feelings are created by our mind and the mind is capable of thinking from the negative ego/fear based/separative aspect or the Spiritual/Christ/Buddha /God Aspect. So they may feel angry and that is their truth! This may be their personal truth, however, it is truth based on being victimized by the negative ego mind, and is not the "Higher Truth" based on God's Reality of Truth! It is "Higher Truth" that often transcends the limited perspectives of truth that people hold to be true! The only way to be aligned with real "Truth" is to transcend all negative ego/fear based/ separative and imbalanced thinking! Then you can see with Spiritual/Christ/Buddha/God eyes and hence be aligned with the "Higher Truth of God!" Most people don't realize that we do not see with our Physical eyes only, but our minds. It is consciousness that governs perception! Truth is a very tricky thing, for integration, balance, level of development, full spectrum prism perspective, the entire context of situation must be considered! However, there are certain principles we hold that are what might be called "Eternal Truths," and this is, in truth, what people should base their lives upon! For example, "God equals man minus ego! Perfect Love casts out fear! Judge not that ye not be Judged! Love the Lord Thy God with all thy Heart and Soul and Mind and Might and love thy neighbor as you love thyself! All suffering comes from attachment! All suffering comes from wrong points of view! The Lord thy God is One!" Allow other people to have their truth, even if it is wrong in your opinion! Many people hold truths in one aspect of their being, but do not manifest in another. This is not truth but disintegration and fragmentation! A person may hold a truth on a conscious level that jealousy and competition is of the negative ego, yet on a subconscious level or in their behavior that is what they are doing! Part of seeking truth is being honest with your self and truly examining your motives for doing all that you do! Part of seeking truth is not defending the negative ego or having a need to defend your truth or having to convince others of following your truth! To do so is a sure sign one is insecure about their truth! If not this the negative ego misusing that truth, to proselytize and force one's truth on another! Often it is better to just be your truth and be the example! Only share your truth, where it is welcome and wanted! Also be Spiritually discerning about who you share your truth with for truth is a very Spiritually precious thing. As the Bible says, "Don't cast your pearls to swine," unconscious souls, who do not appreciate it or will stamp all over it! The most important thing is to always live your truth! For a truth not lived is not really a truth at all. It is an unlived, unbreathed, mental concept! A truth becomes a real truth not only by thinking it, feeling the truth of it, but most importantly by being it, demonstrating it, living it, practicing the presence of it, and fully embodying it in all ways and all things as God would have you do this! "Knowledge that is not put into practice is like food that is not digested." (Sai Baba) It is of the highest importance that we practice what we preach for as we all know actions speak louder than words! It is through demonstrating truth to the best of our ability in our daily lives that truth is "Realized" and we become Living Embodiments of that Integrated and Balanced God Truth on Earth! As the Buddha said, "Follow the truth of the way. Reflect upon it. Make it your own. Live it. It will always sustain you!" "God alone is truth and everything else is transitory and illusory." (Mahatma Gandhi) And Jesus said, "I am the way and the truth and the life. No one come to the father except through me." (John 14:6 NIV)

*   *   *

The Universal Law of Turning the Other Cheek

Master Jesus said, "It has been said, an eye for an eye, and a tooth for a tooth. But I say, do not resist evil. But whosoever smites you on your right cheek, turn to him the other also!" When he said those words, he was speaking both, in a Psychological and Physical sense. A Spiritual Master does not attack back because they also do not allow themselves to become defensive. They are so fully established in their Personal Power, Self-Love, Self-Worth, Wholeness, Christ/Buddha Consciousness, Transcendence of negative ego consciousness, Attunement to GOD, Compassion, Wisdom and Understanding, Protection, and being a Cause of their reality and not an Effect, that when the attack or criticism comes, it just bounces off them like a rubber pillow, and is not allowed to implant itself in the subconscious mind or Emotional Body. The Spiritual Master, understanding that such behavior stems from fear and negative ego control, has compassion, understanding and detachment so as to again respond rather than react and to set a better example. If one were to react, one would be in a sense catching the Psychological disease of the other instead of setting the healthy example. The Spiritual Path is always taking the high road and not the low road. The Spiritual Path is always setting the Christ/Buddha example, not lowering oneself to the level of the lower-self and negative ego. A Spiritual Master is not victimized in the slightest by turning the other cheek. In truth, just the opposite takes place; they are fully empowered because they are staying attuned to GOD and maintaining their Realization of GOD. "A person pure of heart has the strength of ten." In truth, one is a victim when they attack back or allow themselves to be victimized in the first place. This is not to say that at times it is not appropriate to respond to a person who attacks you Psychologically or Physically. The response of the Spiritual Master would always be from a very calm, rational, detached, unconditionally loving, forgiving, compassionate state of consciousness. When attacked Physically, the Spiritual Master turns the other cheek Psychologically and Physically and then walks out the door in total peace, unconditional love and forgiveness. Lord Buddha said, "The worse of the two is he who, when abused, retaliates. One who does not retaliate wins a battle hard to win." (Samyutta Nikaya I, 162) We opened this paragraph with the words of Master Jesus, and we shall seal it thusly, "And if any man sues you at the law, and takes away your coat, let him have your cloak also!"

*   *   *

The Universal Law of Twilight Masters and Cults

A Twilight Master is a Lightworker that is working for both the light and the dark side of life. A Lightworker who is not clear on a personality or Psychological level or in terms of the negative ego often attracts a member of the Dark Brotherhood who overshadows him/her in a way similar to what the Ascended Masters do. Those who are truly full-fledged Twilight Masters, under the domination of the negative ego and opened enough to the forces of darkness to create a very deep and intense gray-zone, are generally masters that are not simply a bit lost and operating out of the subconscious mind, but are consciously and willingly aligning themselves with impure motive. Once this is done, they will do anything and everything in their power to keep their students or 'followers' under their spell. Giving forth mixed messages becomes their greatest tool, both in attracting the student to them and in keeping the ones that they have! To clarify, just because a person is run by their negative ego to a certain extent doesn't mean they are a Twilight Master. The Twilight Master is the next step, so to speak, in the wrong direction and develops when they actually are manipulating people in a negative sense to serve their lower self. These are people who are often Physically attractive and have enormous charisma and even brilliance in a certain Spiritual or Psychological teaching. This is where Lightworkers are most susceptible to getting sucked in. Sometimes it is the glamour of psychic abilities that sucks Lightworkers in. Sometimes it is magician-like Psychological abilities or hypnotic-like abilities that pull people in. Other times still it is profound Spiritual teachings, even of the Ascended Masters or other ancient truths that the Twilight Master uses to snag impressionable and undiscerning Lightworkers. The best and most effective method of recognizing a Twilight Master is first and foremost by being as clear as you possibly can within your own self. The second thing you need to do is to be aware that

Twilight Masters are indeed out there, and do seek to feed off of your own energy fields. It is very easy to become blinded by the light, so to speak, and to think that everyone who uses similar terms, language, expressions as you do is upon the path of Ascension into the center of Light, Love and Power of Source. Although that may be their ultimate destiny, be forewarned that there are many who have taken paths of divergence! Do not judge them, however, do not align with them. When the negative ego, personality, and the need to control is in evidence, stay focused upon your own Integrated Ascension and you will be invulnerable. Do not let them seduce you through the offering of some glamorous project, or by believing they will initiate you into some secret teaching that they alone are privy to. Be aware that a Twilight Master literally gets their energy through zapping into the energy field of another who is firmly rooted within the continuous flow of light, love, power and wisdom. In fact, Twilight Masters can be seen as one of GOD's more creative ways to test an initiates' power of discernment. The equality of discernment and discrimination is one that we need at every step of our journey. Recognize individuals for what they *are*, and not for what they *say* they are. Didn't the Bible warn us, "Be aware of false prophets, who come to you in sheep's clothing, but inwardly are ravening wolves. You shall know them by their fruits." Heed those words! Master Jesus also said, "No man can serve two masters: for either he shall hate the one and love the other, or else he will hold to the one and despise the other. You cannot serve God and mammon." "Choose who ye shall serve," as *A Course In Miracles* says.

*   *   *

The Universal Law of Unconditional Love

Mahatma Gandhi said, "When another person's welfare means more to you than your own, when even his life means more to you than your own, only then can you say you love. Anything else is just business, give and take!" Sai Baba teaches that love is the most important Spiritual practice of all. He says that the way to live is to "start the day with love, fill the day with love, spend the day with love and end the day with love—for this is the way to God." And St. Francis of Assisi is quoted as saying, "It is in giving love that we receive love!" The only condition for loving is to love without conditions! So the key is to love unconditionally—without conditions, judgements, attachments, boundaries, restrictions or attitudes. Jesus revealed, "By this shall all men know you are my disciples, if ye have love one to another." He also said, "The whole law could be summed up as 'Love the Lord thy God with all your heart and soul and mind and might and love your neighbor as you love yourself.'" God would always have us practice unconditional love, the rationale for this being that each person, in reality, is an expression of the One Spirit even if their thoughts, feelings, and behavior are not demonstrating that. As Jesus said, "Love your enemies." It is our lesson to be bigger, to practice innocent perception and forgiveness, for what we give is what we get back. If we want God, we must give God, otherwise we will not realize Him. Everyone is God, however, not everyone realizes God in thought, feeling, and action. Earth is a school to practice realizing God in our daily life. "Love walks the golden trail that leads to God," as Paramahansa Yogananda said. "A new commandment I give to you, that you love one another as I have loved you." (Jesus) Conditional love means that another person must meet some requirement to deserve our love. Unconditional means loving one another unconditionally—without any conditions, with the understanding that every mineral, every animal, plant and human being is an incarnation of God. "Love seeks no reward; Love is its own reward. Man loves because he is love. He seeks joy, for he is joy. He thirsts for God, for he is composed of God, and he cannot exist without him." (Sai Baba) One of the basic principles of *A Course in Miracles* is to give up our attack thoughts. Make a vow to yourself and God never to attack even when you are being attacked by others. Go to any lengths to maintain an attitude of love no matter how you are attacked or ripped off. This is not to say that you don't need to stand up for yourself and stand in your own power. But do it with tough love. It is tied in with the quality of humility and what Christ said about turning the other cheek and loving your enemies. It also relates to seeing everything through your Christ Mind. We are either loving or attacking—there are no neutral thoughts. When we are demonstrating conditional love, we are unconsciously attacking, and the other person experiences that attack on an energetic level. It is like an arrow piercing his aura. If he is weak or a victim, this can affect him quite adversely. We must not forget that all minds are joined. Our thoughts are not contained in our Physical Bodies as though behind a fence. The second we think about another person, whether in a positive or negative way, that thought or feeling hits his energy field. When we indulge in attack thoughts, then by the law of karma we operate within our own minds and live in fear. If we attack, we will be fearful, because we will expect other people to attack us, which makes us afraid. If we live in love, then by the law of karma we will expect love in return, and have nothing to fear. Conditional love is of the ego. Unconditional love is God. In every situation of life we can ask ourselves, "Do I want God or my ego in this situation?" Choose once again! Let's remember the words of Mother Teresa, "Spread love everywhere you go: first of all in your own house. Give love to your children, to your wife or husband, to a next door neighbor... Let no one ever come to you without leaving better and happier. Be the living expression of God's kindness; kindness in your face, kindness in your eyes, kindness in your smile, kindness in your warm greeting." May her wisdom inspire each of us to become a living embodiment of Unconditional Love.

"Love is patient, love is kind. It does not envy, it does not boast, it is not proud. It is not rude, it is not self-seeking, it is not easily angered, it keeps no record of wrongs. Love does not delight in evil but rejoices in the truth. [Love] always protects, always trusts, always hopes, always preserves." (1 Corinthians 13:4-7 NIV)

*   *   *

The Universal Law of Unconditional Self-Love and Self-Worth

The Universal Mind channel Paul Solomon said, "If there is a panacea or cure-all to life, it is self-love." "Love is a medicine for the sickness of the world; a prescription often given, too rarely taken." (Karl A. Menninger) The most important relationship in our lives is our relationship to ourselves. If we are wrong with ourselves, we will be wrong with all other relationships. If we are off center in ourselves, how can we be on center with others? Self-love begins with the understanding that there are two types of love in the world: conditional love and unconditional love. Do you love yourself conditionally or unconditionally? Unconditional self-love is based on the understanding that we have worth and we are lovable because God created us. We are sons and daughters of God, and God doesn't make junk. If we don't have worth, then God doesn't have worth. In other words, our worth and lovableness are a Spiritual inheritance. But the ego says our worth is based on meeting certain conditions. We have to have a certain kind of Physical Body, have to go to college and so forth. Those are for sure noble goals to strive for, however, they have nothing to do with your self-love and self-worth. Self-love and self-worth come from who we are, not what we do. It's our Spiritual inheritance. Self-worth is enhanced by focusing on your victories instead of your defeats. It also is very important to compare yourself only with yourself. Do not compare yourself with others, for each of us carries within us a special puzzle piece of God's plan. So we are totally unique and worthy! There are no conditions we have to meet. We can do everything in our lives right or everything wrong, and our worth and lovableness are the same. The point is that there is a difference between the Soul and behavior. The Soul is always lovable and worthy, the behavior may not always be so. No matter what you have done, you are a child of God and hence are worthy and lovable. We need to love ourselves as God loves us—unconditionally. Jesus said, "You shall love your neighbor as yourself." Love yourself! We also need to learn to allow ourselves to feel God's love. God's love is like the sun. It is always shining. It is just a matter of whether we are going to give ourselves permission to step out of the darkness to receive it. Never forget, our true identity is the Christ, the Buddha, the Atman, the Eternal Self. It is only the ego's false, negative, pessimistic interpretation of us that makes us feel unworthy and unlovable. "Ye are Gods and know it not," as the Bible reveals. If you don't have unconditional self-love within yourself, then automatically you end up seeking it outside yourself. Love is a survival need; children in institutions have been known to die from lack of love. The ideal is to give love to yourself and to allow yourself to receive God's unchanging, unconditional love. If you don't do this, you end up seeking love, approval, and acceptance from other people. But this puts you in a compromised position because other people become your programmers and the creators of your reality. Your worth is then in their hands! Do you want other people to hold this power over you? Ideally, you will give yourself so much love, and allow yourself to feel so much of God's love, that you will go into each day feeling totally powerful and totally loved before you encounter another human being. Now, since one of the single most important Spiritual qualities to develop in life is unconditional self-love and self-worth, here is now a very practical program to achieving and/or increasing your present unconditional self-love and self-worth to the highest level possible. First, you must own your 100% personal power, unconditional love, and wisdom in life at all times. See *The Universal Law of Balancing and Integrating the Three-Fold Flame*. Secondly, you need to learn to parent your inner child properly, with firmness and love. See *The Universal Law of Inner and Outer Spiritual Parenting*. Thirdly, there are two levels or two kinds of unconditional self-love and self-worth—the essence level and the form level. The essence level being that you are unconditionally lovable and have worth because GOD created you, and you are a child of GOD! The form level being our behavior and realization and conscious demonstration of our Godliness. You cannot develop true unconditional self-love and self-worth unless you work on both levels! Righteousness in the eyes of God is trying. Even if you are making mistakes, this is fine with GOD as long as you are trying to practice the Presence of GOD in your daily life. We all know how the negative ego mind can turn gold into garbage. Even though, in truth, from GOD's objective perspective you are doing wonderfully and GOD and your own Mighty I Am Presence are totally pleased with your progress and efforts, your own negative ego is having you "forget" all of your successes and efforts on a form level. Fourthly, recognize that everything that happens in life is just a lesson and not a sin. See *The Universal Law of Everything in Life Being a Spiritual Lesson, Teaching, and Challenge*. Fifthly, learn to turn lemons into lemonade—the Science of Spiritual Alchemy. See *The Universal Law of Spiritual Alchemy*. Sixthly, recognize that just as we are a Spiritual parent for our inner child and/or inner self, GOD and our Mighty I Am Presence and Higher Selves are our Spiritual parents. This way you unconditionally love your inner child and self, and GOD, Christ, the Holy Spirit, your Mighty I Am Presence and Higher Self unconditionally love you. Lastly, maintain your Spiritual vigilance and Golden Bubble of Protection at all times around yourself. See *The Universal Law of Protection*. Follow these simple steps and you shall develop 100% self-love and self-worth! "To love is to return to a home we never left, to remember who we are." (Sam Keen)

*   *   *

The Universal Law of Working with the Ascension Seats

C all to the Cosmic and Planetary Ascended Masters to be taken in your Soul Body or Spiritual Body in a bi-located sense to the various Ascension Seats. The working with these Ascension Seats will literally accelerate your Ascension and Initiation Process a thousand fold if you work with them on any kind of regular basis. To travel to these Ascension Seats is as simple as calling to your own Mighty I Am Presence or the Inner Plane Ascended Master of your choice to be taken there, and you immediately will be! You will also immediately feel the downpouring of Spiritual current. There are not only Planetary Ascension Seats, but also Solar, Galactic, Universal, Multi-Universal, and Cosmic Ones. And if this were not enough, it is even possible to request that the Cosmic and Planetary Masters anchor and activate these Ascension Seats into your actual Physical home! That way you actually live and sleep in the Ascension Seats 24 hours a day, without having to go anywhere! Ask and you shall receive—if it's earned by demonstrating mastery on all levels and service work! That's law!

*   *   *

My Spiritual Mission and Purpose

by
Dr. Joshua David Stone

My Spiritual mission and purpose is a multifaceted process. Spirit and the inner plane Ascended Masters have asked myself and Wistancia (married since 1998), to anchor onto the Earth an inner plane Ashram and Spiritual/Psychological/Physical/Earthly Teaching and Healing Academy! This Academy is called the Melchizedek Synthesis Light Academy! We are overlighted in this mission by Melchizedek, the Mahatma, Archangel Metatron, the Inner Plane Ascended Master Djwhal Khul, Sananda and a collective core group of approximately one million inner plane Ascended Masters and Archangels and Angels, Elohim Masters, and Christed Extraterrestrial Masters who I like to call the "Collective Core Group." Some of these Masters, besides the ones I mentioned, are the Divine Mother, Archangel Michael, Archangel Gabriel, Sai Baba, Vywamus, the Lord of Arcturus, Lord Buddha, Lord Maitreya, Mother Mary, Quan Yin, El Morya, Kuthumi, Serapis Bey, Paul the Venetian, Master Hilarion, Lady Portia and Saint Germain, and a great many others who we like to call the "Core Group"!

I have also been asked by the inner plane Ascended Master Djwhal Khul, who wrote the Alice Bailey books and was also involved in the

Theosophical Movement, to take over his inner plane Ashram in the not too distant future when he moves on to his next Cosmic Position.

Djwhal holds Spiritual Leadership over what is called the inner plane Second Ray Synthesis Ashram. On the inner plane the Second Ray Department is a gigantic three story building complex with vast gardens.

The Ascended Master Djwhal Khul runs the first floor of the Second Ray Department in the Spiritual Hierarchy. Master Kuthumi, the Chohan of the Second Ray, runs the second floor. Lord Maitreya the Planetary Christ, runs the third floor! When Djwhal Khul leaves for his next Cosmic Position, I will be taking over this first floor Department. The Second Ray Department is focused on the "Spiritual Education" of all lightworkers on Earth and is the Planetary Ray of the Love/Wisdom of God. What is unique, however, about the Synthesis Ashram is that it has a unique mission and purpose which is to help lightworkers perfectly master and integrate all 12 Planetary Rays, which is one of the reasons I love this particular Spiritual leadership position and assignment so much! For this has been a great mission and focus of all my work—"Integration and Synthesis"!

Wistancia's and my mission has been to anchor the Synthesis Ashram and Teaching Academy onto the physical Earth, which we have done and are continuing to do in an ever increasing manner on a global level. Currently there are 42 Branches of the Academy that have been set up around the world! The Academy actually first came into existence in 1995! This we have been guided to call the Melchizedek Synthesis Light Academy for the following reasons. It is called this because of the Overlighting Presence of Melchizedek (Our Universal Logos), the Mahatma (Avatar of Synthesis), and the Light which is the embodiment of Archangel Metatron, who created all outer light in our Universe and is the creator of the electron! These three beings, Djwhal Khul, and a very large Core Group of inner plane Planetary and Cosmic Masters help us in all this work.

I have also been asked by the inner plane Ascended Masters to be one of the main "High Priest Spokespersons for the Planetary Ascension Movement on Earth." I have been asked to do this because of the cutting-edge, yet easy to understand nature of all my books and work, as well as certain Spiritual Leadership qualities I humbly possess. In this regard, I represent all the Masters, which works out perfectly given the Synthesis nature of my work. I function as a kind of "Point Man" for the Ascended Masters on Earth, as they have described it to me.

The Masters, under the guidance of Lord Buddha our Planetary Logos, have also guided us as part of our mission to bring Wesak to the West! So, for the last eight years we have held a Global Festival and Conference at Mt. Shasta, California for 2000 people. This, of course, honors the Wesak Festival, which is the holiest day of the year to the inner plane Ascended Masters, and the high point of incoming Spiritual energies to the Earth on the Taurus full moon each year! We invite all lightworkers to join us each year from all over the world for this momentous celebration, which is considered to be one of the premiere Spiritual Events in the New Age Movement!

The fourth part of my mission and purpose is the 40 volume "Easy to Read Encyclopedia of the Spiritual Path" that I have now fully completed. The Ascended Master Djwhal Khul prophesized in the 1940's that there would be a Third Dispensation of Ascended Master teachings what would appear at the turn of the century. The first dispensation of Ascended Master teachings was the Theosophical Movement, channeled by Madam Blavatsky. The second dispensation of Ascended Master teachings was the Alice Bailey books, channeled by Djwhal Khul, and *The "I Am" Discourses* channeled from Saint Germain by Godfre Ray King. My 40 volume series of books is, by the grace of GOD and the Masters, the Third Dispensation of Ascended Master teachings as prophesized by Djwhal Khul. (See listing of 40 Volumes as described on Website.) These books are co-creative channeled writings of myself and the inner plane Ascended Masters. What is unique about my work is how easy to read and understand it is, how practical, comprehensive, cutting-edge, as well as integrated and synthesized. Wistancia has added to this work with her wonderful book *Invocations to the Light!*

The fifth aspect of our work and mission, which is extremely unique, is the emphasis on "Synthesis." My books and all my work integrate in a very beautiful way all religions, all Spiritual paths, all mystery schools, all Spiritual teachings, and all forms of psychology! Everyone feels at home in this work because of its incredible inclusive nature! This synthesis ideal is also seen at the Wesak Celebrations, for people come from all religions, Spiritual paths, mystery schools, and teachings. The Event is overlighted by over one million inner plane Ascended Masters, Archangels and Angels, Elohim Masters, and Christed Extraterrestrials. Wesak, the books, the Academy, and all our work embody this synthesis principle. This is part of why I have been given Spiritual Leadership of the Synthesis Ashram on Earth, and soon on the Inner Plane as well. This also explains our unique relationship to Melchizedek who holds responsibility for the "synthesis development" of all beings in our universe. Our connection to the Mahatma is explained by the fact that the Mahatma is the Cosmic embodiment of "synthesis" in the infinite Universe. This is also why the Mahatma also goes by the name, "The Avatar of Synthesis." Archangel Metatron, who holds the position in the Cosmic Tree of Life of Kether, or the Crown, hence, has a "Synthesis Overview" of all of the Sephiroth, or Centers, of the Cosmic Tree of Life! Djwhal Khul holds Spiritual Leadership of the "Synthesis Ashram" on the Planetary, Solar, and Galactic levels for the Earth! The Core Group of Masters that overlight our mission are, again, the embodiment of the synthesis understanding!

The unique thing about our work is that it teaches some of the most cutting-edge, co-created, channeled work on the planet in the realm of Ascension and Ascended Master Teachings. This can be seen in my books *The Complete Ascension Manual, Beyond Ascension, Cosmic Ascension, The Beginner's Guide to the Path of Ascension, Revelations of a Melchizedek Initiate, How to Teach Ascension Classes,* and *The Golden Book of*

Melchizedek: How to Become an Integrated Christed/Buddha in this Lifetime! Because of my background as a Psychologist and licensed Marriage, Family and Child Counselor, I also specialize in some of the most advanced cutting-edge work on the planet in the field of Spiritual Psychology. In this regard, I would guide you to my books, *Soul Psychology, How to Release Fear-Based Thinking and Feeling, The Golden Book of Melchizedek: How to Become an Integrated Christ/Buddha in this Lifetime, Integrated Ascension, How to Clear the Negative Ego, Ascension and Romantic Relationships*, and *Questions and Answers on the Path of Initiation and Ascension*! Thirdly, I also have humbly brought forth some extremely cutting-edge work on the physical/Earthly level in the field of healing, Spirituality and society, politics, social issues, Extraterrestrials, Spiritual leadership, Spirituality and business, and, of course, the annual Wesak Celebrations. This can be found in my books: *The Golden Keys to Ascension and Healing, Hidden Mysteries, Manual for Planetary Leadership, Your Ascension Mission: Embracing Your Puzzle Piece, How to be Successful in your Business from a Spiritual and Financial Perspective*, and *Empowerment and Integration Through The Goddess* —written by Wistancia and myself.

Adding to this, the 22 new books I have just completed—*The Golden Book of Melchizedek: How to Become an Integrated Christ/Buddha in this Lifetime, How to Release Fear-Based Thinking and Feeling: An In-depth Study of Spiritual Psychology, The Little Flame and Big Flame* (my first children's book), *Letters of Guidance to Students and Friends, Ascension Names and Terms Glossary, Ascension Activation Meditations of the Spiritual Hierarchy, How to Achieve Perfect Radiant Health from the Soul's Perspective, Esoteric Psychology and the Science of the Rays and Chakras of God: A Compilation, Secrets of the Ages as Revealed by Spirit and the Masters, Questions and Answers on the Path of Ascension and Self Realization, Letters of Guidance and Teaching on the Path of Initiation and Ascension, How to Achieve Self Realization through Properly Integrating the Material Face of God: A Compilation, The Bible Revealed from the Ascended Masters'*

Perspective: A Compilation, God's Truth and Wisdom Revealed: Achieving Spiritual Vigilance in the Face of Terrorism, The Story of Creation: A Compilation, and *The Universal Laws of God!*

Currently I have completed 42 volumes in my Ascension Book Series. Fourteen of these books are published by Light Technology Publishers. A newer version of *Soul Psychology* is published by Ballantine Publishers, owned by Random House, which I am quite excited about as well! The other 22 books are all in manuscript form and are also in the process of being officially published by iUniverse.com publishers! My books have also been translated and published in Germany, Brazil, Japan, Holland, and Israel, and this process continues to expand.

Spirit and the inner plane Ascended Masters have told me that because of this unique focus, that what I have actually done in a co-creative way and manner with them, has opened a new Portal to God. This new portal opening stems out of all the cutting-edge Ascension Activations and Ascended Master Teachings, the totally cutting-edge Spiritual Psychology work because of my background as a Psychologist and licensed Marriage, Family and Child Counselor, and the unique ability to ground all the work into the physical/Earthly world in a balanced and integrated manner. Spirit and the Masters have told me that this new Portal to God is on an inner and outer plane level, and continues to be built in a co-creative way with Spirit, the Masters, myself, and certain other Masters and High Level Initiates who are helping me on the inner and outer planes! I have Spiritual leadership, however, in spearheading this project, and it is one of the many exciting projects I am involved in at this time!

In terms of my Spiritual initiation process as I have spoken of in my books, I have currently now taken my 18th major initiation. These are not the minor initiations that some groups work with, but are the major initiations that embody all the minor initiations within them. The Seventh Initiation is the achieving of Liberation and Ascension. The 10th Initiation is the completion of Planetary Ascension and the beginning of Solar Initiation. The 11th Initiation being the first Galactic Initiation. The 12th

Initiation being the first Universal Initiation from an Earthly perspective. Having taken my 18th initiation, what is most important to me is that these initiations have been taken in an "integrated manner," for, in truth, the Masters told me that they are not really into Ascension, which may surprise a great many lightworkers. The Masters are into *"Integrated Ascension"*! There are many lightworkers taking initiations, but many are not doing so in an integrated and balanced manner! They are taking them on a Spiritual level, but they are not being properly integrated into the mental and emotional bodies or psychological level properly. They are also not transcending negative ego/fear-based thinking and feeling and properly balancing their four-body system. They are also not integrating their initiations fully into the Physical/Earthly level, addressing such things as: Grounding their Spiritual Missions; Finding their Puzzle Piece, Mission and Purpose; Fulfilling their Spiritual Contract and personal Divine Blue Print, Leaving their Earthly legacy, fulfilling their Dharma, Prosperity Consciousness and Financial and Earthly Success, Integrating the God/Goddess, Embracing the Earth Mother and the Nature Kingdom, Properly Integrating into Third-Dimensional Society and Civilization in terms of the focus of their Service Mission, enjoying Earth life and loving Earth life. This is just mentioned as a very loving reminder of the importance of an integrated and balanced approach to one's Spiritual Path. The grace to have been able to take these 18 Major Initiations and to be able to have completed my Planetary Ascension process and to have moved deeply into my Cosmic Ascension process, I give to GOD, Christ, the Holy Spirit, Melchizedek, the Mahatma, Archangel Metatron, and the Core Group of Masters I work with. I have dedicated myself and my life to GOD and the Masters' service, and I have humbly attempted to share everything I know, have used, and have done in my Spiritual path and Ascension process with all of you, my Beloved Readers! For I firmly believe in the adage "To Have All, Give All!"

Melchizedek, the Universal Logos, has also inwardly told me that because of the Cosmic work I am involved with that I have taken on the

Spiritual assignment of being one of the "12 Prophets of Melchizedek on Earth." I am very humbled to serve in this capacity. For Melchizedek is the Universal Logos, who is like the President of our entire Universe. In truth, all Religions and Spiritual teachings have their source in Melchizedek and in the Great Ancient Order of Melchizedek. It is my great honor and privilege to serve GOD and Melchizedek in this capacity. This is something I have never spoken of before, although I have known of this for many, many years. I have been guided after all this time to share a little more deeply about my Spiritual mission on Earth at this time.

I have also anchored and activated all my major light bodies and am humbly considered by Spirit and the Masters as an equal full-fledged member of the Spiritual Hierarchy, not only in the ideal, but also in terms of Self Realization of being a full-fledged Ascended Master on Earth! In this regard, the anchoring of the Melchizedek Synthesis Light Academy on Earth is part of the Externalization of the Hierarchy as prophesied would come in the Theosophical Movement and in the Alice Bailey books!

The Academy Website is one of the most profound Spiritual Websites you will ever explore because it embodies this "synthesis nature" and is an ever-expanding, living, easy-to-read Spiritual "encyclopedia" that fully integrates all 12 Rays in design and creation! This is also embodied in the free 100-page information packet that we send out to all who ask who wish to get involved and know more about our work! The information in the information packet is also available by just exploring the Academy Website!

We have also set up a wonderful Ministers Ordination and Training Program, which we invite all interested to read about. I am also very excited about a book I have written called *How to Teach Ascension Classes*. Because I have become so busy with my Spiritual leadership and global world service work, I really do not have the time to teach weekly classes as I have in the past. I firmly believe in the motto "Why *give* a person a fish when you can *teach* them to fish!" In this vein, the Masters guided me to write a book on how to teach people to teach Ascension classes based on my work. I humbly suggest it is a most wonderful channeled book that can teach you in the easiest way and manner on every level to teach Ascension classes in your home or on a larger level if you choose. These classes are springing up now all over the globe and have been successful beyond my wildest dreams and expectations. When I wrote the book I was so involved with the process of writing it, I never fully envisioned the tremendous success it would have on a planetary and global level. Using this book and my other books, I have really done the initial homework for you, which can and will allow you to immediately begin teaching Ascension classes yourself. I humbly suggest that you look into the possibility of doing this yourself if you are so guided!

One other very interesting aspect of our Spiritual mission is something the Masters have been speaking to me about for over 10 years which is what they described as being "Ambassadors for the Christed Extraterrestrials"! I have always known this to be true! This was part of the reason I wrote the book *Hidden Mysteries*, which I humbly suggest is one of the best overviews, in an easy to read and understand manner, of the entire Extraterrestrial Movement as it has affected our planet. If you have not read this book, I highly recommend that you do so. It is truly fascinating reading! My strongest personal connection to the Extraterrestrials is with the Arcturians! The Arcturians are the most advanced Christed Extraterrestrial race in our galaxy. They hold the future blueprint for the unfoldment of this planet. The Arcturians are like our future planet and future selves on a collective level. Part of my work, along with the Ascended Master Teachings I have been asked to bring through, has been to bring through a more conscious and personal connection to the Arcturians, the Ashtar Command, and other such Christed Extraterrestrial races. I also encourage you to read my book *Beyond Ascension*, where I explore some of my personal experiences with the Arcturians and how you may do so as well!

Currently, behind the scenes, we are working on some further expansions of this aspect of our mission, which we will share at a later time! Wistancia has also been involved with "White Time Healing," which is another most wonderful Extraterrestrial healing modality that she offers to the public!

One other aspect of our mission deals with having developed, with help from the inner plane Ascended Masters, some of the most advanced Ascension Activation Processes to accelerate Spiritual evolution that has ever been brought forth to this planet. In this co-creative process with the Masters, we have discovered the "keys" to how to accelerate Spiritual evolution at a rate of speed that in past years and centuries would have been unimaginable! This is why I call working with the Ascended Masters "The Rocketship to GOD Method of Spiritual Growth." There is no faster path to God Realization than working with the Ascended Masters, Archangels and Angels, Elohim Masters and Christed Extraterrestrials! What is wonderful about this process is that you do not have to leave your current Spiritual practice, religion, or Spiritual path. Stay on the path you are on and just integrate this work into what you are currently doing! All paths, as you know, lead to GOD, my friends! This is the profundity of following an eclectic path and path of synthesis! I humbly suggest I have found some shortcuts! I share this with all lightworkers on Earth, for I love GOD with all my heart and soul and mind and might, and I recognize that we are all incarnations of GOD, and Sons and Daughters of this same GOD, regardless of what religion, Spiritual path, or mystery school we are on. We are all, in truth, the Eternal Self and are all God! There is, in truth, only GOD, so what I share with you, I share with you, GOD, and myself, for in the highest sense we are all one! What we each hold back from each other, we hold back from ourselves and from GOD. This is why I give freely all that I am, have learned and have, to you, my Beloved Readers, giving everything and holding back nothing! In my books and audiotapes I have literally shared every single one of these ideas, tools, and Ascension Activation methods for accelerating evolution that I have used and come to understand. My Beloved Readers, these tools and methods found in my books and on the audiotapes will "blow your mind as to their effectiveness," in terms of how profound and easy to use they are! I would highly recommend that all lightworkers obtain the 15 Ascension Activation Meditation tapes I have put together for this purpose. Most of them were taped at the Wesak Celebrations with 1500 to 2000 people in attendance, with over one million inner plane Ascended Masters, Archangels and Angels, Elohim Masters, and Christed Extraterrestrials in attendance, under the Wesak full moon and the mountain of Mt Shasta. You can only imagine the power, love, and effectiveness of these Ascension activation audiotapes. I recommend getting all 15 tapes and working with one tape every day or every other day! I personally guarantee you that these tapes will accelerate your Spiritual evolution a thousandfold! You can find them in the information packets and on our Website. They are only available from the Academy! Trust me on this, the combination of reading my books, Wistancia's book, and working with these audio ascension activation tapes, will accelerate your Spiritual evolution beyond your wildest dreams and imagination!

One other extremely important part of my mission, which is a tremendous Spiritual passion of mine, is the training of lightworkers on Earth in the area of Spiritual/Christ/Buddha thinking and negative ego/separative/fear-based thinking! These are the only two ways of thinking in the world, and each person thinks with one, the other, or a combination of both. If a person does not learn how to transcend negative ego thinking and feeling, it will end up, over time, corrupting every aspect of their lives including all channeling work, Spiritual teaching, and even healing work! One cannot be wrong with self and right with GOD. This is because our thoughts create our reality, as we all know! I cannot recommend more highly that every person reading this book, read my other books: *Soul Psychology, The Golden Book of Melchizedek: How to Become an Integrated Christ/Buddha in this Lifetime, How to Release Fear-Based Thinking and Feeling: An In-depth Study of Spiritual Psychology, How to Clear the Negative Ego,* and *Integrated Ascension!* I humbly suggest that these five books will be five of the most extraordinary self-help books in the area of mastering this psychological area of life. They are extremely easy to read, very practical, and filled with tools that will help you in untold ways. Being a channel for the Ascended Masters and being uniquely trained as a Spiritual Psychologist and Marriage, Family and Child Counselor, as well as being raised in a family of psychologists, has given me an extraordinary ability to teach this material through my books in a most effective manner. The combination of my books on Ascension, and these books on Spiritual Psychology, will literally revolutionize your consciousness in the comfort of your own home! The most extraordinary thing about all this work is how incredibly easy to read and easy to understand it is. It is also incredibly comprehensive, completely cutting-edge, and totally integrated, balanced, and synthesized. It contains the best of all schools of thought in the past, present, and channeled cutting-edge future understanding that is available now! I humbly ask you to trust me in this regard and just read one of these books and you will immediately want to buy the others!

One other aspect of our work and mission is our involvement with the "Water of Life" and the Perfect Science products for the healing of our own physical bodies and the physical body of Mother Earth of all pollution in the air, water and earth. This is the miracle Mother Earth has been waiting for to bring her back to her "original edenic state" after so much abuse. This is not the time or the place to get into this subject in detail; however, I invite you to check out the "Water of Life" and the Perfect Science information in the Information Packet and on the Academy Website! It is truly the miracle we have all been waiting for to help heal the Earth!

One other aspect of our work and mission is a project that the Ascended Masters have asked us to put together on behalf of lightworkers and people around the globe. It is called the "Interdimensional Prayer Altar Program" that the Masters have guided us to set up in the Academy in Agoura Hills, California on the property we live on. We have set up a "Physical Interdimensional Prayer Altar" where people can send in their prayers on any subject and we will place them on this Altar. In consultation with the Masters, Archangels and Angels, Elohim Masters, and Christed Extraterrestrials, we have set up an arrangement with them that all physical letters placed upon this Altar will be immediately worked upon by these Masters. We have been guided by the inner plane Ascended Masters to create 15 Prayer Altar Programs in different areas of life that people can sign up for. For example, there is one for health and one for financial help in your Spiritual mission. Two-thirds of these programs are totally free. There are five or six that are more advanced Spiritual acceleration programs where written material is sent to you to work with in conjunction with these programs so as to accelerate your Spiritual growth. All letters we receive by e-mail, fax, or letter are placed on the Altar by myself or my personal assistant. It is kept 100% confidential and is an extremely special service provided by the inner plane Ascended Masters and Angels to help all lightworkers and people on Earth with immediate help for whatever they need should they desire assistance. Other examples of Prayer Altars are: Building your Higher Light Body, Extra Protection, Relationship Help, World Service Prayers, Help for your Animals, Prayer Altar for the Children, Integrating the Goddess, Integrating your Archetypes, Integrating the Seven Rays and working with the Seven Inner Plane Ashrams of the Christ, Integrating the Mantle of the Christ, Ascension Seat Integration, and Light, Love, and Power Body Building Program! These Prayer Altar Programs have been co-created with the inner plane Ascended Masters as another tool for not only helping all lightworkers with whatever they need help with, but also as another cutting-edge tool to accelerate Spiritual evolution!

In a similar regard, the Masters have guided us to set up a Melchizedek Synthesis Light Academy Membership Program which is based on three levels of involvement. Stage One, Stage Two, and Stage Three! Stage One and Stage Three are totally free. Stage Two costs only $20 for a Lifetime Membership with no other fees required. You also receive free, large colored pictures of Melchizedek, the Mahatma, Archangel Metatron, and Djwhal Khul for joining. It is not necessary to join to get involved in the work; however, it has been set up by the inner plane Ascended Masters as another service and tool of the Academy to help lightworkers accelerate their Spiritual evolution! When joining the different Stages, the Masters take you under their wing, so to speak, and accelerate your evolution by working with you much more closely on the inner plane while you sleep at night and during your conscious waking hours. The joining is nothing more than a process that gives them the permission to work with you in this more intensive fashion! Again, it is not necessary to join to get involved in the work, and is really just another one of the many fantastic tools and services the Academy has made available to you to accelerate your Spiritual, psychological, and Earthly/physical evolution in an integrated and balanced manner!

I had a dream shortly after completing my two new books, *The Golden Book of Melchizedek: How To Become an Integrated Christ/Buddha in This Lifetime*, and my book *How to Release Fear-Based Thinking and Feeling: An In-depth Study of Spiritual Psychology*. In the dream I was being shown the different Spiritual missions people had. My Spiritual mission was the embodiment of the Holy Spirit. I clearly was shown how other people within GOD, Christ, and the Holy Spirit, had missions of being more detached off-shoots of the Holy Spirit and other Masters, and continuing outward from there had all kinds of different Spiritual missions. However, mine was the embodiment of the Holy Spirit on Earth.

My Beloved Readers, I want to be very clear here that in sharing this I am in no way, shape, or form claiming to be the Holy Spirit. There is enough glamour in the New Age Movement and I am not interested in adding any more to it. What I am sharing here, which is being given to more clearly and precisely share my Spiritual mission and purpose, is that which I am here to strive to embody and demonstrate. The Holy Spirit is the third aspect of the Trinity of GOD. I have always greatly loved the Holy Spirit, for the Holy Spirit is like the "Voice of GOD"! It is the "Still, Small Voice Within"! When one prays to GOD, it is the Holy Spirit who answers for GOD. The Holy Spirit is the answer to all questions, challenges, and problems. The Holy Spirit speaks for the Atonement or the At-one-ment! It teaches the Sons and Daughters of

GOD how to recognize their true identity as God, Christ, the Buddha, and the Eternal Self! In truth, there are only two voices in life! There is the voice of the negative ego and the "Voice of the Holy Spirit"! There is the voice of negative ego/fear-based/separative thinking and feeling, and there is the Voice of God/Spiritual/Christ/Buddha thinking and feeling! There is the "Voice of Love" and the voice of fear! There is the "Voice of Oneness" and the voice of separation!

I was given this dream after completing these two books because, I humbly suggest, this is the energy I was embodying in writing them and that I embody at all times in my Spiritual mission and purpose on Earth. This is not surprising in the sense that this has always been my Spiritual ideal and the dream was just an inward confirmation in that moment that I was embodying and demonstrating that Spiritual Ideal in the energy flow I was in, and continue to be in and maintain, in my focus and Spiritual mission on Earth! This is what I strive to do in all my work, be it my Ascension Book Series, Wesak Celebrations, Teaching, Counseling, Videotapes, Audiotapes, and all my work, which is to strive to be the embodiment of a "Voice for God"! By the grace of GOD, Christ, the Holy Spirit, and the Masters, I provide a lot of the "answers" people and light-workers are seeking! I teach people how to "undo" negative ego/fear-based/separative thinking and feeling, and show then how to fully realize God/Christ/Buddha thinking and feeling! I show them how to release and undo glamour, illusion, and maya, and instead seek "Truth, as GOD, Christ, the Holy Spirit, and the Masters would have you seek it!"

My real purpose, however, is not to just be the embodiment of the Holy Spirit on Earth, for I would not be embodying the Voice and Vision of the Holy Spirit if I just focused on this. The Voice and Vision of GOD, Christ, the Holy Spirit, and Melchizedek is that of synthesis! This is the other thing I feel in the deepest part of my heart and soul that I am here to embody! So my "truest and highest Spiritual ideal" that I am here to strive to embody is GOD, Christ, the Holy Spirit, the inner plane Ascended Masters, the Archangels and Angels of the Light of GOD, the Elohim

Councils of the Light of GOD, and the Christed Extraterrestrials of the Light of GOD. I feel in the deepest part of my heart and soul, and what I try to embody every moment of my life, is "All that is of GOD and the Godforce on Earth!" In this regard, it is my Spiritual mission and purpose to strive to be the embodiment of the "synthesis nature of God on Earth"! This is why I have been given Spiritual leadership of the Synthesis Ashram and Academy on Earth and future leadership of the inner plane Synthesis Ashram that governs our planet.

I was also told by the Masters that I had achieved my Ascension in the fullest sense of the term and that I did not need to physically die anymore!

I have also been living on Light the last four years, however, this is not something I would recommend everyone do, for the Masters have told me they would actually prefer that almost all lightworkers live on what they call a partial Light diet, which is a good healthy physical diet and also absorbing Light as well. Because of certain factors that are connected with my particular Spiritual mission and purpose, living on Light has been appropriate for the Spiritual mission, Spiritual blueprint, puzzle piece, Spiritual contract and Service mission that I came to fulfill!

The other thing I strive to do in my Spiritual mission is to embody Spiritual mastery on a Spiritual, psychological, and physical/Earthly level. What most people and lightworkers do not realize is that there are three distinct levels to God Realization. There is a Spiritual level, a psychological level, and a physical/Earthly level! To achieve true God Realization, all three levels must be equally mastered! Another way of saying this is that there are "Four Faces of GOD"! There is a Spiritual Face, a Mental Face, an Emotional Face, and a Material Face! To truly realize God, all four must be equally mastered, loved, honored, sanctified, integrated, and balanced! The "Mental and Emotional Faces of GOD" make up the psychological level of GOD. So, my Spiritual mission and purpose is to fully embody Spiritual mastery and unconditional love on all three of these levels and in all Four Faces of GOD! In a similar vein, my Spiritual mission and purpose is to embody self-mastery and proper integration of all

"Seven Rays of GOD," not just one or a few. For the "Seven Rays of GOD" are, in truth, the true "Personality of GOD"! My Spiritual mission and purpose is to not only strive to embody all levels of GOD, but to also try and develop all my God-given abilities and Spiritual gifts, on a Spiritual, Psychological, and Physical/Earthly level, and in all Four Faces of GOD!

My Beloved Readers, all these things that I have written about in this chapter are what I strive to fully embody and demonstrate on the Earth every moment of my life, and is what I strive with all my heart and soul and mind and might to teach others to do as well!

As the Founder and Director of the Melchizedek Synthesis Light Academy it has been my great honor and privilege, with great humbleness and humility, to share "my Spiritual mission and purpose" in a deeper and more profound manner at this time. I do so in the hopes that all who feel a resonance and attunement with this work will get involved with the Academy's "Teachings" and all that it has to offer. I also share this so that all who choose to get involved might join this vast group of lightworkers around the globe to help spread the teachings and work of the inner plane Ascended Masters. The inner plane Ascended Masters and I, along with the Archangels and Angels, Elohim Councils, and Christed Extraterrestrials, put forth the Clarion Call to lightworkers around the world to first explore this work, then integrate this work, and then become Ambassadors of the Ascended Masters so we may at this time in Beloved Earth's history bring in fully now the Seventh Golden Age in all its Glory!

My Beloved Friends, I am also guided to add here that Spirit and the Masters have told me there are only ten "Integrated Spiritual Masters" who currently are living on this Planet! There are only two beings on this planet that have taken initiations at the level I have spoken of here in this Spiritual Mission and Purpose Statement!

They have also told me that there are only three people on this planet that have fully anchored and activated the full array of their light bodies and all the light bodies spoken about in *The Keys of Enoch*, and even beyond the teachings of *The Keys of Enoch*! As a Special Gift to all of you who are reading this, I will share with you a Revelation from God and the Masters as to what these Light Bodies are: Physical/Etheric Body, Emotional or Astral Body, Mental Body, Buddhic or Causal Body, Atmic Body, Monadic Body, Logoic Body, Monadic Blueprint Body, Mayavarupa Body, Electromagnetic Body, Epi-Kinetic and Eka Body, Gematrian Body, Higher Adam Kadmon Body, Overself Body, Zohar Body of Light, Annointed Christ Overself Body, Galactic Son Overself Body, Body of the Brotherhood of Light, Paradise Son's Body, Elohistic Lord's Body, Lord's Mystical Body, and the Sonship Star Light Body.

My Beloved Friends, the words I speak in this Spiritual Mission and Purpose Statement are not just theoretical words, they are, I very humbly share with you, words of a fully Realized Integrated Spiritual Master who shares these things with you from personal experience and from having Realized the things I am sharing with you, not just as an academic theoretical exercise! My Beloved Friends, you have found Spiritual Gold of a most refined and purified form in finding this work! Take advantage of my Website, all my books, meditations, tapes, prayer altar programs, sessions, articles, Wesak, and all the services the Academy has to offer, for it, I very humbly share with you, my friends, if followed, will take you in the most efficient, quickest, easy to understand and practical manner to the "Promised Land" that you seek, and which it is my job to help you find! Share this work with all your friends, family and students! For within this work, my friends, is the Revelation for the New Millennium and the Keys and Secrets to the unfolding of the Seventh Golden Age on this Planet! So be about the Father's Business and do your Spiritual Homework and study these Books, Tapes, Services and Tools, and they will bring you a "peace that passeth understanding!" I end this Spiritual Mission Statement with words from the Master Jesus/Sananda who said, "Be ye faithful unto death, and I will give thee a Crown of Life"!

So let it be Written! So let it be Done!

Kodoish, Kodoish, Kodoish, Adonai T'sabayoth!
Holy, Holy, Holy is the Lord God of Hosts!

Adonai in the Light and Love of God and the Masters!
Love and Light,
Dr Joshua David Stone

About the Authors

Dr. **Joshua David Stone** has a Ph.D. in Transpersonal Psychology and is a licensed Marriage, Family and Child Counselor, in Agoura Hills, California. On a Spiritual level he anchors *The Melchizedek Synthesis Light Academy and Ashram*, which is an integrated inner and outer plane ashram that seeks to represent all paths to God! He serves as one of the leading spokespersons for the Planetary Ascension Movement. Through his books, tapes, workshops, lectures, and annual Wesak Celebrations, Dr. Stone is known as one of the leading Spiritual Teachers and Channels in the world on the teachings of the Ascended Masters, Spiritual Psychology, and Ascension! He has currently written over 42 volumes in his Ascension Book Series, which he also likes to call "The Easy to Read Encyclopedia of the Spiritual Path"!

For a free information packet of all Dr. Stone's workshops, books, audiotapes, Academy membership program, and global outreach program, please call or write to the following address:

Dr. Joshua David Stone
Melchizedek Synthesis Light Academy
28951 Malibu Rancho Rd.
Agoura Hills, CA 91301

Phone: 818-706-8458
Fax: 818-706-8540
e-mail: drstone@best.com

Please come visit my Website at:
http://www.drjoshuadavidstone.com

Rev. **Gloria Excelsias** is a Minister, Spiritual Teacher, Healer and Author, who works at the Melchizedek Synthesis Light Academy as one of Dr Stone's main key assistants. Gloria is a celebrator and lover of Life and God! She is determined to dream and live the impossible dream and make this life the most glorious she has ever lived on Earth! Her name fully embodies and describes her energy! Gloria Excelsias, which is her Spiritual and Earthly embodied name, has its roots in Latin and means Highest Glory to God! Gloria's philosophy every moment of her life is to try to embody the Highest Glory of God, which shall take her to Glorious Heights!

0-595-21334-0

Printed in the United States
4712